Growth of the Medical Tourism Industry and Its Impact on Society:

Emerging Research and Opportunities

Manjeet Singh
Central University of Jammu, India

Subbaraman Kumaran
Alliance University, Bangalore, India

A volume in the Advances in Hospitality, Tourism, and the Services Industry (AHTSI) Book Series

IGI Global
PUBLISHER of TIMELY KNOWLEDGE

Published in the United States of America by
IGI Global
Business Science Reference (an imprint of IGI Global)
701 E. Chocolate Avenue
Hershey PA, USA 17033
Tel: 717-533-8845
Fax: 717-533-8661
E-mail: cust@igi-global.com
Web site: http://www.igi-global.com

Library of Congress Cataloging-in-Publication Data

Names: Singh, Manjeet, 1986- editor. | Kumaran, Subbaraman, 1963- editor.
Title: Growth of the Medical Tourism Industry and Its Impact on Society : Emerging Research and Opportunities / Manjeet Singh and Subbaraman Kumaran, editors.
Description: Hershey, PA : Business Science Reference, 2021. | Includes bibliographical references and index.
Identifiers: LCCN 2019053035 (print) | LCCN 2019053036 (ebook) | ISBN 9781799834298 (ebook) | ISBN 9781799834274 (hardcover) | ISBN 9781799834281 (paperback)
Subjects: LCSH: Medical tourism.
Classification: LCC RA793.5 (ebook) | LCC RA793.5 .G56 2021 (print) | DDC 362.1--dc23
LC record available at <https://lccn.loc.gov/2019053035>

This book is published in the IGI Global book series Advances in Hospitality, Tourism, and the Services Industry (AHTSI) (ISSN: 2475-6547; eISSN: 2475-6555)

British Cataloguing in Publication Data
A Cataloguing in Publication record for this book is available from the British Library.

Advances in Hospitality, Tourism, and the Services Industry (AHTSI) Book Series

ISSN:2475-6547
EISSN:2475-6555

Editor-in-Chief: Maximiliano Korstanje, University of Palermo, Argentina

MISSION

Globally, the hospitality, travel, tourism, and services industries generate a significant percentage of revenue and represent a large portion of the business world. Even in tough economic times, these industries thrive as individuals continue to spend on leisure and recreation activities as well as services.

The Advances in Hospitality, Tourism, and the Services Industry (AHTSI) book series offers diverse publications relating to the management, promotion, and profitability of the leisure, recreation, and services industries. Highlighting current research pertaining to various topics within the realm of hospitality, travel, tourism, and services management, the titles found within the AHTSI book series are pertinent to the research and professional needs of managers, business practitioners, researchers, and upper-level students studying in the field.

COVERAGE

- Sustainable Tourism
- Leisure & Business Travel
- Tourism and the Environment
- Service Design
- Customer Service Issues
- Hotel Management
- Destination Marketing and Management
- Health and Wellness Tourism
- Food and Beverage Management
- Casino Management

IGI Global is currently accepting manuscripts for publication within this series. To submit a proposal for a volume in this series, please contact our Acquisition Editors at Acquisitions@igi-global.com or visit: http://www.igi-global.com/publish/.

The Advances in Hospitality, Tourism, and the Services Industry (AHTSI) Book Series (ISSN 2475-6547) is published by IGI Global, 701 E. Chocolate Avenue, Hershey, PA 17033-1240, USA, www.igi-global.com. This series is composed of titles available for purchase individually; each title is edited to be contextually exclusive from any other title within the series. For pricing and ordering information please visit http://www.igi-global.com/book-series/advances-hospitality-tourism-services-industry/121014. Postmaster: Send all address changes to above address.

Titles in this Series

For a list of additional titles in this series, please visit: http://www.igi-global.com/book-series

Global Development of Religious Tourism
Emilia Alaverdov (Georgian Technical University, Georgia) and Muhammad Waseem Bari (Government College University, Faisalabad, Pakistan)
Business Science Reference • © 2021 • 366pp • H/C (ISBN: 9781799857921) • US $195.00

Innovation and Entrepreneurial Opportunities in Community Tourism
Jakson Renner Rodrigues Soares (Universidade da Coruña, Spain & Universidade Estadual do Ceará, Brazil)
Business Science Reference • © 2021 • 358pp • H/C (ISBN: 9781799848554) • US $195.00

Handbook of Research on Human Capital and People Management in the Tourism Industry
Vânia Gonçalves Costa (School of Hospitality and Tourism, Polytechnic Institute of Cávado and Ave, Portugal & CiTUR, Portugal & GOVCOPP, University of Aveiro, Portugal) Andreia Antunes Moura (Polytechnic Institute of Coimbra, Portugal & CiTUR, Portugal & GOVCOPP, University of Aveiro, Portugal) and Maria do Rosário Mira (Polytechnic Institute of Coimbra, Portugal & CiTUR, Portugal & GOVCOPP, University of Aveiro, Portugal)
Business Science Reference • © 2021 • 472pp • H/C (ISBN: 9781799843184) • US $285.00

Handbook of Research on the Role of Tourism in Achieving Sustainable Development Goals
Filipa Brandão (GOVCOPP, University of Aveiro, Portugal) Zélia Breda (GOVCOPP, University of Aveiro, Portugal) Rui Costa (GOVCOPP, University of Aveiro, Portugal) and Carlos Costa (GOVCOPP, University of Aveiro, Portugal)
Business Science Reference • © 2021 • 385pp • H/C (ISBN: 9781799856917) • US $285.00

Role and Impact of Tourism in Peacebuilding and Conflict Transformation
Jorge Tavares da Silva (GOVCOPP, University of Aveiro, Portugal) Zélia Breda (GOVCOPP, University of Aveiro, Portugal) and Fabio Carbone (Centre for Trust, Peace, and Social Relations, Coventry University, UK & GOVCOPP, University of Aveiro, Portugal)
Business Science Reference • © 2021 • 402pp • H/C (ISBN: 9781799850533) • US $195.00

Strategies for Promoting Sustainable Hospitality and Tourism Services
Maximiliano Emanuel Korstanje (University of Palermo, Argentina) Babu George (Fort Hays State University, USA) and Alexandru-Mircea Nedelea (Stefan cel Mare University of Suceava, Romania)
Business Science Reference • © 2020 • 243pp • H/C (ISBN: 9781799843306) • US $195.00

IGI Global
PUBLISHER of TIMELY KNOWLEDGE

701 East Chocolate Avenue, Hershey, PA 17033, USA
Tel: 717-533-8845 x100 • Fax: 717-533-8661
E-Mail: cust@igi-global.com • www.igi-global.com

Table of Contents

Foreword

Medical Tourism is not a recent global phenomenon. It dates back to thousands of years, when Greek pilgrims travelled from the eastern Mediterranean to a small territory in the Saronic Gulf called Epidauria, a form of medical tourism destination of that era. With the advent of globalisation and culture of consumerism there is an increasing tendency among people to travel in search of better quality and affordable health option.

Medical tourism includes medical treatments, wellness and alternative medicines and is gradually transitioning towards medical value travel, that also includes capturing of patient's healthcare seeking behaviour as well as the wider economic impact on the countries hosting them.

Over the last decade, India has grown to become a sought-after destination for medical tourism. Today, it is one of the top ten medical tourism destinations in the world and being one of the fastest growing destinations, India is predicted to drive higher with time.

Modern healthcare facilities, skilled doctors, low cost of treatment and Government's initiative to ease the travel process for international medical tourists, have made India a popular hub, attracting a large number of medical travellers every year.

This Book, titled "Growth of the Medical Tourism Industry and Its Impact on Society" having eight chapters, contributed by academicians and medical practitioners from India and other countries, gives a global overview of medical tourism, with focus on fast emergence of India as a major destination. The book has given a comprehensive account of future growth of medical tourism market in the world and has also highlighted the competitive advantage, that India has, compared to other medical tourism destination countries. The proposal of initiating domestic medical tourism and yoga tourism in India and the concept of medical tourism index, suggested in the book are novel and innovative.

Vinod Zutshi
Ministry of Tourism, Government of India, India

Preface

An Englishman travel to India for cardiovascular surgery at a one tenth of price he would pay in London. A Canadian prefers to visit Costa Rica for Cosmetic surgery because the waiting time period is more than year in their home country. An American chose to get medical treatment in Malaysia to get cost effective treatment because he does not have health insurance in USA. Europeans travels to Thailand for elective eye surgery at a fraction of the treatment cost he would pay in their home country. The general perception of the Westerners about the developing countries like India, Thailand, Costa Rica are poor in infrastructure, hot climate, unhygienic environment, huts and hungry children. Most Westerners who have visited India, Thailand, Malaysia and Costa Rica are travelled on a Western Airlines, stayed in Western hotels that offer modern conveniences and ate restaurants food modified to western tastes. During their stay, they have limited interaction with local people.

For people with such an experiences, the idea that India and Thailand might have state-of-art hospitals where highly skilled medical professionals offering high-tech services to international patients seems absurd. Yet it is true. Offering high-tech medical services to foreigners is currently a reality in numerous developing countries. The act of providing medical treatment to foreign patients is called Medical Tourism. It is the combination of tourism and medical treatment. In 2006, it has captured the attention of governments, policy makers, academics and the press both in destination and sending countries. It is an economic activity that entails trade in services and represents the splicing of at least two sectors: medicine and tourism.

International patients from United States travel to Asia for cosmetic surgery, organ transplants, and artificial insemination; patients from South America, the Middle East and other parts of Asia travel to India, Thailand, Malaysia and Singapore for cost effective medical treatment. West Europeans and Canadians prefer the hospitals in Asia to get better treatment and to avoid the long waiting time in their country.

Moreover, the international patients who buy health care usually in the form of package which includes treatment cost, air ticket, transfers, accommodation and post operative vacations. According to World Health Organisation, it is a growing trend with enormous economic implications. According to a report by Organisation for Economic Cooperation and Development (OECD), the trade in health services provided developing countries with a competitive opportunity in this arena, given their abundance of labour and availability of capital and skills in medicine. As long as they can maintain quality levels, they might be able to generate significant growth.

In 1997, the United Nations Conference on Trade and Development (UNCTAD), which monitors trade between countries, noted for the first time that trade in services, including health services, could be beneficial for developing countries. A growing number of these countries have the requisite manpower, the investment capital, the know-how and the motivation to supply medical tourist facilities. In Asia, the countries like India, Thailand, Malaysia, Singapore, Philippines are leading medical tourism destinations. In the Western hemisphere Cuba, Argentina, Costa Rica is providing best medical treatment for international patients. The Baltic states of former Soviet Union has high skilled labour force to lure the Western European to their health care facilities.

In 2003, around 1 million Americans crossed their border for seeking medical treatment: weight loss surgery in Mexico, heart-valve replacement in Thailand, Cardio vascular surgery in India, proton therapy in Korea, fertility treatment in Israel, face lift in Costa Rica, restorative dentistry in Mexico. Nearly fifty countries involve in medical tourism activities and took medical care for 14 million international patients through their hospitals and clinic each year. The main reason for international patients goes abroad for medical treatment is cost savings, better quality care, improved patients experience, exclusive treatments, speciality treatments, shorter waiting periods, more inpatient friendly, the lure of new and different.

According to new report by Grand View Research Inc, the global medical tourism market is expected to reach US$ 179.6 billion by 2026. In Asia, countries like India, Thailand, Singapore, Malaysia and South Korea are leading medical tourism providers. Thailand treated more than 3 million international patients in 2019. India treated 495056 international patients and generated revenue of $3 billion in 2017 and it is expected to reach $9 billion by 2020. The major destination for medical tourism in India is Delhi, Chennai, Mumbai, Bangalore, Hyderabad, and Kolkata. Mumbai attracts more than 20 percent of the medical tourists; Chennai treats nearly 15 percent of the international patients while Kerala handles around 5 percent. The major markets for India are the South-East Asian countries, the Middle East, Africa, and SAARC countries. More than 50 percent of medical tourists are coming from Bangladesh to India. In India the international patients are taking treatment in Cardiology, Dentistry, Ophthalmology, Oncology, Orthopaedics, and other general surgery.

By understanding the importance of medical tourism, this book titled "Growth of the Medical Tourism Industry and Its Impact on Society" was written. The main aim of this book is to have better understanding about cost effective medical tourism and facilities and services offered by hospitals in India.

This book mainly focuses on background of medical tourism and profile of the medical tourists visiting India and other Asian countries over the developed countries for varied reasons. The profile includes sex, age, occupation, type of treatment underwent, accompany details etc. The facilities and services offered by hospitals like type of treatment offered, hospitals experience, accommodation detail, hospitality care, patient care, hospital accreditation, Medical human resource detail and activities of medical tourism department are provided. The average cost of various medical treatments in India and other countries like Singapore, Malaysia, Thailand, UK, USA, and Canada has been assessed. The benefits of taking treatment in India and other Asian countries rather than developed nations are also highlighted. The health care crisis in United States of America, Branding Inbound International Medical Tourism and Institutional role in promoting medical tourism in India also included in this book. To understand the perception of the inbound international patients about the services and facilities provided in the hospitals, various chapters by the authors have showcased the outcomes of their research related to medical tourism. These authors have very diligently described the issues and challenges that are occurring in their native places on account of medical services and even how medical tourism can be a win-win situation for the patients from developed countries and medical practitioners as well as service providers from developing countries. Based on the findings of the research, suggestions are provided for better development of medical tourism practices. The outcome of their studies are highly useful for the students pursuing hospital and medical tourism education, and tourism researchers in academic institutions, medical tourism planners and strategic managers in hospitals dealing international patients.

Acknowledgment

We are greatly thankful to all the contributors of the book who have enriched the book with their academic insights and contributed to the success of this book. We are equally thankful to the IGI Global's publishing team for their impeccable support and guidance to make this book a reality.

Chapter 1
Medical Tourism:
History, Global Scenario, and Indian Perspectives

Kumaran Subbaraman
Alliance University, Banaglore, India

Manjeet Singh
https://orcid.org/0000-0002-4842-4393
Central University of Jammu, India

Inder Puneet Johar
Kashmir University, India

ABSTRACT

India has been coming up as a growing destination in terms of medical tourism. Medical tourism in India at present is valued around $7-8 billion dollars. High quality services in medical context at an affordable cost have made India one of the prominent destinations of medical tourism. Medical tourism in India is exponentially growing at a rate of 30% every year. Chennai is termed as the "Health Capital of India" being the region with highest footfall in terms of medical tourists with highest number of hospitals with multi- and super-specialty services offering highest quality healthcare treatment at the lowest cost. Ministry of Tourism and Ministry of Health and Family Welfare are working collaboratively to promote India as a premier medical tourism destination. To facilitate the easy movement of patients for medical tourism, m-visa (medical visa) has been launched and is being promoted, which gives the patients an opportunity to stay in India for the period of their treatment.

DOI: 10.4018/978-1-7998-3427-4.ch001

INTRODUCTION

Tourism is the activity of travelers to see the different tourism attractions and observe the different culture for the purpose of leisure, business, medical treatment and others. During their travel if they stay in places outside their usual environment for not more than one consecutive year to fulfill their purposes. According to United Nations World Tourism Organization, more than 1400 million people travelled internationally in the year 2018 and generated one in ten jobs and contributed 10 percent of the GDP. According to Ministry of Tourism, Government of India, the total number of foreign tourists arrived in 2018 was 10.56 million and also it foreign exchange of 1.94 lakh crore. WTTC (World Travel and Tourism Council) predicts that the travel sector creates 300 million jobs and contributes 9.6 percent to GDP by 2020.

According to the objectives and purpose of the visits, the types of tourism are classified as Pilgrim tourism, leisure tourism, adventure tourism, fairs and festival tourism, rural tourism, eco-tourism, medical tourism etc. Among the various type of tourism, medical tourism is gaining importance at global level. Medical tourism is defined as the act of travelling nationally and internationally for the purpose of taking medical treatment as well as visiting tourist attractions. According to World Tourism Organization (2014), medical tourism is termed as tourist services which take medical care, sickness and health, health and recreation as main themes. It is also termed as the patients crossing their borders to get quality medical treatment at affordable prices. Balaban & Marano (2010)Medical tourism is the provision of cost effective medical treatment in collaboration with tourism industry as well as health care hospitals. It is a travel to destinations to undergo medical treatment like surgery and other specialist interventions. Medical tourism is a travel that seeks to enhance personal health and well-being, including through authentic and location-based therapies. The process of providing quality medical treatment for international patients is now becoming an emerging business at global level. Before 1990, the international patients from developing and under developed countries cross the border to take quality treatment in developed countries due to lack of facilities at their home country. After 1995, the health facilities have improved in developing economies, a reverse flow takes place due to high treatment cost.

OBJECTIVES

The main objectives of this research paper are to analyze the historical background of medical tourism and to find out the global scenario of medical tourism. Finally to assess the issues and challenges faced by Indian medical tourism industry.

HISTORY OF MEDICAL TOURISM

The concept of medical tourism is not new one and it is existing as old as medicine itself. This is practiced more than centuries, though the concept of travelling for taking treatment has gained huge acceptance in recent years. This practice of travelling for health treatment can be traced back to Greek pilgrims, who travelled to the small Mediterranean town of Epidauria in the Saronic Gulf. It is called as sanctuary of Asclepios, the god of healing, so Epidauria emerged as world first medical travel destination (Balaban & Marano 2010)[1]. Some research study indicates that the medical tourism is practiced in the early 4000 BC itself in Egypt, Rome, India, China and Japan.

From the ancient culture it is observed that there is close relationship between religion and healthcare, which dates backs thousands of years. Mineral thermal springs and sacred temple baths are considered as healing effects for many medical problems and it is well recognized by ancient civilization. In 2000 BC, Sumerians constructed health complexes alongside mineral water springs which include elevated temples and flowing pools. During Bronze Age 2000 BC, hill tribes near present–day Saint Moritz, Switzerland gathered around to drink and bath in iron rich mineral springs. The drinking cups of Bronze age have also been found in thermal springs in France and Germany as well as in Celtic mineral wells, which could signify health pilgrimages within these cultures.

EARLIEST MEDICAL TOURISM CENTERS

Earliest medical tourism center were built by Persians, Greeks, ancient Romans, Europeans and Indians.

Greek Medical Tourism

The Greeks were the first to lay foundation for medical tourism at global level. The Asclepia temples built to honor the Greek God Asclepius were acted as healing Centre for the patients from around region for healing purposes. The numerous Asclepia temples were constructed along the mineral springs to treat the patients. Most temple complexes also had snake nurseries where serpents were farmed for spiritual and healing rituals. At Epidaurus, the Asclepia temple complex included bathing springs, a dream temple, gymnasium, exercise area and a snake farm large enough to supply nearby villages. Patients at temple were attended by assistants of priest and caretakers and finally granted appointment by head priest. Until fourth century AD, the Asclepia temples flourished and treatments were less ritualistic and more clinical. The old "sleep and dream" formula was popular in certain parts of the Mediterranean. Other spa temples like Sanctuary of Zeus at Olympia and the spa multiplex at Delphi were flourished throughout ancient Greece, while not like Asclepia temples.

Early Roman Medical Tourism

In ancient Rome hot water baths are familiar to heal the medical problems. This is called as Thermae. It is not only for medicinal benefits, but it was used for important social gathering of elite people in the society. Romans are not believers in Spartan healing and they could spend money lavishly for their treatment at hot springs and bath. The Roman treatment centers were high class establishments and included facilities like theaters, lounges, art galleries, conference halls, brothels and sports stadiums. The establishment was able to accommodate 3000 patients and patrons at a time. These Thermae were hardly considered as medical tourism spots since most tourists were one day visitors. Later the Roman Empire slowly expanded facilities and made pilgrims, diplomats and kings from various parts of the world visited the Mediterranean to get medical counsel and health treatments. As a result of active trade with Africa, Asia and Persia, this healing art was expanded by Rome. Later Ayurveda massage, Chinese medicine and various aspects of Buddhist spiritual healing became common features at Roman healing centers (Oberhelman, 2014.).

Islamic Medical Tourism

The Islamic nations were contributed well in the field of medicine and healing. They had well established health care system especially for foreigners by creating Mansuri Hospital in Cairo (1248 AD). This hospital had capacity to accommodate 8000 people as in-patient and it was considered as largest hospital at that time. The hospital complex had facilities like separate wards for women, a pharmacy, a library and numerous lecture halls. There was a facility for undergoing surgery and separate department for eye related diseases. The patients from international community's treated equally and there was no limit for stay in hospital. There is numerous welfare driven hospitals in Syria and Baghdad for weary travelers from abroad. The facilities at hospitals are donated by nobles and princes who were inspired by the Islamic principles of charity.

Japanese Healing Therapy

In olden days Japan discovered the healing powers of hot water mineral springs which are called as Onsen, used for relieving pain and tend their wounds. The bubbling was used by hunters as well as animals to relive their pains. The healing property of water enriched with volcanic soil pulled the international tourists from all over the world. The hunters, fishermen and elderly farmers used this water for treating arthritic aches. The various soldier groups visited this hot springs to lessen pain, heal wounds, recuperate and replenish their energy.

Indian Medical Tourism

A 5000 years old Yoga retreats, Buddhist pilgrimages and meditation centers were the indicators for the existence of medical tourism in India in the past. Ever since yoga's birth, India received constant medical travelers and spiritual students from foreign countries hoping to master the benefit of alternative medicine. After the emergence of Buddhism in India, it became epi-center of Eastern cultural, spiritual and medicinal progress. Even after the development of western clinical medicine, the India's spiritually healing center become Mecca for alternative medicine practitioners. The new age movement in the US and flower child movement made the health tourism industry to become flourishing and made to develop India's healthcare infrastructure.

European Health Tourism

Until 16th century, much of the Europeans are pilgrimages of other medical tourism destination. The Europeans medical tourism started only after the rediscovery of Roman baths in Italy. Entire communities sprung up around spa towns like Baden Baden, Aachen and Bath. The emergence of Bath or AquaeSulis as a major medical tourism destination for Europe and it became famous wellness center and recreation place for rich and executives. In 1720s, the nobles and grantees of leisure from other parts of Europe were flooded to Bath for healing and cleansing. England was not only the place for medical tourism in Europe. In 1326, a small village in East Belgium became very famous after the discovery of iron-rich hot springs. And it became town of waters and it developed as a full-fledged resort only in the 16th century. Visitors from all over Europe flocked to this village for relief from gout, rheumatism and intestinal disorders. Peter the Great and Victor Hugo were beneficiaries of the iron-rich springs. The spa means "salude per aqua" (health through waters) was coined around this time and it was applied to any health resorts which did not practice traditional clinical medicine.

MEDICAL TOURISM IN 21ST CENTURY AND BEYOND

During 18th and 19th century Europeans and Americans continued to travel to spa towns in Europe for curing disease like tuberculosis. During 20th century, rich people traveled to Europe and USA to receive high class medical treatments available. In 1933, the American Board of Medical Specialties was established to set the standards for medical treatment at global level. In 1958, European Union of Medical Specialties was established to improve health care facilities of their member countries. During 1960s India became famous destination for pilgrims from abroad. Due to lack of quality health care in developing nations, the patients travel to Europe and USA to get treatment. In 1997, due to economic crisis in most of the countries in Asia, the government officials were asked to market their countries for medical tourism activities and make effort to create premiere destinations for international healthcare. Thailand offered plastic surgery at one tenth of cost charged by Western countries.

The Joint Commission International (JCI) was to confirm the international standards due to emergence of health providers around the world. In 2000s, nearly 150000 US citizens traveled to medical tourism destinations in Asia and Latin America for dental and cosmetic treatment. During this period, India, Thailand Malaysia and Singapore became medical tourism destination due to JCI accreditation. In 2007, the number international patients cross their border became three lakhs, the largest ever in medical tourism history. In 2008, several health care insurance companies in USA, started tie up with hospitals in Asia and South America for non-emergency procedures. Now India, Malaysia, Singapore and Thailand became familiar medical tourism destination at global level and able to attract international medical tourists from all the continents in the world.

Medical Tourism at Global Level

At global level the medical tourism industry is developing at faster rate and it is commonly observed that patients from developed countries travelling to regions once characterized as "third world", where high quality health treatments are available at affordable price. As per the assessment made by International Medical Travel Journal, the worth medical tourism business at global level is US$ 13 billion and the number of medical tourists to all countries in 2017 was estimated at 14 to 16 million. At global level, the medical tourism business expected to reach US $ 179.6 billion by 2026, registering at 21.9 percent CAGR between the year 2017 and 2026. According to patient beyond border, a medical travel advocacy group for consumers, 14 to 15 million patients travelled outside their countries to seek medical treatment in 2017.In India, the medical tourism industry is showing considerable growth since

2010. The number of international patients taken medical treatment in India during 2017 was 495056, which is more than doubled compare to previous year.

The Top 25 Medical Travel Destination

Among the top 25 countries in medical tourism business the first five places are captured by USA, South Korea, Turkey, Thailand and Germany. In Asian continent Thailand plays a leading role. The main reason for attracting international patient to Thailand is competitive cost of treatment, JCI accredited hospitals, quality health care and zero waiting time. In Asia, India stood second position in medical tourism business. The international patients from USA, UK, Canada, Gulf region and Bangladesh are taking medical treatment regularly. The Ministry of Tourism and Ministry of Health, Government of India taking initiatives to promote medical tourism business in India. India is able to attract more one lakh of international patients every year.

Table 1. Top twenty five medical travel destinations

Rank	Country	US$ in Millions
1	USA	3500
2	South Korea	655
3	Turkey	600
4	Thailand	600
5	Germany	575
6	India	450
7	UK	350
8	Malaysia	350
9	Mexico	350
10	Iran	315
11	Jordan	300
12	Taiwan	300
13	UAE	300
14	Poland	300
15	Spain	240
16	Hungary	225
17	Switzerland	175
18	Singapore	150
19	Belgium	150

continues on following page

Table 1. Continued

Rank	Country	US$ in Millions
20	Israel	135
21	Costa Rica	125
22	South Africa	120
23	Brazil	100
24	Czech Republic	30
25	Australia	28
	Total	10430

The above table indicates that more than sixty percent of the total business was achieved by six countries: USA, South Korea, Turkey, Thailand, Germany and India.

Source: International Medical Travel Journal

Mexico

It is Latin American country located at the border of USA, offering specialties include plastic surgery and dentistry. The cost of treatment for dental procedures in Mexico is one-fifth of treatment cost in USA, while other procedure cost a third what they would in the USA. Because of less treatment costs in Mexico, the number USA patients crossing the border to take treatment are increasing every year. This variation in the cost of dental treatment is severely affecting the dental business in USA. Despite the US based dentist horror stories of rampant infections and undetected cases of oral cancer, the business in Mexico are growing with positive feedback from US patients. In Texas, the legislators explored the possibility of allowing health maintenance organization to operate on the both sides of the borders. But US dentist opposed the move and denied to compete with low cost Mexican dentist. Also they claimed that the Mexican legal system does not allow suing Mexican Doctors for malpractice. However majority of the patients took treatment in Mexico expressed their satisfaction about the treatment provided to them. Indeed some US dentist have accepted to the competition and opening offices in Mexico to take advantage of lower cost. More health insurers in US are providing only 60 percent of the actual medical cost. Remaining 40 percent the patient has to spend from their pocket. Due to continuing rise in medical treatment cost in US, many employers in Southern California are having tie-up with insurance companies in Mexico and started sending their employees for routine health care. The number of employees taking treatment in Mexico is more than 5000 every year. In addition to plastic and dental surgeries, the hospitals in Mexico offering bariatric surgery for weight loss, which is not covered by some of the insurers in US. Mexican healthcare providers have big opportunity in their business by treating retired people from US and Canada, who are searching for low cost drugs, dental care and physician services. The cost of treatment is 40 percent lesser than US and most of the uninsured Americans can find better deals on medical procedures in Mexico.

Thailand

Thailand is fast growing destination in medical tourism and it stood first in Asia and it is the fourth largest medical facilities provider for international patients at global level and its revenue is 600 million US$ every year and it is estimated that Thailand receives 3,50,000 medical tourists every year. It has 64 JCI accredited medical facilities, which is three times more than Singapore and six times more than Malaysia.

Price Comparison of some popular procedures is shown in Table 2.

Table 2. Cost of treatment in Thailand

Procedure	Treatment Costs in US $		
	USA	Singapore	Thailand
Coronary Angioplasty	28200	13500	4200
Heart Bypass	123000	17200	15000
Hip Replacement	40300	12000	17000
Gastric Bypass	25000	13700	16800
Hysterectomy	15400	10400	3650
LASIK	4000	3800	2310
Dental Implant	2500	2700	1720
Breast Augmentation	6400	8400	3500

Source: Medical Tourism.com

From the above table, it is observed that the cost of Coronary Angioplasty in Thailand is 85 percent lesser than that of USA. The cost Heart bypass is 88 percent lesser than that of in USA. The other treatment is also comparatively lesser than cost in USA and Singapore.

United States of America

Since the cost of treatment in USA is higher than other developed and developing countries, lakhs of Americans travel to other country for taking medical treatment. The uninsured Americans also seek low cost medical treatment in South America and

Asia. According to a 2015 report by US International Trade Commission between 150000 and 320000 Americans travel abroad every year to receive health care. Due to quality health care, advanced medical technology and trained physicians the hospitals in America attracts more than one lakh of patients from other country every year. Several hospitals in USA has exclusive international department to treat foreign patients. Most of this hospitals offers, service assistance, nursing assistants, and accommodation facilities for accompany, finances and transportation including air ambulance service.

South Korea

The medical tourism activities in South Korea is growing at faster rate due to high tech facilities in hospitals and providing cost effective quality health care to the international patients. Most of the hospitals in Korea are private and the Doctors working there are internationally qualified. The hospitals are equipped with latest technology and medical equipment. The treatments like cosmetic surgery, dental, eye care, medical check-up and cancer treatment. Majority of the international patients are from Russia, Japan, Kazakhstan, Mongolia and USA. According to Korea Health Industry Development Institute, the number of international patients took treatment in 2016 is 364000, which is up from 60000 in 2009. South Korean government expects one million international patients' visits by 2022.

Turkey

Turkey's medical tourism is one the fastest industry and it is estimated to contribute $ 4 billion to the country's economy annually.Accoriding to Istabul International Health Tourism Association,, Turkey was able to attract 75,000 international patients in 2007 and it is increased to 700000 in 2017 over a period of ten years. Due to increased health care cost in Europe, people travel thousands of mile to take treatment and they can save up to 90 percent on the cost of treatment. The main motivating factor for medical tourism growth in Turkey is low cost medical treatment (the average cost for heart valve replacement in US is $150000, whereas it is just $17000 in Turkey), shorter waiting times (18 months for knee replacement in UK, whereas it just two weeks in Turkey). The ministry of Health,Turkey, planned to attract two million patients fromabroad .

According to Healthcare Travel Council, Turkey has treated 746000 international medical tourists in 2016and generated $5.8 billion revenue. This revenue is expected to increase $5 billion by 2020. Turkey earned this revenue, with 90% from medical operations and remaining ten percent from cosmetic surgery and hair transplants. Among the total number of patients underwent for eye surgery, majority are from

Europe. Turkey government encourages and support private business organization to start medical tourism hospitals to achieve their goal.

Germany

Due to high quality medical care, advanced medical technology, strict ethical standards and quick access to medical specialists, Germany become popular destination for international patients. There are two main reasons for patients traveling to other nations for medical treatment is low cost and access to treatment which is not available in their home country. The cost of treatment in Germany is significantly lower than in many industrialized nations. The standards of health care in Germany hospitals are extremely high and the Doctors and Nurses are properly trained and continually educated to update the latest developments in their field. German hospitals are equipped with high-tech imaging technology such as 3D ultrasound and MRI etc. German clinics have surgical robots, heart catheters and targeted radiation therapies for cancer patients. Germany has formulated strict laws to protect patient safety and maintain hygienic conditions in hospitals and created a transparent system in medical treatment and comprehensive follow-up care. There is no exact statistics about number of international patients' visits to German hospitals. But it is estimated that 150000 to 250000 international patients are visiting Germany every year.

The range of treatments offered by German hospitals to international patients is Cancer, fertility treatment, Cardiology and cardiac surgery, orthopedic surgery, Neurology and neurosurgery, Obesity treatment, treatment for kidney ailments, alternative treatment for maladies and Ophthalmology. There is facility for diagnostic work as well as comprehensive health and wellness check-ups. Germany has health spas, wellness resorts and rehabilitation centers, which attracts millions of tourists each year. The waiting times for taking surgical treatments are less and most of the Doctors and nursing staff speak English which could make to attract patients from English speaking countries. Majority of the international patients are from Middle East and USA to take orthopedic treatment as well as Cardio related treatments.

Singapore

Singapore is one of the leading medical tourism destinations in Asia. The hospitals in Singapore are high-quality and equipped with advanced medical technology. Singapore health care hospitals are JCI accredited and the cost of treatment is low when compare to USA,UK and Canada. The private hospitals have well trained Doctors and nursing staff and it has English speaking environment. Singapore has set up International Patient Service Centers (IPSCs) and it act like medical tourism agent. It facilitates international patients and expatriates coming to Singapore for taking treatment. This IPSC is attached to each medical tourism hospitals and it would provide cost of treatment and coordinate appointments with healthcare specialists. Singapore treats international patients who come under international health insurance plan. As per the Ministry of Health, the cost of treatment for various medical ill is given in Table 3.

Table 3. Cost of treatment in Singapore

Sl. No.	Procedure Detail	Cost of Treatment in Singapore Dollars
1	Normal Delivery	6048 - 11264
2	C-section delivery	9024 -17125
3	Gall bladder removal surgery	5500 - 8600
4	Hemorrhoidectomy	3000 - 3500
5	Hand, wrist or finger surgery	4300 - 7200
6	Heart bypass surgery	16050 - 25000
7	Hernia repair	4400 - 8000
8	Hip Replacement	8550 – 12850
9	Hysterectomy for benign conditions	6400 - 9500
10	Arthroscopic knee surgery	8550 - 10700
11	Knee replacement surgery	11750 - 17100
12	Urinary stones with lithotripsy	3200 -5150
13	Tonsillectomy and/or Adenoidectomy	4050 - 5350
14	Breast Lump removal biopsy	5450 - 10700

Source: www.moh.gov.sg

Majority of the international patients are coming from Indonesia Malaysia and China. Australia, UK, Hong Kong and Thailand are the other source market for Singapore medical tourism. Singapore has hospital capacity to treat more than 5 lakh international patients annually.

Malaysia

Malaysia is providing quality health care to the international patients and became medical tourism hub of Asia. Well-equipped, trained Doctors and nursing staffs from UK and USA and low cost of treatment are the main reason for attracting international patients to Malaysia. It has more than seventy private hospitals for providing health care to international patients. Most of the hospitals are internationally accredited by agencies like the Joint Commission International (JCI), Malaysia Society for Quality in Health, Australian Council on Healthcare Standards (ACHS) and the Reproductive Technology Accreditation Committee (RTAC) of Australia. Malaysia has treated 643000 international patients in 2011. With quality healthcare, patient safety, affordable and easy accessible, it has able to attract 12 lakhs patients in 2018. The revenue generated also surged from US$127 million to US$ 362 million. The main source of patients to Malaysia is Indonesia, Philippines, China, Singapore, Australia, Japan, UK and USA. The medical tourism sector has recorded a compound annual growth rate of 16 to 17 percent over the last five years. It is ahead of global average 10-12 percent.

Table 4. Medical tourism in other countries

Sl. No.	Name of the Country	Treatment Detail	Source Country
1	Costa Rica	Dental, Cosmetic, Preventive Medicine and other surgery.	North America and Canada
2	Brazil	Cosmetic	USA,Canada
3	Spain	Ortho, Dental, Cosmetic, Eye	UK, USA.
4	Hungary	Dental. Cosmetic	European countries.
5	Poland	Dental, Ortho, Dermatology, Eye, Cardio	European Union.
6	Iran	Cosmetic, Ophthalmology, Cardiac surgery, Spine and organ transplant.	Turkey, Iraq, Pakistan, Oman and Afghanistan.
7	Jordan	Ortho, Stem cell, Cardio.	Palestine, Iraq, Saudi Arabia, Libya, Nigeria, Kazakhstan
8	Israel	Cosmetic .Born marrow treatment, Heart surgeries, Spine surgery, Organ transplant and infertility treatment.	Russia, Ukraine, East European countries, Cyprus
9	UAE	Orthopedics, Dermatology and Ophthalmology.	Asian Countries, Arab and GCC countries and Europe.
10	Belgium	Orthopedic treatment of hips and knees, Heart surgery, Caesarean sections and hysterectomies.	Netherland, France, Germany Luxembourg. UK, and Italy
11	Switzerland	Medical Spa treatments, Cosmetic surgery,IVF treatment, Neuro surgery, and Orthopedic.	Brazil, Russia, India, China, Middle Eastern countries.
12	Czech Republic	Cardio surgery, Dentistry, Eye surgery, Neuro surgery, Oncology, Orthopedics and Plastic surgery.	UK, Germany and Russia.
13	Taiwan	Coronary Artery Bypass Grafts, Hip replacement, Facelift, IVF, Gastric bypass and Dentistry.	Asia, USA, Europe.
14	Australia	Dentistry, Cosmetic surgery, Surrogacy, Neurology, Orthopedics, Weight loss surgery.	Papua New Guinea, New Caledonia, NZ, China, Bamgladesh.
15	South Africa	Cosmetic surgery, Dentistry, Ophthalmology, Orthopedics and others.	USA, Britain, Western Europe and Middle East.
16	UK	Ortho, Dental, Organ Transplant, Heart surgery.	UAE, Irish Republic, SPAIN, France, Gibraltar.

Source: www.health tourism.com

Medical Tourism in India

Medical Tourism industry in India is growing exponentially and becoming one of the major players in worldwide. Increasing medical cost, high medical insurance cost, increasing number of uninsured and underinsured in developed nations, long waiting time in the home country and lack of quality care in their home country are main factors for international patients traveling to India. The quality health care at affordable rate, cheaper air fare, internet facilities and tourism attractions are considered as major driving force for patients to cross border for medical treatment (Reddy & Qadeer 2010).

Number of International Patients Visits to India and FEE

According to Ministry Tourism's written reply, it is observed that the total number of medical tourists visit India in 2017 was 495,000 and the number had stood at around 2.34 lakh in 2015 and that of in 2016 was 4.27 lakh. The foreign exchange earned during 2015, 2016 and 2017 are 135193 crores, 154146 crores and 177874 crores.

Table 5. Number of medical tourists and foreign exchange earned

Sl. No.	Year	Number of Medical Tourists	Foreign Exchange Earned in Crores
1	2017	495000	177874
2	2016	427000	154146
3	2015	234000	135193

Source: Ministry of Tourism, Government of India.

Bangladesh and Afghanistan are major source countries for India in terms of medical tourism. The number of medical tourists visit India in 2015, 2016 and 2017 are 1.2 lakh, 2.1 lakh and 2.21 lakh respectively. Likewise the number of medical tourists from Afghanistan to India in 2015, 2016 and 2017 are 27505, 61231 and 55681 respectively. The other countries from where major numbers of international patients taking treatment in India are Oman, Iraq, Maldives, Yemen, Sudan and Uzbekistan. The NitiAayog has identified medical value travel as a major source of FEE and India has 18% of the global medical tourism market. By 2020, India will get 20 percent global market share in Medical Tourism and achieve 9 billion worth business. The major medical treatment offered in India for international patient is cardiology, orthopedics, transplants and ophthalmology. India has high credibility in wellness, preventive and alternative medicine.

Medical Tourism in India

Progress to promote medical tourism in India initiated in the late 2002 when the McKinsey-CII outlined the potential for Medical tourism. In the same year, when the country was planning to develop tourism, the then Finance Minister Jaswant Singh called for country to become a global health destination and urged for airport infrastructure to ease the arrival of international patients. Then government has modernized and developed airports and road infrastructure for tourism development. Government has declared 45 hospitals as center of excellence for treating international patients and introduced medical visa for medical tourists. Ministry of Health and Family welfare created a board called National Accreditation Board for hospitals and declared medical tourism as service export and provided tax concessions.

Gupta, (2008) in his study found that the states like Karnataka, Gujarat, Tamil Nadu, Maharashtra and Kerala took effort to promote health care tourism and announced a separate policy for medical tourism. Hospitals were upgrading the technology on par with international standards and started provided separate department for international patients. Hospitals are involved in the process of continuous innovation of products, services and focusing on cost effective-customer oriented technology. Many healthcare hospitals are increasingly participating in international trade fairs and exhibitions to attract international customers. Currently more than 38 hospitals are JCI accredited hospitals in India and spread across Indian major cities like Delhi, Mumbai, Chennai, Bangalore, Hyderabad, Kolkata and Chandigarh. There are 662 NABH accredited hospitals are available in India. Out of different purpose of visit by foreigners in India, the percentage of tourists visiting for medical tourism is ranging from 2.7 percent to 3 percent.

Cost Competitiveness

The cost of various medical treatments in India is compared with different countries as shown in Table 6.

From the above table, it is observed that the cost treatment in India for procedures like Heart bypass, Heart valve replacement, Hip replacement, Knee replacement, Facelift and Lap Gastric bypass in India is compared with countries like USA, UAE, Costa Rica, Mexico, South Korea, Malaysia, Singapore and Thailand is compared. Shanmugam, K. (2013) the cost of treatment in India is comparatively less. The cost of Heart bypass surgery in USA is US$ 133000 and that of in India is US$ 7000. The cost of Heart bypass treatment in India is just 5.26 percent of cost in USA. The cost treatment in India is lesser than the cost of treatment in other Asian countries like Singapore, Malaysia and Thailand.

Table 6. Cost competitiveness in US$

Procedure	USA	India	Thailand	Singapore	Malaysia	South Korea	Mexico	Costa Rica	UAE
Heart Bypass	133000	7000	22000	16300	12000	31700	27000	24100	40900
Heart valve Replacement	140000	9500	25000	22000	13400	42000	30000	30000	50600
Hip Replacement	57000	7020	12700	1200	7500	10600	13900	11400	46000
Knee Replacement	53000	9200	11500	9600	12000	11800	14900	10700	40200
Face Lift	16000	4800	5000	7500	6400	6600	11300	4900	NA
Lap Gastric Bypass	52000	9300	13000	16500	12700	9300	11000	NA	NA

Source: https://www.researchgate.net/publication/259375271

Opportunities for Medical Tourism in India

The cost of quality healthcare treatment in India is one tenth of cost in USA and also it lesser than the cost in other neighboring countries. Due to well qualified and experienced Doctors and English speaking staff become major attraction for international patients. India is already familiar with natural treatment like Ayurveda Unani and Siddha. After entering into global market, India receives lot of foreign tourists as well as employees from abroad for the international companies. The Non Resident Indians are another major source for medical tourism. Doctors in the western countries started prescribing Indian system of medicine to their patients and this make many patients to visit for medical treatment. Soaring medical cost, high insurance premiums, large number of uninsured/under insured and long waiting time in developed countries makes the people to cross the border for medical treatment. Insurance companies and employers are preferred to send their customers to abroad where the medical cost is less. Demand from countries which has poor healthcare facilities also increases. The main opportunity for medical tourism is contribution to healthcare economies. Due to this, other infrastructure like road, transport, pharmaceuticals, hotels and restaurants are also developing and creating job opportunity in Tourism sector.

CHALLENGES AND ISSUES

The main challenges of Indian Medical Tourism industries are as follows:

1. Lack of coordination among various players like hospitals, airline and hotels.
2. The government support to medical tourism is not encouraging.
3. Lack of sanitation facilities, cleanliness and hygienic conditions in the hospitals and other tourism places.
4. Lack of uniform pricing policy for different treatments is different for hospitals.
5. The city traffic becomes major constraint for international patient to reach hospital from airport.
6. Lack international insurance policy for patients from abroad and no MOU with foreign insurance companies and Hospitals in India.
7. Lack of medical specialists in healthcare industries.
8. The availability of hotels and cost of accommodation is another hindrance to middle-level international travelers visiting India.
9. Low investment in hospital infrastructure development.

CONCLUSION

Medical tourism is not new concept; it was practiced in the early 4000 BC itself in Egypt, Rome, India, China and Japan. In 2000 BC Sumerians offered healthcare facilities mineral water springs. A 5000 year old Yoga retreats and meditation cetres were the indicator for existence Indian medical tourism. Among the top twenty five destinations at global level USA, South Korea, Thailand, Turkey and Germany stood first five places in providing medical treatment to international patients .In Asia, Malaysia, Singapore and India are the developing medical tourism destinations. After 2000, India has emerged as growing medical tourism business center it has capacity to treat more than four lakhs of international patients every year. The main reason for the development of medical tourism in India is due to quality healthcare at affordable cost, good infrastructure, less waiting time, cheaper air fare, internet facility and tourism attractions. India has 662 NABH and 38 JCI accredited hospitals and well qualified and experienced medical specialists. By sorting out the challenges of medical tourism by the Indian government, India can able to get 20 percent global market share by 2020 and achieve 9 billion worth business. Due to quality healthcare facilities available in most of the leading countries in the world, the medical tourism business is expected to reach US$179.6 billion by 2026.

REFERENCES

Balaban, V., & Marano, C. (2010). Medical tourism research: A systematic review. *International Journal of Infectious Diseases, 14*, e135–e135. doi:10.1016/j.ijid.2010.02.1784

Gupta, A. S. (2008). Medical tourism in India: Winners and losers. *Indian Journal of Medical Ethics*, *5*(1), 4–5. doi:10.20529/IJME.2008.002 PMID:18630244

Oberhelman, S. M. (2014). Anatomical votive reliefs as evidence for specialization at healing sanctuaries in the Ancient Mediterranean World. *Athens Journal of Health*, *1*(1), 47–62. doi:10.30958/ajh.1-1-4

Reddy, S., & Qadeer, I. (2010). Medical tourism in India: Progress or predicament? *Economic and Political Weekly*, 69–75.

Shanmugam, K. (2013). *Medical Tourism in India: Progress, opportunities and challenges*. Madras School of Economics.

Chapter 2
Medical Tourism:
Understanding the Phenomenon

Oğuz Doğan
Antalya Bilim University, Turkey

Nedim Yüzbaşıoğlu
Akdeniz University, Antalya, Turkey

ABSTRACT

The number of travels around the world to benefit from health services provided abroad is increasing every year. The high level of global demand for health services has influenced the rapid development of the medical tourism industry. Due to these developments in the industry, a global market has emerged, the medical tourism market. Countries operating in the industry are also striving to gain share from this large market or to increase their existing market shares. In this study, different perspective on global phenomenon, medical tourism, medical tourism market, and leader destinations in the industry are examined in detail.

INTRODUCTION

Tourism is a dynamic industry that is constantly changing and renewing itself. The rapid changes in the industry have affected the change of tourism preferences and the emergence of new types of tourism. The new types of tourism have contributed to the diversification of the tourist profile and the emergence of tourism industries that serve different tourist profiles (Durgun, 2007). One of these industries is the medical tourism industry.

DOI: 10.4018/978-1-7998-3427-4.ch002

Medical tourism emerging from the combination of health services and tourism services, can be defined as travelling abroad to get health services that are not available or expensive for individuals in their home countries. Individuals can also benefit from the tourism services provided in the countries where they have travelled to receive health services. Although the demand for medical tourism has increased in recent decades, travels to be healthy are as old as human history. For example, in the Middle East tradition, it is believed that Cleopatra established one of the world's first SPA centers in BC 25. Also, it is stated that there were many SPAs and thermals built by Romans in Europe, Middle East, and North Africa between BC 54 and AD 450 (Erfurt-Cooper & Cooper, 2009).

Today, medical tourism has become a global phenomenon. Millions of patients travel abroad every year and the number of these patients are increasing very fast. Moreover, many destinations providing high-quality medical tourism services at low prices have emerged. Therefore, it is important to understand the dynamics of this phenomenon. For this purpose, in this chapter different opinions on the term medical tourism, motivational factors driving medical tourism, medical services offered in the industry, and leader destinations are discussed.

THE CONCEPT OF MEDICAL TOURISM

Globalization has contributed to emergence of medical tourism (Roy et. al, 2018), which is a way to offer healthcare services to foreign patients in a host country (Rydback & Hyder, 2018). Medical tourism is a kind of niche tourism arising a result of the rapid rise of the number of travels abroad to access to medical services (Suess et. al, 2018). Thus, it has become a global phenomenon in the few decades (Chew & Darmasaputra, 2015).

There is no consensus on the definition of medical tourism (Lee & Spisto, 2007) but it can be defined as travelling across international borders with the intention of obtaining healthcare services (Roy et. al, 2018) in order to find a solution to health problems or improve the health conditions. Although there is a debate whether traveling abroad for obtaining healthcare services should be called as "health tourism" or "medical tourism", Pocock & Phua (2011) stated that there is a consensus in the related literature that medical tourism is a subset of health tourism. Smith and Puczko (2009) stated that health tourism is composed of medical tourism and wellness tourism, which means that medical tourism is a subset of health tourism. Garcia-Altes (2005) used the term "health tourism", as an umbrella term, to explain the all health-related tourism activities. Connell (2006) expressed that there should be a differentiation between medical tourism and health tourism, as medical tourism is a correct term used in cases requiring medical operations. Saiprasert (2011) specified that medical tourism and health tourism are two different terms, but the terms are related to each other because medical tourism is conceptually a subset of health tourism. From this point of view, medical tourism is used as a general term in cases involving more aggressive methods (surgeries, etc.) and medical controls where obtaining better health conditions is an essential component of travelling abroad (Connell, 2013). However, Labonté (2013) advocated that the term medical travel is more suitable to explain the phenomenon because medical tourism can mean an add-on to holiday package, which cause misunderstanding that holiday is primary purpose. Although there are many debates on the term, medical tourism is widely accepted to explain this new phenomenon.

Some researchers in the field of anthropology (Inhorn, 2009; Kangas, 2010; Song, 2010) criticized the term medical tourism because according to them the term is insufficient to describe the different types of medical travel that people take, suggested recreational activities, pains and sufferings of the patients, and their experiences. Instead of the term medical tourism, therefore, some researchers suggested different terms. For example, Matarros (2005) suggested the term "medical migration", Milstein and Smith (2006) suggested the term "medical migrants", and Kangas (2010) suggested the term "biotechnological or biomedical pilgrims". According to these researchers, these terms are more accurate in explaining the practices performed in this type of tourism. These researchers approached medical tourism from anthropological perspective and examined the phenomenon of people performing medical tourism movements. It is considered that those suggested terms are covered by the term medical tourism. On the other hand, economists describe the phenomenon as "medical value travel export" or "medical tourism export". Because according to economists, the money leaved by the foreign patients in the country could be taken into consideration as export earnings (Labonté, 2013).

Some researchers in medical journals advocated that medical tourism only consists of health care services (Yu and Ko, 2012). However, unlike these researchers, Jagyasi (2008) asserted that medical tourism is often a long-distance or overseas travel movement beneficial health care services that are directly or indirectly related to a person's recreation, business or other purposes, while Heung et. al (2010) asserted that medical tourism includes relaxation, recreation and leisure activities as well as healthcare services. Bookman and Bookman (2007) indicated that patients buy packages that include airport transfer, accommodation, and a post-operative holiday in addition to treatments. Thus, medical tourism is a synthesis of healthcare services and tourism services. People can consider tourist attractions of a destination where they seek health care services and decide accordingly. Additionally, the countries use their tourist attractions to attract patients. In their advertisement activities, tourist attractions and health care services are synthesized.

New countries which provide better quality and affordable health services have emerged due to growing of world population, improvement of life quality, and increase of costs of health services in some countries. The reasons for increasing demand for medical tourism are 1) to get rid of long waiting lists, 2) to get better quality services in less time, 3) to reach the high health technology, 4) to decrease healthcare costs, 5) lack of specific treatments in the country of residence 6) willingness to travel and culture visits as well as treatment, 7) people's desire to survive (Connell, 2013; Turkey Health Foundation, 2010). In fact, the primary reason for participating in medical tourism is economic reasons. Therefore, medical tourism can be summarized as "accessing first class services at third class prices" (Connell, 2013). Thus, health care services have become a global service, and the medical tourism industry has been a rapidly growing industry (Yıldırım & Altun, 2006).

Medical tourism can be divided into three categories, depending on where patients go as tourists to receive some form of medical services (Deloitte, 2008a);

- *Outbound medical tourism* involves domestic patients travelling to other countries.
- *Inbound medical tourism* is in which international patients travel to the country.
- *Intrabound medical tourism* involves only domestic travels of patients.

It is emphasized in some medical tourism definitions that medical tourism means travel from the host country to another country (e.g. Johnston et. al., 2010; Lunt and Carrera, 2010). However, medical tourism also includes domestic travels to get healthcare services. Voight et al. (2010) noted that people travel in their own countries to obtain medical treatments. But, they also maintained that these individuals should benefit from tourism services such as accommodation, sightseeing, etc. after a treatment so that they can be called as medical tourists as individuals participating in other types of medical tourism.

Although there is no consensus about the term used to describe travelers travelling to protect and improve their health, individuals combining tourism services and medical treatments can be called as medical tourist (Cohen, 2008; Helble, 2011). Munro (2012) stated that medical tourists are international patients who are travelling from one country to another. Cohen (2008) advocated that in the statistical data about medical tourists belonging to any country, all foreign patients treated in that country are included as medical tourists, but not all foreigners treated in this data can be called as a medical tourist. Because data includes foreigners who are expatriates or have lived in the country for a long time, which are not considered as a tourist (Cohen, 2008).

MOTIVATIONAL FACTORS DRIVING MEDICAL TOURISM

Travel motivation is one of the important elements of tourism. Understanding why people travel and which factors are important in choosing a particular destination is very useful in tourism planning and marketing. Dann (1997), one of the researchers studying on this subject, revealed that the concept of push and pull factors (Doshi, 2008). Push and pull factors are defined as different aspects of travel motivations (Froelich, 2012). Push factors that are briefly reasons for travel, are the internal reasons enable individuals to search for activities to meet their needs such as desire to escape from the place of residence, search for innovation, search for adventure, desire to fulfill dreams, self-discovery, recreation and leisure, desire to be healthy, prestige and socialization (Doshi, 2008; Froelich, 2012; Saiprasert, 2011). Pull factors that are the aspects of a destination and attract tourists can be defined as tangible and intangible features such as natural and historical attractions, physical environment, infrastructure, sport and entertainment facilities, goods and services offered (Doshi, 2008; Saiprasert, 2011). Push factors decisive in the desire to travel, while pull factors decisive in the choosing a destination (Froelich, 2012).

Push Factors in Medical Tourism

Push factors for medical tourism can be stated as healthcare costs, long waiting lists, lack of specific services, and privacy and confidentiality (Eissler, 2010; Cannon Hunter, 2007; Altın et al., 2011; Sarwar et al., 2012).

- *Healthcare Costs:* There are numerous factors influencing the individuals' motivations to participate in medical tourism movements in the related literature. The most important one of this factors are high healthcare costs which are frequently emphasized in the literature (Eissler, 2010). Price differences for different medical treatment and the desire to save costs are the primary factors for medical tourism. The cost factor is particularly important for millions of patients who have no health insurance and have health insurance in developed countries that cover simple operational treatments but do not cover the costs of treatments received in the international industry (Altın et al., 2011). The healthcare costs in developed countries are higher than in developing countries. The costs are primary motivation for participation in medical tourism for many American patients (Sarwar et al., 2012). Eissler (2010) asserted that the costs of some orthopedic and cardiac treatments in USA are higher that between 40% and 90% compared to the costs of the same procedures in other countries. Sarwar et al. (2012) stated that the rapid increase in the number of destinations providing medical tourism services and the low cost due to the high level of competition in the industry as the most motivating factor in the participation of patients in medical tourism movements in order to benefit from health services abroad.

- *Long Waiting List:* The long waiting periods for health services in the country of residence are another reason affecting the motivation to participate in medical tourism movements (Eissler, 2010). Altın et al (2012) maintained that the healthcare system of some developed countries, such as UK and Canada, waiting periods for some treatments may exceed 18 months. The cost of this kind of services provided by private clinics can be high (Altın et al., 2011). Waiting periods for minor operations such as knee reconstruction, for example, may exceed 18 months in the UK and 2 years in Australia and Canada (Connell, 2011). The large number of options in global healthcare industry allows patients to receive the same treatments in any country, rather than waiting long for the treatments in their home country (Eissler, 2010). Therefore, patients seek alternative health services abroad (Altın et al., 2011)
- *Lack of Specific Services:* Patients travel abroad in order to reach the treatments not available in their home country (Eissler, 2010). Altın et al. (2012) stated that restrictions imposed by society and legal institutions on certain treatments, such as stem cell treatments, surrogacy, organ transplants, determination of sex of unborn child, lead to the need to travel abroad for such treatments.
- *Privacy and Confidentiality:* Patients have concerns about confidentiality as far as health care is provided in their home country. For instance, although medical records in USA are protected by law, such as by insurance companies and courts, they can be accessed by others. Privacy and confidentiality is needed for some treatments such as drug rehabilitation, plastic surgery, gender reassignment (Altın et al., 2012). For this reason, patients can participate in medical tourism movements in order not record their services.

Pull Factors in Medical Tourism

Pull factors for medical tourism can be stated as goods/services quality, easy access to information needed, employer/insurance company, and attraction of a holiday (Sarwar et al., 2012; Altın et al., 2011).

- *Goods/Services Quality:* Quality has become a complementary element in the rapidly developing and customer-oriented healthcare industry. People living in wealthy countries travel to less developed countries for high quality health services as well as low costs. The quality can be examined in medical tourism in two categories: 1) technical quality, that is the quality of equipment used in facilities, 2) service quality, that is the quality of services provided by medical personnel and facility managers to patients. The service quality is more important than technical quality for patients (Sarwar et al., 2012, s.3).

- *Easy Access to Information Needed:* The internet is one of the major push factor driving medical tourism (Gan & Frederick, 2011). Medical tourists can access the information they need about the healthcare services provided in destinations where they have no information about them via internet. Through the internet, they can easily access to hospitals' websites, travel agencies and the patient who previously benefited from the services provided in the destination. This is another factor effective in patients' participation in medical tourism (Altın et al., 2011).
- *Employer/Insurance Company:* Upon the realization of financial savings thanks to medical tourism, some companies and insurance firms have made agreements with clinics in other countries for the provision of health care abroad. For example, the Blue Cross Blue Shield insurance company in South Carolina has an agreement with Bumrungrad International Hospital in Thailand and Apollo Hospital in India. The company covers the costs of the patient and a person accompanying him (Altın et al., 2011). Some Gulf countries and Middle East countries which do not have the necessary infrastructure, technology, and specialized labors needed provide support to their citizens for receiving health care abroad, and cover the costs of the patient and those accompanying him (Connell, 2011).
- *Attraction of A Holiday:* The attraction of the location of a destination is an advantage in the marketing of medical tourism with sea, beach and coastal attractions, which can be very important for medical tourist (Bookman & Bookman 2007). Complex and costly healthcare services in developed countries push people to receive health services abroad by combining them with a holiday (Cannon Hunter, 2007). The idea of combining the healing process with an exotic holiday with the health service can attract most people (Altın et al., 2011).

Gan & Frederick (2011) examined a number of different studies to determine the main pull and push factors in medical tourism. They divided pull and push factors into two categories. The pull factors comprise of globalization and institutional factors. *Globalization* includes "convenience of using the internet to gather information, ease of travel between countries, and emergence of low-cost telecommunication and economy air travel". *Institutional factors* include "favorable, bonuses and cash incentives by employers, and incentives by insurance companies". The push factors consist of consumer-specific factors and country-specific factors. *The consumer-specific factors* include "cost savings (lower bureaucratic and administrative fees, lower labor and training costs, lower malpractice insurance or litigation costs, and lower pharmaceutical charges), minimal waiting lists, more personalized care, availability of treatments, and greater privacy and confidentiality". *The country-specific factors* include "political concerns, social and cultural compatibility, freedom from disasters, bioethical legislation, international accreditation and reputation, quality of care, and advanced medical technology and equipment" (Gan & Frederick, 2011).

Numerous hospitals have started to operate in different countries that want to get a share from the medical tourism market. However, the reliability of these hospitals and whether they meet the standards has become an important issue in the industry. For this reason, Joint Commission International (JCI) was established in 1994 (Turkey Health Ministry, 2012). JCI is a sub-branch of The Joint Commission on Accreditation of Healthcare Organizations (JCAHO) which is the best-known health care accreditation group in the United States. Today, there are over 220 accredited health institutions worldwide (Taleghani et al., 2011). This accreditation is important for medical tourists and it can be a pull factor for the tourists. Individuals seeking health care abroad can look for a JCI accreditation in hospital selection process.

MEDICAL TOURISM MARKET

The medical tourism market is defined as a group of consumers that affect the individual's expectations and needs and share certain characteristics that make it the potential recipient of the health service or product (Thomas, 2005). Due to the aging population in developed countries and high healthcare costs, the demand for healthcare has increased and led to the emergence and rapid development of medical tourism market. Kotler et al. (2008) advocated that the firms operating in medical tourism market could not realize this rapid development, however they perform some activities to obtain a market share in recent years. They described these activities as (Kotler et al., 2008);

- Hospitals advertise in newspaper and magazines about the services they provide, the physical properties (facilities, technology, etc.) they have, along with tourism products of the destination to attract customers (Kotler et al., 2008; Johnston et al., 2010).
- Some hospital managers can participate in television shows to provide information about their services.
- Some doctors open clinics with interesting office arrangement in the places where patients may be interested and try to attract new patients through the treatment methods.

Bookman & Bookman (2007) examined the medical tourism services in three categories, namely, *i. invasive* (dental procedures, plastic surgery, etc.), *ii. diagnostic* (blood screening, bone density testing, etc.) and *iii. lifestyle* (antiaging, wellness, stress reduction, etc.). Persic & Jankovic (2012) listed the services offered in medical tourism market following *i. cosmetic surgery* (arm lift, breast augmentation, breast lift-mastopexy, breast reduction, buttocks implants, chemical peels, chin surgery, ear pinning, ear reshaping, eye-bag removal, eyelid lift, face-lift, etc.), *ii. dental procedures* (dental bondings, dental fillings, dental implants, etc.), *iii. medical procedures* (cancer treatment, cardiology procedures, etc.) and *iv. alternative medicine* (acupressure, acupuncture, aromatherapy, ayurveda, balneotherapy, etc). Lee & Spisto (2007) examined the medical tourism services in four categories; *i. treatment of illness* (medical check-ups, health screening, dental treatment, joint replacements, heart surgery, cancer treatment, neurosurgery, transplants, etc.), *ii. enhancement* (cosmetic surgery, facelifts, liposuction, etc.), *iii. wellness* (SPA, thermal and water treatments, acupuncture, aromatherapy, herbal healing, yoga, etc.), and *iv. reproduction* (fertility related treatments). Although there are different categorizations, invasive medical treatments, dental treatments, and alternative traditional treatments are mainly offered in the medical tourism market. Beside these services, medical tourism also includes accommodation, food and beverage services, transportation, entertainment, and other components of destinations such as landscape, attractions, know-how, human resources, etc. (Ile & Tigu, 2017). Additionally, when the websites of some medical tourism providers are examined, it can be seen that medical tourism service packages include medical treatments and emergency medical services, personalized leisure and recreation packages that will help the healing process, interpreters, luxury accommodation during the treatment process, car rental services, and visa procedures (Caballero Danell & Mugomba, 2007).

Labonté (2013) maintained that the size of the medical tourism market is not known exactly. A few countries track the number of medical tourists they host. For instance, The Bumrungrad Hospital-Thailand asserts to host nearly 400 thousand foreign patients annually. However, according to McKinsey (2008) report estimated that the number of medical tourists are not more than 60.000 to 80.000 per year (Labonté, 2013). Merrell et al. (2008) claimed that 500.000 Americans traveled abroad to obtain medical treatments in 2007 and in 2008 Bauer (2009) advocated that 2 million Americans participated in medical tourism (Eissler, 2010). Deloitte (2008a) estimated the number of Americans traveling abroad for medical issues is 750.000 in 2007. Nicolaides (2011) asserted that since 1960's, the health expenditures in OECD countries have been 2% higher than their global domestic products. This shows that OECD countries increasingly spend their national incomes on healthcare services. If this tendency persists, it can be stated that OECD countries will spend at least 25% of their global domestic products on health care services by 2050 (Nicolaides, 2011).

As seen from these different estimations, Connell (2006) stated that the measurement of medical tourist flow varies. This derives from difficulties in the classification of data and lack of statistical information that distinguishes medical tourists from other tourists. The most prominent research was carried out in 1991 in Costa Rica. The findings of the research revealed that %14 of tourists visiting the country to get some medical services such as aesthetic operations and dental treatments (Connell, 2006).

MEDICAL TOURISM DESTINATIONS

Previously patients from developing countries were travelling overseas for obtaining medical services, when a health care needed was inadequate or un available at their home countries (Pocock & Phua, 2011). Nowadays however, the direction of medical travels changed toward developing countries because of some problems in health system of developed countries such as long waiting lists, high costs, and quality problems etc. (Yıldırım & Altun, 2006; Pocock & Phua, 2011). Now, there are intensive patient migrations from developed western countries or wealthy gulf countries to less developed or developing countries in the industry (Connell, 2013; Yeoh et al., 2013).

Medical tourism destinations are located in North and South America, Europe, Asia, and Africa. Destination countries differ in providing health care services. For example, Eastern European countries are preferred for organ transplantations and fertility treatments, South American countries specialized in aesthetic operations, and Asian countries provide traditional treatments for health protecting or promoting (Eissler, 2010). Especially, Asian countries dominate the industry (İçöz, 2009). Asia is the leader in the industry and it can be accepted as the heart of medical tourism (Deloitte, 2008b). Thailand, India, and Singapore attracting the most medical tourists are located in Asia (TÜSİAD, 2009). There two main reasons why the region is a leader in the industry, healthcare cost and up-to-date technology infrastructure. A healthcare service in Asia is sometimes 20% to 30% of the same procedure in the USA or UK. Thailand, India and Singapore, healthcare institutions provide quality services to their patients by investing in the latest medical technologies (Deloitte, 2008b). However, the number of destinations providing medical tourism services is rapidly increasing worldwide (İçöz, 2009; Eissler, 2010).

Thailand

Medical tourism is an integral part of Thailand's tourism and healthcare industry (Heung et al., 2011). The country has become one of the known countries for medical tourism since the beginning of 1970s. Thailand specialized in gender reassignment (Connell, 2006) offers a wide range of medical services, from heart operations to organ transplants, in modern facilities at lower prices than Western countries (Heung et al., 2011). Gender reassignment is very popular among foreign patients. Aesthetic operations and dental care are the main attractive medical services of the country (Reisman, 2010). Thailand's medical industry has developed and expanded since the 1980's, merging with tourism activities. The main reason why the country is successful in medical tourism is the development of medical tourism industry through differentiation strategy supported by the government and national tourism board (Kim et al, 2011). Besides, the advantage of Thailand that maintains its success in the industry and increases its competitiveness is its healthcare services' prices (Heung et al., 2011). The costs of accommodation and health care are cheaper than in other countries (Kim et al., 2011). For example, health care costs are half of the service in Singapore, one-third of service in Hong Kong and one-tenth of service in the USA and Europe (Heung et al., 2011).

Bumrungrad hospital is the first JCI accredited hospital in Asia among the many private hospitals in Thailand. The hospital has 554 bed capacity and employs 1000 doctors, many of whom have trained or worked in countries abroad, most notably in the USA and Japan (Reisman, 2010). The hospital also employs 200 surgeons certified by USA, 70 interpreters. And all the staff can speak English (Connell, 2006). About 60% of medical tourists visiting the country in 2005 received treatment at Bumrungrad hospital (Deloitte, 2008b). The hospital also served 55.000 patients from the USA in 2005 (İçöz, 2009). In 2007, a total of 430,000 foreign patients, 60,000 of whom were from the United States, were treated at the hospital. About half of the patients from the US are Thai immigrants living in the US, while the other half are US citizens who come as medical tourists. In the same year, the hospital received more than $ 110 million in revenues, accounting for about half of the treatment of foreign patients (Reisman, 2010).

Phuket Hospital, another hospital in Thailand, provides translation services in 15 languages and hosts approximately 200,000 international patients annually (Connell, 2006). Bangkok Hospital, one of the most popular destinations for medical tourism, employs 70 interpreters and provides translation services in 26 languages. All of the staff speak English. 200 doctors working in the hospital are certified from USA (Connell, 2011).

India

India, a major destination after Thailand for medical tourism activities in the Asia (Nicolaides, 2011), is seen as modern global center of medical tourism (Connell, 2011). The country has positioned itself as a priority medical destination offering a wide range of services ranging from alternative therapies to highly complex medical procedures (Heung et al., 2011). India offers the highest quality health care at the lowest costs among medical tourism destinations (Kim et al., 2011).

India has become a popular medical tourism destination through the low prices for advanced treatments such as heart operations, articular operations, etc. in addition to simple treatments (Heung et al., 2011). Medical tourists visit the country because of low health care prices (Reisman, 2010). Because main attractiveness of the country is low prices (Heung et al., 2011). For example, heart valve replacement surgery in USA is $200.000, while in India the same procedure is about $10.000 (Reisman, 2010). Besides, India has a well-trained and skilled human capital of well-known doctors and nurses (Heung et al., 2011). Moreover, in the country, 20.000 to 30.000 highly qualified doctors and nurses graduate from medical school every year (Nicolaides, 2011). There is no communication problem between medical tourists and employees, since English is widely spoken in the country (Heung et al., 2011). Nevertheless, the reasons why prices are not high is that half of the country's population is under 25 years of age and labor costs are low (Reisman, 2010).

The country's medical tourism increases by 30% annually (Heung et al., 2011) and it is expected that the country will develop significantly in coming years. India gives special visas to medical tourists in order to support this development. The special visa, called M-visa, is given to medical tourists and individuals accompanying them for their long stay (Eissler, 2010). However, most medical tourists still use a standard tourist visa. This is because medical tourists who medical visa must register with the Foreign Registration Office (FRO) and all medical tourists do not stay in the country for a long time (Connell, 2011).

The Apollo Hospitals chain in India is one of the hospital chains whose reputation has crossed national borders (Connell, 2011). India has 43 hospitals and six of them have JCI accreditation. The country also has in excess of 1.000 pharmacies and nursing school, in excess of 100 tele-medicine services. Approximately 70% of doctors working in hospitals have studied or worked abroad, especially in the USA, UK or Australia (Reisman, 2010). The Apollo hospital advocated that they treated 100.000 patients, most of whom were intra-bound medical tourists (Connell, 2011).

Singapore

Singapore is one of the important destinations in Asian medical tourism with its excellence quality, reliability and internationally accredited hospitals (Heung et al., 2011). The country has become a famous destination in complicated and advanced surgical procedures as well as orthopedic procedures, neurological procedures, oncologic and organ transplant procedures. For example, in 2000, doctors working at the Singapore Hospital successfully separated 10-year-old Nepalese conjoined twins with a successful operation, thus attracted international public attention (Stolley & Watson, 2012).

The Singapore government has defined the medical tourism sector as a new growth area and has strongly supported the sector (Heung et al., 2011). The government has pioneered in making the country a developing medical tourism destination in the region as a biomedical center and attracting high-income patients to the country (Connell, 2011). The country has signed state-level agreements with some states in the Middle East, such as the United Arab Emirates, to provide health services to these states. Singapore has become more attractive for foreign investor due to these agreements (Heung et al., 2011). The country hosts medical tourists from developed countries such as USA, and neighboring countries such as Indonesia and Malaysia (Heung et al., 2011, s.998), and provides private health services for royal families from Middle East and Europe (Kim et al., 2011).

Singapore has the highest number of hospitals accredited by JCI in Asia. The country has 16 hospitals having JCI accreditation. Singapore has one of the highest health care system in Asia. In 2000, World Health Organization (WHO) ranked the country as number one healthcare system in Asia and sixth ahead of USA worldwide (Stolley & Watson, 2012). Connell (2011) stated despite the country's technological superiority and advanced health systems, it is difficult to compete with other destinations in the region. For example, the cost of a service in Thailand is 15-20% cheaper than the cost of the same service in Singapore. Even citizens of the country go to Thailand because of the low cost even for non-essential treatments such as check-ups and teeth whitening, although they have access to high-tech hospitals (Connell, 2011).

Malaysia

Malaysia has entered quite late into the medical tourism market. However, the country has rapidly developed due to its high-quality hospitals with international accreditations and its cultural relationship with Muslim countries. Malaysia offers a wide range of healthcare services including highly demanded healthcare services such as heart surgery, cancer and eye surgery (Connell, 2011). While only 3 hospitals in the country have JCI accreditation (Reisman, 2010, p.174), as of mid-2012, the number of JCI accredited hospitals reached eight (Malaysia-Asia, 2012).

Thanks to its political and economic stability and the government's efforts to improve the medical tourism sector, the country has become an important destination for medical tourism. The number of medical tourists visiting the country increased by an average of 23.6% annually between 2003-2011. The country's market share increased 8-fold compared to its market share in 2003 (International Medical Travel Journal, 2012). In order to encourage medical tourists seeking health services abroad to come to the country, Malaysian government has implemented the "second home" project, a program that enables medical tourist to enter and exit the country for five years (Doshi, 2008). In addition, medical tourists visiting the country are entitled to extent their visas up to six months (Malaysia-Asia, 2012).

Malaysia generally hosts medical tourists from neighboring countries (Connell, 2011). The reasons of this situation can be that Malaysia has good infrastructure, specialized medical staff and many nice touristic places, and that the spoken native language is similar to each other (Malaysia-Asia, 2012). Two-thirds of the medical tourists visiting the country are Indonesian patients, while the remaining are from Brunei, Singapore and Japan (Connell, 2011). Reismann (2010) asserted that 70% of medical tourist treated in the country are Indonesian patients and the number of patients from developed countries such as USA and England, and Middle East are increasing. He also asserted that Singapore and Malaysia are competing for the Indonesian market. Because it is estimated that between 200.000 and 1.000.000 Indonesian travel abroad for obtaining health services and they have spent in excess of $1 billon. Malaysia is advantageous in this competition because Malaysia is more similar to Indonesia as a spoken language and culturally. In addition, the cost of accommodation, entertainment and health services in the country is cheaper than Singapore (Reisman, 2010).

Israel

Israel is rapidly advancing to become a leading country in the medical tourism industry. Many medical tourists travel to the country for benefiting from cheap health care services (Discover Medical Tourism, 2011). Israel's world-class health standards and the impressive proportion of healthcare facilities and doctors and health professionals it has made make Israel a popular destination for medical tourists. There are many quality private health facilities in Jerusalem (Medical Tourism Company, 2013).

Israel's healthcare system ranks 28th worldwide. The country is renowned for its state-of-the-art healthcare facilities. The health services provided by the country are oncology and cancer treatments, reproductive and in vitro fertilization (IVF) treatments, neurosurgery and orthopedic surgery (Israel Medical Tourism Journal, 2013). Israel is the capital of the world in the IVF method. Approximately 28,000 IVF treatments are administered annually in Israel (New York Times, 2011). The hospitals in the country have a high success rate in IVF treatments and the cost of this treatment is cheaper than Western countries (Medical Tourism Company, 2013). Medical tourism services provided by Israel are very popular among African, Middle Eastern and European medical tourists. Some American patients and some Jewish patients living in Western Europe also prefer the country for medical tourism (Israel Medical Tourism Journal, 2013).

Hungary

Hungary is one of the important medical tourism destinations in Europe. Hungary is an attractive destination for tourists seeking health services and wellness treatments. The country has become the European hot spot for dental treatment, especially for Western and Northern Europeans (Pitu, 2018). The main reason why Hungary is an important destination in the European medical tourism is that the country has important and long experience and practice in the international market. Hungary's success story began in the 18th century when German and Austrian patients began to seek high-quality dentistry and dental prosthesis services. After the country's accession to the European Union, medical tourism services have become more diverse and more international (International Medical Travel Journal, 2013).

Hungary is known as the capital of dental treatment. Patients travel to the country for dental treatment with the latest medical knowledge and technology (Szabo, 2012). The country generates approximately $2 million income a year thanks to dental treatments it provides (Turkey Health Ministry, 2012). Hungary especially hosts medical tourists from UK. The costs of services in Hungary is nearly 30% cheaper that the costs of same services in UK. It is estimated that 25.000 patients traveled to Hungary for dental treatments in 2007 (Connell, 2011). Hungary offers not only dental treatments but also aesthetic operations, hair transplantation, dermatology. and obesity treatments. In addition, gynecology, radiological examination services and eye surgery are among the services offered. Therefore, Hungary tries to change its image that provides only oral and dental treatments. For this reason, it intensively promotes the other treatment services offered (International Medical Travel Journal, 2013). Hungary does not have any JCI accredited health facilities. But some facilities are recognized by the Care Quality Commission, the independent regulator in England (Care Quality Commission, 2019) and the International Organization for Standardization (ISO). The costs of health services provided by the country are between 40% and 70% of the costs in the UK, USA and Scandinavian countries

(International Medical Travel Journal, 2013). Hungary is a very convenient destination for foreign patients due to the favorable exchange rates (Szabo, 2012).

Turkey

Turkey is among the countries subsequently began competition in the medical tourism market. Despite its late entry into the market, the country has made significant progress in a short time due to its unique advantages (Aktepe, 2013). Turkey, located in the center of Middle East, Europe, Balkans, and Africa, has an important potential in the medical tourism industry thanks to its well-educated and well-trained doctors and medical staff, ease of transportation, visa-free travel with 62 countries, and high health technology (Health Tourism Department, 2012).

Turkey, especially past 20 years period, has achieved significant progress and today, it has started to compete with countries such as India, Malaysia, Thailand and Hungary which are considered as the most successful countries in the medical tourism industry in the world. MedRetreat, the most reliable medical tourism company in the USA, specified India, Thailand, Malaysia, Brazil, Argentina, Turkey, and Northern Africa as important medical tourism destinations which can offer exotic and high-quality health services with affordable prices (Zengingönül et al., 2012). Medical tourism services offered in Turkey are oncology, cardiology and cardiovascular surgery, orthopedics and traumatology, plastic surgery, ophthalmology, obstetrics, organ transplantation, and oral and dental treatments (TÜSİAD, 2009). The number of JCI accredited hospitals in Turkey is higher than in other countries in the industry (Connell, 2011). In the country, 47 hospitals have JCI accreditation (Health Tourism Department, 2012). The number of accredited hospitals in the country is approximately 10% of all accredited hospitals in the world (Zengingönül et al., 2012).

The number of medical tourists visiting Turkey is increasing annually. The one of the main reasons for this increase is that modern operations performed in developed countries with modern methods are performed at affordable prices in Turkey (İçöz, 2009). However, being cheaper than European countries is not the only reason for preferring of the country for health services. For example, one of the reasons for patients who chose the country for IVF treatment is that the success rate on the first attempt in Turkey is higher than in European countries. Patients from Middle Eastern and European countries prefer the country for cancer treatment as well as IVF treatment. One of the devices used only in five countries in Europe is located in Turkey which made significant progress in cancer research and treatment (Şahbaz et al., 2012).

Other Destinations

Mexico is especially very popular medical tourism destinations among American medical tourists (Connell, 2013). In the middle of 1990s, approximately 250.000 Mexican immigrants living in USA crossed the Mexican border to reach affordable health services in Mexico, and in the same year, 50.000 Mexicans traveled to California-San Diego for the same reasons (Bookman and Bookman, 2007). Although American patients generally visit Mexican hospitals for plastic surgeries, they can visit the country for getting other health services. In 2009, 80-90% of patients admitted to dental clinics in border cities were American and 60% of these patients were over 50 years old. It is estimated that in 2010, 650,000 medical tourists visited Mexico to seek health care (Connell, 2011).

Cuba and Costa Rica are another important medical tourism destinations. Cuba has become a successful in the medical tourism industry in the middle of 1990s due to its geographical proximity to the United States and Latin American countries. The country is mainly preferred by patients from Spanish-speaking regions of Caribbean, and patients from Latin American countries such as Argentina, Dominican Republic and Venezuela. 20.000 medical tourists visited the country in 2006. Costa Rika is specialized in aesthetic operations and dental treatments. In 2006, 150.000 medical tourists visited the country (Connell, 2011).

Jordan is one of the prominent countries in the Middle East where medical tourism is developing slowly. Jordan serves patients, who do not have enough economic power means to travel to distant countries, from neighboring countries such as Iraq, Palestine and Syria. In 2007, 200.000 medical tourists from 84 countries visited the country. However, this statistical data cannot be verified. But, according to statistical data recorded by Jordan, in 2007 190.000 medical tourists, in 2008 200.000 medical tourists and in 2009 220.000 medical tourists visited the country (Connell, 2011). Dubai, a member of the United Arab Emirates, has embarked on developing its own medical tourism sector to reverse the flow of medical tourists in the region. Dubai has established a new "health city" (BAKA, 2011) in order to gain a share in the Middle East market and reduce the dominance of Asian countries in the sector (Connell, 2006).

CONCLUSION

Medical tourism is one of the new types of tourism. In this type of tourism, patients from developed countries travel to developing countries to get affordable and high-quality health services. Medical tourism was examined in different academic disciplines. Therefore, there is no consensus on the definition of the term medical tourism. Some researchers advocate that the term medical tourism is insufficient in explaining this kind of movements. Different types of term are proposed for medical tourism such as medical travel, medical pilgrims, medical value export, etc. However, the term medical tourism is widely used to define the phenomenon in the related literature.

The direction of medical tourism travels is from developed countries to developing countries. The long waiting lists, health care costs, and unavailability of some health services in developed countries push patients to seek health services abroad. Low costs, High-quality services offered in a medical tourism destination, easy access to information, low travel costs, and touristic attractions in a destination pull patient to participate in medical tourism.

Patients participating in medical tourism can reach high-quality services at low prices. Especially, some health services in developing countries are cheaper than in developed countries. Therefore, the demand for medical tourism is very high and the level of demand is increasing year by year. For this reason, there are many destination offering medical tourism services. Destinations offer different kind of health services, for example, destinations in Eastern Europe offer organ transplantation and fertility treatments while destinations in South America offer aesthetic operations. However, Asia is the leader in the industry. It is possible to say that Asia is the heart of medical tourism industry. Thailand, India, Singapore, and Malaysia are famous medical tourism destinations in the region. These countries are visited millions of medical tourist every year. Israel, Hungary, Turkey, Cuba, Mexico are among other famous medical tourism destinations.

The number of destinations offering medical tourism services is increasing. New destinations are entering the market year by year. From this point of view, it can be state that the competition level is quite high in the industry. Countries trying to gain competitive advantage must understand dynamics of the industry, and provide high-quality services at low prices.

REFERENCES

Aktepe, C. (2013). Sağlık turizminde yeni fırsatlar ve Türkiye'de yerleşik sağlık işletmelerinin pazarlama çabaları [New Opportunities and Marketing Efforts of Healthcare Companies in Turkey]. *İşletme Araştırmaları Dergisi, 5*(1), 170-188.

Altin, M. M., Singal, M., & Kara, D. (2011). *Consumer decision components for medical tourism: A stakeholder approach*. Academic Press.

Bookman, M. Z., & Bookman, K. R. (2007). *Medical tourism in developing countries*. Springer. doi:10.1057/9780230605657

Caballero-Danell, S., & Mugomba, C. (2007). *Medical Tourism and its Entrepreneurial Opportunities-A conceptual framework for entry into the industry*. Master Thesis.

Cannon Hunter, W. (2007). Medical tourism: A new global niche. *International Journal ofTourism Sciences*, *7*(1), 129–140. doi:10.1080/15980634.2007.11434599

Care Quality Commission. (2019). https://www.cqc.org.uk/about-us

Chew, Y. T., & Darmasaputra, A. (2015). 12 Identifying research gaps in medical tourism. *Destination Marketing: An international perspective*, 119.

Cohen, E. C. E. (2008). Medical tourism in Thailand. *AU-GSB E-Journal, 1*(1).

Connell, J. (2006). Medical tourism: Sea, sun, sand and... surgery. *Tourism Management*, *27*(6), 1093–1100. doi:10.1016/j.tourman.2005.11.005

Connell, J. (2011). *Medical tourism*. Cabi. doi:10.1079/9781845936600.0000

Connell, J. (2013). Contemporary medical tourism: Conceptualisation, culture and commodification. *Tourism Management*, *34*, 1–13. doi:10.1016/j.tourman.2012.05.009

Deloitte. (2008a). *Medical Tourism - Consumers in Search of Volume*. Deloitte Center for Health Solutions.

Deloitte. (2008b). *Medical Tourism: The Asian Chapter*. Deloitte Center for Health Solutions.

Doshi, D. R. (2008). *Health tourism: An exploratory study on motivation, satisfaction and consumption behavior ofhealth tourists in Malaysian private hospitals* (Doctoral dissertation). University of Malaya.

Durgun, A. (2007). Isparta turizminin SWOT analizi [SWOT analysis of Isparta's tourism]. *Süleyman Demirel Üniversitesi Sosyal Bilimler Enstitüsü Dergisi*, *5*, 93–109.

Eissler, L. A. (2010). *The lived experience of seeking healthcare through medical tourism: an interpretive phenomegical study of alaskan patients traveling internationally for medical and dental care* (Unpublished PhD Thesis). University of Hawai'I, School of Nursing, Manoa.

Erfurt-Cooper, P., & Cooper, M. (2009). *Health and wellness tourism: Spas and hot springs*. Channel View Publications. doi:10.21832/9781845411138

Froelich, N. C. K. (2012). *Medical tourism–A study about motivational factors and the prerequisites for creating a competitive offer–with a Swedish perspective* (Doctoral dissertation). Södertörn University.

Gan, L. L., & Frederick, J. R. (2011). Medical tourism facilitators: Patterns of service differentiation. *Journal of Vacation Marketing, 17*(3), 165–183. doi:10.1177/1356766711409181

Garcia-Altes, A. (2005). The development of health tourism services. *Annals of Tourism Research, 32*(1), 262–266. doi:10.1016/j.annals.2004.05.007

Health Tourism Department. (2012). *Sağlık turizmi Türkiye'de en hızlı gelişen hizmet sektörüdür* [Health tourism in Turkey is the fastest growing service sector]. Retrieved from https://docplayer.biz.tr/1854616-Saglik-turizmi-turkiyede-en-hizli-gelisen-hizmet-sektorudur.html

Helble, M. (2011). The movement of patients across borders: Challenges and opportunities for public health. *Bulletin of the World Health Organization, 89*(1), 68–72. doi:10.2471/BLT.10.076612 PMID:21346893

Heung, V. C., Kucukusta, D., & Song, H. (2010). A conceptual model of medical tourism: Implications for future research. *Journal of Travel & Tourism Marketing, 27*(3), 236–251. doi:10.1080/10548401003744677

Heung, V. C., Kucukusta, D., & Song, H. (2011). Medical tourism development in Hong Kong: An assessment of the barriers. *Tourism Management, 32*(5), 995–1005. doi:10.1016/j.tourman.2010.08.012

İçöz, O. (2009). Sağlık turizmi kapsamında medikal (tibbi) turizm ve Türkiye'nin olanakları [Medical tourism within the scope of health tourism and Turkey's possibilities]. *Journal of Yasar University, 4*(14).

Ile, F. L., & Ţigu, G. (2017, July). Medical tourism market trends-an exploratory research. In *Proceedings of the International Conference on Business Excellence* (*Vol. 11*, No. 1, pp. 1111-1121). De Gruyter Open. 10.1515/picbe-2017-0114

Inhorn, M. C., & Patrizio, P. (2009). Rethinking reproductive "tourism" as reproductive "exile". *Fertility and Sterility, 92*(3), 904–906. doi:10.1016/j.fertnstert.2009.01.055 PMID:19249025

International Medical Travel Journal. (2012). *Asian medical tourism: Research and statistics update*. Retrieved from https://www.imtj.com/news/asian-medical-tourism-research-and-statistics-update/

International Medical Travel Journal. (2013). *Hungarian Tourism promotes medical tourism.* Retrieved from https://www.imtj.com/news/hungarian-tourism-promotes-medical-tourism/

Jagyasi, P. (2008). Defining medical tourism. Another approach. *Medical Tourism Magazine*, *6*, 9–11.

Johnston, R., Crooks, V. A., Snyder, J., & Kingsbury, P. (2010). What is known about the effects of medical tourism in destination and departure countries? A scoping review. *International Journal for Equity in Health*, *9*(1), 24. doi:10.1186/1475-9276-9-24 PMID:21047433

Kangas, B. (2010). Traveling for medical care in a global world. *Medical Anthropology*, *29*(4), 344–362. doi:10.1080/01459740.2010.501315 PMID:21082482

Kim, Y. H., Boo, C., Demirer, I., & Kim, M. (2011). A case study of health tourism in the Jeju Province, South Korea. *Hospitality Review*, *29*(1), 4.

Kotler, P., Shalowitz, J. I., & Stevens, R. J. (2008). *Strategic marketing for health care organizations: building a customer-driven health system*. John Wiley & Sons.

Labonté, R. (2013). *Overview: Medical tourism today: What, who, why and where. Travelling well: Essays in medical tourism*. Institute of Population Health, University of Ottawa.

Lee, C., & Spisto, M. (2007). Medical tourism, the future of health services. In *Proceedings of the 12th International Conference on ISO* (*Vol. 9000*, pp. 1-7). Academic Press.

Lunt, N., & Carrera, P. (2010). Medical tourism: Assessing the evidence on treatment abroad. *Maturitas*, *66*(1), 27–32. doi:10.1016/j.maturitas.2010.01.017 PMID:20185254

Malaysia-Asia. (2012). *Medical tourism in Malaysia*. Retrieved from http://blog.malaysia-asia.my/2013/02/medical-tourism-in-malaysia.html

Matorras, R. (2005). Reproductive exile versus reproductive tourism. *Human Reproduction (Oxford, England)*, *20*(12), 3571. doi:10.1093/humrep/dei223 PMID:16308333

Merrell, R. C., Boucher, D., Carabello, L., Herrick, D. M., Lazzaro, V., Ludwick, L., Toral, R., Woodman, J., & Doarn, C. R. (2008). Medical tourism. *Telemedicine Journal and e-Health*, *14*(1), 14–20. doi:10.1089/tmj.2008.9995 PMID:18328021

Milstein, A., & Smith, M. (2006). America's new refugees—Seeking affordable surgery offshore. *The New England Journal of Medicine*, *355*(16), 1637–1640. doi:10.1056/NEJMp068190 PMID:17050886

Munro, J. W. (2012). *What is medical tourism. Toward a practical understanding of medical tourism and medical travel, wellness tourism, health tourism and health travel. Best Practices in medical tourism.* Medical Travel Quality Alliance.

Nahai, F. (2009). It's procedure, not tourism. *Medical Tourism, 1*, 106.

New York Times. (2011). *Where families are prized, help is free.* Retrieved from http://www.nytimes.com/2011/07/18/world/middleeast/18israel.html?pagewanted=all&_r=1&

Nicolaides, A. (2011). Lessons for South Africa from Asia on medical tourism's practice and potential: Peer reviewed special article. *Medical Technology SA, 25*(2), 7–16.

Peršić, M., & Janković, S. (2012). The assessment of opportunities and assumptions of the Croatian health tourism development. *Journal of Business and Management, 6*(2), 88–104.

Pitu, L. (2018). *Holidays with the doctor: Medical tourism in Hungary.* Retrieved from https://www.dw.com/en/holidays-with-the-doctor-medical-tourism-in-hungary/a-45857567

Pocock, N. S., & Phua, K. H. (2011). Medical tourism and policy implications for health systems: A conceptual framework from a comparative study of Thailand, Singapore and Malaysia. *Globalization and Health, 7*(1), 12. doi:10.1186/1744-8603-7-12 PMID:21539751

Reisman, D. A. (2010). *Health tourism: Social welfare through international trade.* Edward Elgar Publishing. doi:10.4337/9781849805537

Roy, J., Chatterjee, K., Bandyopadhyay, A., & Kar, S. (2018). Evaluation and selection of medical tourism sites: A rough analytic hierarchy process based multi-attributive border approximation area comparison approach. *Expert Systems: International Journal of Knowledge Engineering and Neural Networks, 35*(1), e12232. doi:10.1111/exsy.12232

Rydback, M., & Hyder, A. S. (2018). Customization in medical tourism in the Philippines. *International Journal of Pharmaceutical and Healthcare Marketing, 12*(4), 486–500. doi:10.1108/IJPHM-07-2017-0035

Şahbaz, R. P., Akdu, U., & Akdu, S. (2012). Türkiye'de medikal turizm uygulamaları; İstanbul ve Ankara Örneği [Medical tourism applications in Turkey; Istanbul and Ankara example]. *Balıkesir Üniversitesi Sosyal Bilimler Enstitüsü Dergisi, 15*(27), 267–296.

Saiprasert, W. (2011). *Examination of the medical tourists motivational behavior and perception: A structural model* (Doctoral dissertation). Oklahoma State University.

Sarwar, A. A., Manaf, N. A., & Omar, A. (2012). Medical tourist's perception in selecting their destination: A global perspective. *Iranian Journal of Public Health, 41*(8), 1. PMID:23113218

Song, P. (2010). Biotech pilgrims and the transnational quest for stem cell cures. *Medical Anthropology, 29*(4), 384–402. doi:10.1080/01459740.2010.501317 PMID:21082484

Stolley, K. S., & Watson, S. (2012). *Medical tourism: A reference handbook*. ABC-CLIO.

Suess, C., Baloglu, S., & Busser, J. A. (2018). Perceived impacts of medical tourism development on community wellbeing. *Tourism Management, 69*, 232–245. doi:10.1016/j.tourman.2018.06.006

Szabo, A. (2012). *Medical Tourism and SPAs in Hungary, Hungarian Tourism Plc.* Retrieved from https://en.calameo.com/read/0050564400b1ffaecaf6d

Taleghani, M., Chirani, E., & Shaabani, A. (2011). Health tourism, tourist satisfaction and motivation. *Interdisciplinary Journal of Contemporary Research in Business, 3*(4), 546–555.

Thomas, R. K. (2005). *Marketing health services*. Health Administration Press.

Turkey Health Foundation. (2010). *Dünya'da ve Türkiye'de Sağlık turizmi durum tespit raporu ve çözüm önerileri [Health tourism in the world and Turkey due diligence report and solutions]*. Efil Yayınevi.

Turkey Health Ministry. (2013). *Türkiye medikal turizmi değerlendirme raporu* [Turkey medical tourism assessment report]. Retrieved from http://saglikturizmi.gov.tr/uploads/8565562-tr-medikal-turizm.pdf

Turkish Industry and Business Association (TÜSİAD). (2009). *Türkiye için yeni bir fırsat penceresi: tıp turizmi - görüş belgesi* [A new opportunity for Turkey: medical tourism – position paper]. Retrieved from https://tusiad.org/tr/saglik-cg/item/4844-turkiye-icin-yeni-bir-firsat-penceresi-tip-turizmi-gorus-belgesi

Voigt, C., Laing, J., Wray, M., Brown, G., Howat, G., & Weiler, B. (2010). *Health tourism in Australia: supply, demand and opportunities*. Sustainable Tourism.

West Mediterranean Development Agency (BAKA). (2011). *Sağlık turizmi sektör raporu* [Health tourism sector report]. Retrieved from https://www.baka.gov.tr/uploads/48947588121518SAGLiK-KATALOG-TURKCE-16MAYiS-3.pdf

Yeoh, E., Othman, K., & Ahmad, H. (2013). Understanding medical tourists: Word-of-mouth and viral marketing as potent marketing tools. *Tourism Management, 34*, 196–201. doi:10.1016/j.tourman.2012.04.010

Yıldırım, H. H., & Altunkaya, Ü. (2006). Türkiye'nin sağlık turizmi potansiyeli ve güçlükler [Turkey's health tourism potential and challenges]. *Hastane ve Yaşam Dergisi, 2*(12), 120–123.

Yu, J. Y., & Ko, T. G. (2012). A cross-cultural study of perceptions of medical tourism among Chinese, Japanese and Korean tourists in Korea. *Tourism Management, 33*(1), 80–88. doi:10.1016/j.tourman.2011.02.002

Zengingönül, O., Hamdi, E. M. E. Ç., İyilikçi, D. E., & Bingöl, P. (2012). *Sağlık turizmi: İstanbul'a yönelik bir değerlendirme [Health tourism: an assessment for İstanbul]*. İstanbul Kalkınma Ajansı.

Chapter 3
Indian Medical Tourism Industry Basics and Its Competitive Positioning:
Case Study

Nadeem Ahmed Bashir
https://orcid.org/0000-0001-5741-6291
Department of Management, King Saud University, Saudi Arabia

Premkumar Balaraman
MBA Department, Veltech Rangarajan Dr. Sagunthala R&D Institute of Science and Technology, India

Aroop Mukherjee
https://orcid.org/0000-0003-2991-8686
Department of Aviation and Management, Prince Sultan University, Saudi Arabia

ABSTRACT

Medical tourism (MT) may be described as a journey outside the country of residence to receive medical assistance. It must be taken into account that specialized healthcare involves the participation of specialists in the field of medicine such as surgeons, who differentiate medical tourism from wellness and spa tourism. There can be two main forms of medical tourism: surgical and therapeutic. The chapter mainly aims to understand the fundamentals of medical tourism in perspective to focused on its definition, categories, growing trends, drivers, challenges, and quality standards. The specific case of the Indian medical tourism industry and its competitive position is also being discussed in this chapter.

DOI: 10.4018/978-1-7998-3427-4.ch003

1. INTRODUCTION

The idea of health tourism has traditionally originated from countries that have spa, coastal and indigenous care practices. Medical tourism represents the broader concept of health tourism. The overall trend of health and medical tourism is viewed with different emphasis. It includes healthcare, healthcare suppliers, distributors, consultants, web-based health services, conferences, and media members. These various actors are playing a vital role in developing the health tourism market globally.

Medical tourism attempts to understand its fundamentals, different types, driving factors, quality standards, challenges, and global trends. The act of medical tourism in foreign countries is known to include treatment and care, ranging from highly invasive (hip, chest, plastic surgery, resurfacing) to less invasive (dental) and wellness (Reddy, York, & Brannon, 2010). Despite the fact that, medical tourism trend was wrongly perceived to be driven by cosmetic procedures seeking travelers, it is evident that more critical health procedures (such as cardiac operations or knee transplantation) are provided and considered as key drivers in destinations such as India, Thailand, Singapore, Taiwan, and Malaysia (Singh, 2013).

In India, which has become the world's universal healthcare destination in general, growth is not limited to particular hospitals but also got benefits that are derived from the advancement in number of different healthcare services providers, such as naturopathic, ayurvedic, homeopathic and yoga institutions. According to Mochi (2013) analyzed that India's position in the medical industry is growing daily. According to previous research, the international health industry increases by approximately $3 billion, owing to its services and facilities, and by providing India's as healthcare brand equity. The medical expertise of India in the globe is the highest compared to other countries worldwide, and doctors in India support by providing better services everywhere. The main reason for India's success as an important medical destination is due to its prestige as the world-class Indian healthcare center. Mohanty and Madhav (2006), found that Indian health companies began to emerge as the main tourism destination compared to other countries of the world simply because Indian Industry improves its expertise, ability, fasters and deeper understanding of many advanced medical practices and humanizes its reputation with regard to pricing and excellence. Because of its natural and ayurvedic practitioners only India is one of the most well-known and popular destinations in international patients compared to western and also more respected medical treatment worldwide.

There are many qualities of a destination that tourists who visit a specific type of tourism can draw. This means that the characteristics that lead tourists to choose between destinations must be identified. Ayurvedic treatments are an ancient practice considered to be the best natural healing method in the Indian subcontinent that was formed some 5,000 years ago. As we all know, ayurvedic medicines are a natural process of repairing, healing, and developing human beings ‘ cognitive, physical and emotional state. Ayurveda is a way of life that helps all to enhance their way of life and recognize the various changes that take place in their bodies. The primary destination for Ayurveda Health Tourism is Kerala in India. Ayurvedic medicine is the oldest medical system in Kerala where it is historically practiced until now. The state is fair for therapeutic and rejuvenation therapies, the natural wealth of forests, and the hot monsoons season, which are best suited for. Humidity in the atmosphere and on the skin surface, making it an ideal place to work successfully with natural medicinal products at their highest levels. In Kerala the soil is rich in "alkaloid," which improves the potency and efficacy of many Ayurvedic medicines, in contrast with other states with different soil composition (Padmasani & Remya, 2015).

Kerala is fast becoming a global destination for medical tourism, attracting travelers and foreign parties to the state, and appreciating its centuries-old tradition of ancient Indian Ayurveda. According to Kerala Tourism Secretary, the government has decided to increase the aspects of health care and therapeutic activity along with their wellness program in the monsoon to increase tourism in the traditional and authentic way of Kerala (PTI, 2013).

Ayurveda has become a major selling point, and it is promoted by the state as part of the international medical tourism market for Kerala Tourism Industry. Today, Kerala Ayurveda is so popular within tourists around the world that Ayurvedic treatment becomes an important aspect of decision making to travel to Kerala. Ayurvedic holiday packages are offered in the entire state through various resorts and hospitals. According to Tourism Survey (2012-2013) it was confirmed that 3.1% of international tourists and 3.71 percent of domestic tourists traveled to Kerala for health care. The main reason for this increase can be the aggressive media campaigns of the government and word of mouth advertised by the tourists visiting earlier and low prices.

In Kerala, there are a number of family business that has specialized in some type of remedies including Uzhieil (massage), Marmachikitsa (treatment of certain vital parts of the body) and Balachikitsa (pediatric), Netracikitsa (Opthalmology), Visa Ciqitsa (toxicology), Bhutapasmara Pratividhi (Psychiatric treatment). The family is also involved in the care of the treatment of wounds and bruises. The symptoms of diseases such as arthritis, nerve disorders, Parkinson's disease, asthma, and skin conditions are treated in a traditional way because the atmosphere is dust-free and cool. Despite Ayurveda's is increasing fascination, the private sector has become a major player in the spa industry and can be seen from the number of wellness resorts, hotels, and resorts in Kerala.

People's health and beauty consciousness have opened the way for health tourism to become ever more relevant. According to Remya (2015), service quality and capacity were the reasons why the attributes of destination are highly acceptable;

the overall study thus shows that Kerala could establish its reputation as a tourist destination for Ayurvedic Health. Providing companies with a broader scope to support Ayurveda-based health tourism. Destination managers and service providers must develop a well-planned promotional campaign which will entail needed changes in order to attract domestic visitors, focusing on the quality of services and opportunities in Kerala.

Tourists experience a mix of Ayurveda, Yoga, Acupuncture, Herbal oil massage, Nature treatments, and Ancient Indian medical procedures, including Vedic care, alternative medical treatment, and healthcare. The price benefit is Indian modern medicine's appealing value that is 10-15 times less than anywhere in the world. States like Andhra Pradesh, Karnataka, Kerala, Tamil Nadu, Maharashtra, and New Delhi are fast emerging as the best medical centers of India with a number of hospitals and health centers in India. The Middle East, America, Europe and neighboring countries like Bangladesh, Pakistan, and Afghanistan are attracting many medical tourists from India. Because of its infrastructure and technology and India is a popular destination for medical tourists worldwide. Throughout Ayurveda, people often follow normal and authentic lifestyles. Ayurveda provides the following to balance and pacifies the toxins in the body by -

- A healthy way of life free from diseases and pressures
- A beautiful skin in which natural beauty is restored
- Total relaxation
- Enhances the strength of the body and improves the destressing cycle
- Provides a natural way to lose weight

The Ayurvedic forms and means are based entirely on the principles and learning of the Vedic culture. Ayurvedic treatments help improve the quality of life and show how much a balanced life is evaluated. Ayurvedic based treatments are those that follow the natural healing methods to improve a person's health. Numerous purification procedures are used to remove the toxins from the hair so that the body can respire freely.

The destination's appeal has a big influence on deciding the destination, expectations/ satisfaction, re-visit plans, perceptions of benefits and opportunities, the amount of money spent, and the length of stay of an individual. Countries around the world consider a wide variety and strive hard to attract a large number of tourists with specific attributes and a wide range of tourists to win a large market share. The rivalry for India as the major players, such as Thailand, Costa Rica in the health tourism industry has been immense. Therefore, it is time to know their destination's competitive advantage, attracting visitors. It is always assumed that the most desirable destination will be favoured and revisited.

India is classified as one of the top five medical tourism destinations. YES Bank estimates that the domestic tourist movements will increase by 118% over the period (2008-2020) and foreign tourist inflows by 71.87% over that same period. The latest FICCI-Yes Bank study estimated the presence of over 3,371 medical hospitals, and approximately 750,000 have registered medical practitioners (Chandra, Sharma, Masih, Jamaluddin & Scharma, 2013). According to Patil et. al. (2015) including the growing demand for health care in developed nations, an increase in the population over the age of 60, a rise in the life expectancy of all countries, inability to provide health care systems to cope with increasing demand, a reduced service rates, and long waiting lists. In 2013-2019, the global medical tourism industry will expand at a compound annual rate of 17.9% to 32.5 billion US dollars. The global demand for health services is increasing due to population factors like higher mortality and higher birth rates. The Organization for Economic Co-operation and Development (OECD) predicts that the figure is more than double, from 4% in 2010 to almost 10% by 2050, and Organization for Economic Co-operation and Development claims the number is more than double (KPMG, 2018). In view of the high demand for health tourism, the fundamentals of health tourism and its guiding forces and challenges need to be revisited and understood.

When compared with neighboring countries, India is increasingly developing as an affordable healthcare destination. Tourism and health care may go hand in hand, but this idea is not completely new. The initiative now consists of institutionalizing and bringing patients to Indian hospitals from foreign markets. Value-added facilities have been designed to meet all clients as patients recover and their families enjoy sights and shops in the hospital. In key foreign countries the corporate hospital's group has opened information centers to attract medical visitors. India has become the international healthcare map and thanks to its experience in modern medical services from cardiac surgery to photonic cataract removal. Every year, it attracts approximately a lakh of foreign medical tourists. Thus, health care organizations have recognized the connection between all points in the patient care range. To maximize the real-world re-engineering activities, the whole system and data must be incorporated into or throughout the organization. For the last couple of years, the entry of Western health tourists, particularly the United Kingdom, the USA, and certain European countries has increased. The main reasons for the rise of Western traffic are price differences and affordability of care, coupled with efficiency of physicians shown in Table 1. Thus, the main aim of the case study was to understand the fundamentals of Medical Tourism and to assess India's CASE and its competitive position in the field of medical tourism.

Table 1. Reasons for Foreign Exchange Earrings

Year	Foreign Exchange Earnings (Rs in Crores)	Percentages of Increase	Total Revenue Generated From Tourism (Rs in Crores)	Percentages of Increase
2001	535.00	1.85	4500.00	9.58
2002	705.67	31.90	4931.00	20.45
2003	983.37	39.35	5938.00	12.83
2004	1266.77	28.82	6829.00	15.01
2005	1552.31	22.54	7738.00	13.31
2006	1988.40	28.09	9126.00	17.94
2007	2640.94	32.82	11433.00	25.28
2008	3066.52	16.11	13130.00	14.84
2009	42671	21.23	1056.74	14.86
2010	5761	22.25	14.30	36.55
2011	7576	37.67	5783.25	130739
2012	4027	37.67	37.31	37.710
2013	56219	27.927	49.67	38.80
2014	7561	37.616	187.144	49.75
2015	99574	49.41	245.21	49.96
2016	96856	48.4	0.49971	103.24
2017	11756	58.28	28.29	48.54
2018	11761	58.5	0.2998	51.247

Source: Medical Tourism (2019)

2. HEALTH / WELLNESS TOURISM DEFINITION

Goeldner (1989) first connected and described the various elements of tourism in the health resort (medical treatments, relaxation, enjoyment, motivated health). All pleasure-oriented tourism involving a stress relief component could be seen as health tourism (Benner at al., 2004 in Puczkó, 2010). Health tourism is known to be the coordinated tour outside the local environment for preserving, enhancing or restoring the well-being of individuals and their bodies (Carrera and Bridges, 2006). The term includes medical tourism, which is restricted to coordinated travel outside the jurisdiction of a natural health authority to improve or restore the health of the person by medical procedure.

Wellness tourism deals with all aspects of medical, health, sports / fitness, adventure, or transformation, and it is an all-encompassing way of journeying that integrates the search for health, longevity, spiritual awakening, nature and a connection to God (Seldon & Bushell, 2009).

McKercher (2016) has identified 5 large families of medical needs, including 27 brand categories, 90 customer classes (pleasure, personal quest, human effort, nature, and business). Medical / wellness service forms include procedures (McKercher, 2016). Certain styles include medical procedures (routine evaluation, general interventions, physical cures; non-surgical) and wellness services, (spa, massage, beauty treatment); surgical procedures (surgical, optic, eye and cosmetic fashion, dental, mild invasive; major invasive treatment) (transplants; gender reassignment)

3. MEDICAL TOURISM DEFINITION

The word medical tourism is used to accept all facets of customers seeking treatment, enhancement and change through medical or wellbeing activities provided they go beyond the international borders to do so, according to Munro (2012), the medical tourism defines the act of people making healthy choices and receiving health services across borders.

Medical tourists can be described as traveling outside the residence to receive medical help; specialist medical services, including surgeons, should be included, which differentiate medical tourism from health and spa tourism. medical tourism should be described as traveling outside the country of residence (Lucy, 2014). Wellness tourism in a slightly different way means travel to ensure the well-being and satisfaction of patients through safe care experiences and the quality of life (Fernandes & Fernandes, 2013). The use of medical tourism is more common in-patient movements through their own will and, therefore, it is better for medical tourists to exercise their European rights rather than their rights as consumers rather than people "the phenomenon is commonly called cross-border care" (Lunt & Carrera, 2010).

4. MEDICAL TOURISM TYPES

The Puczkó and Smith study (2008) there is a number of medical tourism which vary from necessary surgery (e.g. cancer, heart disease) to more esthetics but sometimes unnecessary procedures (e.g. orthodontic and plastic operations) and cosmetic operations that are physiologically relevant but still are necessary. Three large and six categories (Cormany 2008), as defined in Table 2, will be included in a system of classification for medical tourism.

There is also another group, called "circumvention-tourists" (Stolley & Watson, 2012, p. 60), who travel to seek treatment at home or who receive special legal benefits in other countries. Customers of Ireland who travel to Hong Kong for abortion, couples visiting India for pregnancy surrogates, people visiting Switzerland for euthanasia, or continental Chinese births to Hong-Kong to circumvent family laws and to provide Hong Kong children with a residence in Hong Kong for the benefit that they will benefit from at a later date of existence. Diverse health-tourism procedures include (Lunt et al., 2011): cosmetic procedure (liposuction, breast, face), dentistry (cosmetic, reconstruction), cardiac / cardiac operation (ventilation replacement, bypass), fertility / reproductive systems (IVF), orgeopathy (gastric bypass, gastric bandage), orthopedic operation (hip / knee substituting), resurfacing, joint operation, and body care.

Table 2. Medical Tourism Classification

Medical Tourism Category	Subcategory
Three sub-categories for Intrusive medical procedures	Elective or prompted surgery because of the patient's wishes. These include cosmetic surgery, cosmetic dentistry, gender reassignment, and reproductive support.
	"Quality of life" is characterized as medically necessary or prescribed operation in cases that do not immediately pose a life risk, such as dental, bariatric, or joint replacement conditions.
	"Life-Saving Surgery" for those procedures for life-threatening conditions medically necessary or approved, such as cardiac operations, organ transplantation and oncology
External testing approaches	One class, including stress testing, screening, cat scanning, electrocardiograms and "executive" for example
Procedures of lifestyle (two subcategories)	Spa treatments and addictions management counseling, stress relief, and relaxation training.
	Non-Surgical alternative therapies for certain disorders (such as acupuncture, Botox injection, Ayurveda, and herbal remedies)

Source: Cormany (2008)

5. GROWING TRENDS IN MEDICAL TOURISM

Important economic, social, and political developments in recent decades have created a more transnational and global position for the development of health policy. The movement of human beings, goods, capital, and ideas includes these national interconnections (political, economic, social, and technical) that offer new opportunities and challenges for the provision and regulation of health care. Especially, the Regulatory aspects of WTO's GATS - General Agreement on Trade in Services, global spreading of transnational diseases, increased patient mobility (low-cost transport, ICT, changing cultural attitudes towards abroad treatment locations), Industry growth factors support the viewpoint of increased national level connectivity. The four growing trends identified in the Medical Tourism Magazine are, under Aircare1 (2017):

- Private health cities with multi-specialty hospitals are attracting foreign investment
- Expansion of Asia (increased hospitality and low-cost standards and technical services)
- Expert translators, facilitators, advanced medical training centers, and the development of professional professionals, including doctors and surgeons.
- New destinations, including Greece, Taiwan, and the UAE, promise beautiful scenery for patients during their stay.

Medhekar and Haq, (2018), highlight the emerging trend in the halal medical tourism niche group, in which the sharia regulations are observed to draw medical tourists, primarily from the Islamic countries; Halal medical tourism hospitals, health facilities, pharmacy, products, and services are being branded and accepted as a new phenomenon to meet the needs of Muslim countries. In the fields of cosmetics, obesity and plastic surgery, several middle and south American countries have been identified according to Woodman (2007). In cardiovascular surgery and orthopedic surgery, the top players are India, Singapore, and Thailand. Compared to all destinations, India has a better cost advantage, whereas, in the case of countries like Belgium, Canada, Germany, Israel, and Italy, they excel in areas of complex surgery and other advanced health services. The various specialties of Medical Tourism are detailed in Table 3.

5.1 Medical Tourism Index (MTI)

The MTI (Medical Tourism Index) consists of three main dimensions (medical, social, industry, and national), with 34 underlying indicators. The MTI is multidimensional. It is the first index that helps countries, policymakers, the health and tourism industry, marketers and underlying organizations and persons to assess their role as a tourism destination in the field of medicine. The MTI demonstrates how attractive countries are as destinations of medical tourism and also shows the country's role in Medical Tourism (IHRC, 2018). According to MTI (2016)., the various top destinations and the MTI ranking for the year 2016 is presented in Table 4 and 5

Table 3. Medical Tourism Specialties

Medical Tourism Specialties	Types
Cosmetic Surgery	- Plastic Surgery Breast enlargement / mastopexia / breast reduction - Facelift / blefaroplast - Liposuction / bodybuilding
Organ and tissue transfer	Solid-organ transplantation - Kidney - Liver Transplantation of Bone Marrow - Stem cell therapy - Heart Failure - Neurologic diseases
Dentistry	- Cosmetic dentistry - Tooth repair / replacement
Cardiology and Heart Surgery	- Coronary artery bypass surgery - Cardiac valve replacement /again - Percutaneous coronary angioplasty /stent - Stem cell treatment for heart failure
Eye	- Laser eye surgery
Orthopedics and Spine Surgery	- Hip replacement - Knee Arthroplasty - Arthroscopy / in joint reconstruction - Laminectomy / spinal decompression - Disk area reconstruction / changing disk
Obesity	- Gastric bypass - Laparoscopic adjustable gastric banding (Lap-Band; Inamed / Allergan, Inc.; Irvine, California) - Contouring body after excessive weight loss
Infertility	- Transurethral resection / Prostatectomy - Sex inversion - In vitro fertilization - Hysterectomy

Source: Woodman (2007)

Table 4. Top 5 Medical Tourism Destinations

Overall Rank	Destination Environment	Medical Tourism Industry	Quality of Facilities and Services
1. Canada 76.62	1. Canada 78.69	1. India 75.94	1. Israel 81.60
2. UK 74.87	2. UK 77.29	2. Colombia 74.96	2. Germany 77.88
3. Israel 73.91	3. Singapore 73.26	3. Mexico 74.17	3. India 77.10
4. Singapore 73.56	4. Israel 66.56	4. Canada 74.13	4. Canada 77.02
5. India 72.10	5. Germany 67.50	5. Dominican Republic 73.85	5. UK 76.94

Source: MTI (2016)

Table 5. Overall MTI Ranking

1. Canada 76.62	16. Dubai 67.54	31. Morocco 59.77
2. UK 74.87	17. Jamaica 67.17	32. Turkey 59.49
3. Israel 73.91	18. Thailand 66.60	33. Jordan 57.02
4. Singapore 73.56	19. Philippines 66.40	34. Russia 57.01
5. India 72.10	20. Taiwan 66.28	35. Oman 56.90
6. Germany 71.90	21. Argentina 65.37	36. Tunisia 56.78
7. France 71.22	22. Brazil 65.22	37. Kuwait 52.69
8. South Korea 70.16	23. China 64.78	38. Saudi Arabia 52.43
9. Italy 69.50	24. Poland 63.79	39. Bahrain 51.99
10. Colombia 69.48	25. Abu Dhabi 63.65	40. Lebanon 49.92
11. Spain 68.29	26. Malta 62.97	41. Iran 36.00
12. Japan 68.00	27. South Africa 62.20	
13. Panama 67.93	28. Egypt 60.92	
14. Costa Rica 67.67	29. Mexico 60.70	
15. Dominican Republic 67.58	30. Qatar 60.07	

Source: MTI (2016)

5.2 Medical Tourism - Pricing Comparison

According to the Medical Tourism Association (MTA, 2019), the various country-wise Cost Comparison of specific medical procedures are summarized in Table 6. And from Figure 1 it is inferred that India stands in the top position in terms of cost advantage in almost most of the categories of Medical procedures. Turkey and Malaysia can be considered to hold the second position, followed by Thailand and Singapore.

6. MEDICAL TOURISM DRIVERS

The Medical Tourism Association's (MTA, 2018) demonstrates the various factors in the demands of medical tourism: cost savings, efficiency, safety, medical trip spending, air travel, and insurance. Pollard's "destination attraction model," which includes seven important factors such as cultural proximity, destination infrastructure, destination setting, geographical proximity, destination picture, risk and reward, and cost, does not include technology or comparisons for potential patients. (Franzensberg, 2012).

Figure 1. Radar Chart – Cost Comparison of Low-Cost Medical Destinations

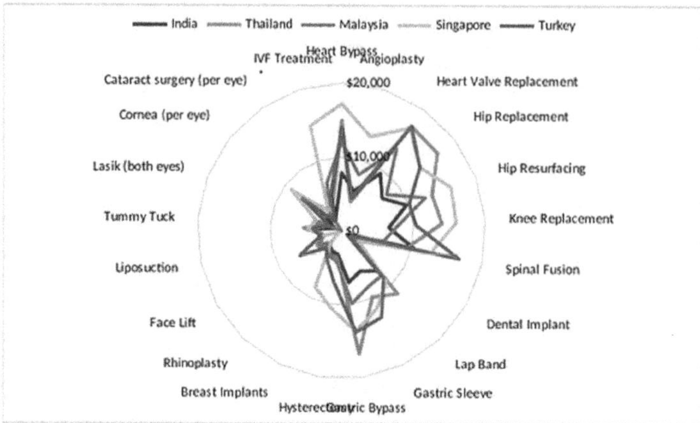

The five factors found in Glinos et al. (2006) that lead to the increasing demand for medical services the abroad include familiarity, accessibility, price, reliability, and bioethics legislation (international travel in abortion services, fertilization treatment, and euthanasia services). Expatriates travel back to home country due to the familiarity factor, but the reasons may be varied, long waits in foreign countries for specific treatments, legality issues, advanced technology available at low cost, etc. Tourist visits are often related to medical treatment (tourist attractive, environment, food, culture) and are seen as a major driver for growth in this sector (MacReady, 2007; Ramírez de Arellano, 2007). The various key medical tourism drivers are detailed in Table 7.

7. MEDICAL TOURISM CHALLENGES

The lack of portability of medical care coverage abroad (Smith, Chanda & Tangcharoensathien, 2009) constitutes the global most significant obstacle to tourism exports. Similarly, in the sense of restrictions and limitations on foreign investments in the health sector, there are possible barriers. In assessing GATS commitments, one of the services sectors in which WTO members made the least commitments seems to be the health sector overall (Adlung, 2009).

The possible risks in all healthcare and surgical procedures are the client, facilitator agent, employer and destination provider, irrespective of whether the patient is being handled in his / her home country or abroad and regardless of the skills or abilities of the practitioner. (Dianne & Linda, 2007). Medical tourism actually refuses to follow regulations on privacy and data transfer in hosting countries.

Table 6. Country Wise Cost Comparison of Specific Medical Procedure

Medical Procedure	USA	India	Jordan	Mexico	Thailand	Malaysia	Poland	Singapore	Turkey
Heart Bypass	$123,000	$7,900	$14,400	$27,000	$15,000	$12,100	$14,000	$17,200	$13,900
Angioplasty	$28,200	$5,700	$5,000	$10,400	$4,200	$8,000	$5,300	$13,400	$4,800
Heart Valve Replacement	$170,000	$9,500	$14,400	$28,200	$17,200	$13,500	$19,000	$16,900	$17,200
Hip Replacement	$40,364	$7,200	$8,000	$13,500	$17,000	$8,000	$5,500	$13,900	$13,900
Hip Resurfacing	$28,000	$9,700	$9,000	$12,500	$13,500	$12,500	$9,200	$16,350	$10,100
Knee Replacement	$35,000	$6,600	$9,500	$12,900	$14,000	$7,700	$8,200	$16,000	$10,400
Spinal Fusion	$110,000	$10,300	$10,000	$15,400	$9,500	$6,000	$6,200	$12,800	$16,800
Dental Implant	$2,500	$900	$900	$900	$1,720	$1,500	$925	$2,700	$1,100
Lap Band	$14,000	$7,300	$7,000	$6,500	$11,500	$8,150	$6,700	$9,200	$8,600
Gastric Sleeve	$16,500	$6,000	$7,500	$8,900	$9,900	$8,400	$9,400	$11,500	$12,900
Gastric Bypass	$25,000	$7,000	$7,500	$11,500	$16,800	$9,900	$9,750	$13,700	$13,800
Hysterectomy	$15,400	$3,200	$6,600	$4,500	$3,650	$4,200	$2,200	$10,400	$7,000
Breast Implants	$6,400	$3,000	$4,000	$3,800	$3,500	$3,800	$3,900	$8,400	$4,500
Rhinoplasty	$6,500	$2,400	$2,900	$3,800	$3,300	$2,200	$2,500	$2,200	$3,100
Face Lift	$11,000	$3,500	$3,950	$4,900	$3,950	$3,550	$4,000	$440	$6,700
Liposuction	$5,500	$2,800	$1,400	$3,000	$2,500	$2,500	$1,800	$2,900	$3,000
Tummy Tuck	$8,000	$3,500	$4,200	$4,500	$5,300	$3,900	$3,550	$4,650	$4,000
Lasik (both eyes)	$4,000	$1,000	$4,900	$1,900	$2,310	$3,450	$1,850	$3,800	$1,700
Cornea (per eye)	$17,500	$2,800	$5,000	N/A	$3,600	N/A	N/A	$9,000	$7,000
Cataract surgery (per eye)	$3,500	$1,500	$2,400	$2,100	$1,800	$3,000	$750	$3,250	$1,600
IVF Treatment	$12,400	$2,500	$5,000	$5,000	$4,100	$6,900	$4,900	$14,900	$5,200

Source: Medical Tourism Association (2019)

Table 7. Medical Tourism Drivers

Medical Tourism Driver	Details
Technology	The key services of the sites are divided into five main functions: as a data portal, accessibility, evaluation / promotion, commercial and communicable opportunities, and connected to the web-based tools to provide customers with information, advertising and market destinations to allow connectivity to healthcare clinics, brokers, according to Lunt et.al. (2010).
Broker	Companies and consultancies that provide brokering arrangements for services and provides prospective patients with web-based data on available services and choices that allow patients to measure costs, negotiate and decide appropriately.
Insurance	Insurance products that cover medical tourists during travel for surgery have been created for those contingencies. Emerging insurance products cover the costs of further care, which may be required following surgery abroad due to complications and dissatisfaction.
Service Providers	They are mostly private but also public (e.g. in Singapore and in Cuba). they are based in the public sector. Private hospitals, agents, hospitality facilities are the major service providers.
National Strategies	Includes a number of national government departments and policy initiatives to encourage and facilitate tourism in their countries. medical tourism for example, the governments of Thai, Indian, Singapore, Malaysia, Hungary, Poland and Malta have sought, through ads in the overseas press and official support for activities within the scope of its economic development and tourism policy, to promote their comparative advantage as destinations for health tourism at major international trade events (Reisman, 2010).

Source: Lunt, Smith, Exworthy, Green, Horsfall, & Mannion (2011)

Shimazono (2007) states that the EU (EU) data guidelines protect personal and medical information and also forbid the transfer for EU data to a non-EU recipient except where the recipient state offers protection equal to that of the EU (Shimazono, 2007). Similarly, the US has its own laws, the HIPAA, which covers all medical data (individual health record, payment information, written and digitally recording of disclosures) (Turner 2009). The USA also has its own legislation. There is no appropriate global coordinated process to settle legal conflicts of medical tourists at international level.

According to Christopher (2008), the major challenges in medical tourism includes the areas of Safety (Food preparation, Water, Ambience), Quality Control (Staff Credentials, Actual Service Quality), Accreditation (Standard Assessment / Monitor), Provision for follow-up care and resolution of complications (Patient Consent / Policies and Procedures). In Asian context, the grey areas or challenges of medical tourism includes, infrastructure Development, retention of health human resources, convincing foreign medical tourist on domestic medical / patient safety matters, need for maintaining International standards and accreditations like JCI, improve service quality perceptions, promotion, increased access to non-personal data sources such as blogs, search engines, advertising, newspapers and magazines (McArthur Baker, 2015).

The specific challenges of Indian Medical Tourism include, poor Government Support in areas of private investment, Slow Visa process, fewer accreditations, lack of uniform pricing, etc. (Sharma, 2013); Other Challenges faced by abroad Patients in India includes difficulty in finding good interpreters /translators, obtaining visa, getting insurance covers, follow-ups and monitoring care, behavior of tour operators, corruption, differential pricing policies, and inadequate lodging arrangements. (Gupta et al. 2015). Other pertinent challenges are Commercialization of the profession (missing of doctor-patient relationship), extensive aftercare requirements in the case of orthopedic or heart bypass surgery, issue of insurance cover, poor power supplies even in hospitals, no industry standards, disparities in government and private health services, brain drain from government to private sectors, raise medical costs for local people (Vivekanand & Hundekar, 2017).

8. MEDICAL TOURISM STANDARDS AND QUALITY

The consumer-driven trend of medical tourism involves facilities that are low-cost, reliable, and easy clinical care choices for individuals all over the world. The two main components of service quality in the healthcare sector are according to Grönroos (1990): technological and mechanical products; and serviceable and operational quality. In the medical industry, the center of the screening of patients is specialized equipment and other related systems for medical diagnosis. The service offered by healthcare centers (includes medical services, physicians, offices, doctors ' treatment to the patient, and their assistants) tests functional quality. Given the value of technical quality for the correct diagnosis, various health research shows that patients give priority to functional quality. (Swan & Köhler, Bowers, 1994).

According to Kacha et al., (2016) minimum standards of care and services (addressed by the Joint Commission International and Health on the Net Foundation, HON), compensation and cost considerations (due diligence protection before and after treatment), and provision of a patient-centered approach (Common Patient Cover) are included in the context of the international medical travel quality frameworks.

8.1 Joint Commission International (JCI) Standard

The JCI standards define the expected performance, structures, or functions for a JCI-accredited hospital. International Patient Safety Goals (IPSGs) by JCI are taken into account and checked as standards; the purposes of the standard help to explain the full meaning of the standard. It sets the intent and rationale of the test, sets the specification criteria and measures a standard specifies as to what will be assessed and be assigned to score during the on-site surveying process. The measures a standard describes the requirements for full compliance with this provision for each tier (JCI, 2014). The key components of the standards are listed in Table 8, as specified by JCI (2017), with brief details of each component.

Table 8. Joint Commission International (JCI) Standards – Overview

JCI Standard	Sub / Component	Details / Focus Areas
Accreditation Participation Requirements (APR)	Nil	The core aspects of these standards revolve around the binding commitment of hospitals on data reporting, timeliness, patient care, and safety, public reporting on patient care, Translation and interpretation services, Employee reporting on patient care issues, etc..
Patient-Centered Standards	International Patient Safety Goals (IPSG)	The standard component revolves around the accuracy of patient identification, Effective Communication (Telephonic/ Diagnostic Tests), High-Alert Medications, Ensure Safe Surgery, Reduce the Risk of Health Care-Associated Infections, Reduce the Risk of Patient Harm Resulting from Falls
	Access to Care and Continuity of Care (ACC)	Includes patient screening, matching, processing events, treatment continuity, discharge, referral, follow up, patient transfer, transportation (quality / safety). transportation services.
	Patient and Family Rights (PFR)	Processes are established that support the rights of the patient and the family, support the integrity of the patient, comply with patient values and beliefs and respond to requests for spiritual and religious consideration, the privacy and security of patient property, theft, information about the care of organs, tissue donation, etc.
	Assessment of Patients (AOP)	Deals with Detailed patient assessment procedures, Laboratory Services / Blood Bank and/or Transfusion Services / Radiology and Diagnostic Imaging Services / All these Services Must Meet Local standards, regulation, and managed by qualified personnel.
	Care of Patients (COP)	Provides support for all patients, provision of risk services, identification of changes in patient status, resuscitation services, treatment for feed and food, pain management, end-of-life care, provision of organ-or-tissue donation services, transplant programs
	Anesthesia and Surgical Care (ASC)	Organization and Management (Adhering to Regulation, Laws, Standard Procedures), Anesthesia Care / Surgical Care (Patient Assessment / Documentation / Protocols)
	Medication Management and Use (MMU)	Organization and Management (Adhering to Regulation, Laws, Standard Procedures), Selection and Procurement (Medical List / Availability), Storage, Ordering and Transcribing, Preparing, and Dispensing (Safety / Cleanliness), Administration, Monitoring.
	Patient and Family Education (PFE)	Education to Support patient and family participation in care decisions and care processes.
Health Care Organization Management Standards	Quality Improvement and Patient Safety (QPS)	Active system for continuous improvement and protection of patients in the hospital Data analysis and Sustainable development. presence of a Successful plan.

continues on following page

Table 8. Continued

JCI Standard	Sub / Component	Details / Focus Areas
	Prevention and Control of Infections (PCI)	Revolves around the responsibility (training, education) of individuals on infection prevention and control activities, Resources (Scientific Knowledge, Laws), Medical Equipment, Devices, and Supplies (cleaning, disinfection, sterilization, and storage process), Infectious Waste (Disposal), Food Services, Construction Risks, Transmission of Infections (Barriers / Isolation procedures), Quality Improvement and Program Education
	Governance, Leadership and Direction (GLD)	Hospital management emphasis, Chief Executive Accountability(s). Medical personnel associations and accounting services; Hospital divisions and operations directorate; administrative and medical ethics; health profession educational; human subjects: Hospital governance; Hospital leadership management for performance and patient safety; Hospital leadership in contract / resource decisions; Hospital staff management and accounting
	Facility Management and Safety (FMS)	It covers leadership and preparation (fire safety, inspection), security and safety, hazardous materials, disaster preparedness, medical equipment / services network, facilities management, and security program, staff training, and supervision.
	Staff Qualifications and Education (SQE)	Involves the scheduling, registration of medical personnel (licensing), and the allocation of the health care professionals (credential verification) on the supervision and evaluation, reassignment, and renewal of clinical privileges.
	Management of Information (MOI)	Focuses on Planning and Design of Hospital Information Systems and Management (Technology, Medical Records,)
Academic Medical Center Hospital Standards	Medical Professional Education (MPE)	Hospital involvement in the provision of medical training.
	Human Subjects Research Programs (HRP)	Is accountable for the protection of human research subjects.

Source: JCI (2017)

9. MEDICAL TOURISM IN INDIA – CASE INSIGHTS

According to IMTJ (2017), 460,000 foreign patients in total were in Indian hospitals in 2015-16, compared to less than half of the statistics on medical visas. Out of three foreign patients in Indian hospitals one is from Bangladesh, at 165,000 - only 58,300 of these were true medical tourists on a medical visa. Other top nations for medical visas includes, Afghanistan: 29,492, Iraq: 9,131, Nigeria: 5,994, Kenya: 3,240 and Pakistan: 1,921. Orthopedics, cardiology, and neurology as among the top reasons for foreign patients gong to India. For the year 2015 to 2016 the highest average revenue per patient for foreigners in India is $2,906, led by Pakistan ($2,084), the nations ($1,950), Russia ($1,618) and Iraq ($1,530) of the CIS (company of independent States).

According to IBEF (2018), the Factors Driving Health Tourism in India includes, Medical Personnel (Skilled doctors and specialists with Global Exposure, High Quality of Nursing), Modern Medical Infrastructure and Resources (Modern Technology, World-Class Medical Supplies, high-quality implants), Low Cost and Quality Treatment, Diverse geography (numerous tourism destinations), No waiting period for international patients, Alternative Medicines for Curing Chronic Ailments, Emergence of multi-specialty hospitals, Favourable exchange, cheaper international travel, English speaking people, extensive use of facilities only accessible to English interpreters, International medical insurance providers, Global banking services, and web-based access to data.

The Government of India is also responsible for providing medical visas and "M-visas" to health tourists. The State Government / Regional Registry Offices (FRRO) can be extended for one year on the basis of professional qualifications or guidance from well-known or recognized national hospitals. International patients prefer Indian for cardiology, gastroenterology, pediatrics, orthopedics oncology, Joint repair, limited access procedures, dentistry, cosmetics, ophthalmology, gynaecology, and obstetrics in general. International tourists including Yoga, Ayurveda, Siddha, Acupuncture, Skincare, Other Indian practices, etc., have also provided complementary medical treatments.

According to the KPMG Medical Value Travel in India publication (KPMG, 2014), the factors that help promote medical tourism includes Economical accessibility, quality healthcare, direct service, anonymity, enhancement in communications, opportunities to fly, and wealthy patients.

On a comparative level of Global JCI standards, the National Accreditation Board for Hospitals & Healthcare Providers (NABH), which is a constituent board of Quality Council of India, provides services for hospitals on quality assurance and quality improvement frameworks. Patient safety and quality of care are the major focus areas of the standards. Focus on. Continuous Monitoring and Integrated Corrective Action Plan are the foundations that lead to Organization Quality Culture across varied functions.

As is the case with JCI, NABH covers broad fields of Patient-Centered Quality, such as Access, Assessment and Care Continuity (AAC), Patient Care (COP), Medicine Management (MOM), Patient Rights and Education (PRE), Continuous Quality Improvement (CQI), Responsibilities for Management (ROM), Facility Management and Security (FMS), Human Resources Management (HRM), Hospital infections management (HIC) and Information Management System (IMS) are a number of organizations that have been adopting the Centered Principles (NABH, 2019)

9.1 Top Medical Tourism Destinations and Hospitals in India

Skyscanner (2018), reports the top Indian Medical Tourism destinations as below:

1. Chennai - Confederation of India Industry study has found that some 40 percent of individuals choose high-quality care in Chennai in bone marrow transplantation, cardiac bypass, eye surgery, hip replacement, and alternative medicines
2. Mumbai - made up of super specialist hospitals, research, and diagnostics for orthopedic studies and weight-loss surgical procedures, which are also known as cosmetic surgery and treatments in Ayurveda
3. New Delhi - Several private hospitals offer service / packages in General surgery, Eye Surgery, Heart Care, and Neuro Surgeries
4. Goa - Mostly focused on Health and Wellness Tourism
5. Ahmedabad - Has world-class amenities, Home to Civil Hospital -one of the largest in Asia, SAL hospital, and others

Medical Tourism (2019) gives a glimpse of the top hospitals in India based on their facilities and Specialties in the forthcoming section in Table 9.

Table 9. Top Hospitals in India

Indian Hospital	Facilities	Specialties
BLK Super Specialty Hospital, Pusa Road, New Delhi	Modular operation Rooms, electronic security system, modern fire-management systems, medical record transfer, online doctor consultation, personal assistance / concierge, private rooms for patients' available, special dietary requests accepted	Anesthesiology, Ayurveda, Bariatric, and Adv. Laparoscopy Surgery, Dental & Maxillofacial Surgery, Dermatology, Emergency & Acute Care Medicine, Endocrinology and Endocrine Surgery, ENT & Cochlear Implant, External Counter Pulsation, General and Minimal Access Surgery, Gynecology & Obstetrics Hepato Pancreato Biliary Surgery, etc.
Fortis La Femme, Delhi	Foetal & Genetic Medicine, High-Level Diagnostics (Ultrasound, Mammography & Bone Densitometry), Mamma Mia: Wellness, Fitness & Education for New & Expecting Mothers, A variety of rooms to choose from, Cafeteria, Gift Shop	High-Risk Pregnancy Care, Advanced New-born Care (NICU), Minimal Access General & Gynecological Surgeries, Fertility Clinic & IVF, Aesthetic & Cosmetic Surgery, etc.
Columbia Asia Referral Hospital, Yeshwanthpur, Bengaluru	Histopathology, Clinical Pathology, Cytology, Biochemistry, Microbiology, Pathology, 24 Hours Cafe at Ground Floor, Out Patient Cafe at 4th Floor, Inpatient dining, Speech Therapy, Swallowing Therapy, Voice Therapy	Anesthesiology, Bariatric Surgery, Cardiology and Interventional Cardiology, Cardiothoracic and Vascular Surgery, Critical Care Medicine, Dermatology, Emergency Medicine, Endocrinology, ENT, Head and Neck Surgery, Gastroenterology, General Surgery, Infectious Diseases, Internal Medicine, Liver Transplant & Hepatic Surgery, Maxillofacial Surgery, Medical Oncology & Clinical Hematology, Minimally Invasive Gynecology, Psychiatry, Pulmonology and Sleep Medicine, Renal Transplant, Rheumatology, Surgical Gastroenterology, Urology, Vascular and Endovascular Surgery etc.

continues on following page

Table 8. Continued

Indian Hospital	Facilities	Specialties
VPS Rockland Hospital, Dwarka, New Delhi	Blood Bank, Trauma Care, Ambulance, Laboratory, Pharmacy, Radiology & Imaging, Preventive Health Checks, Cancer treatment, Pediatrics, Clinical psychology, Anesthesiology, Internal medicine, Pain Management Clinic, Dermatology, Pulmonology and sleep medicine, Respiratory medicine and critical care, Department of physiotherapy and rehabilitation, Preventive health check-ups	Center of Excellence for Cardiology, Orthopedics and Spine care, Neurosciences, Renal Sciences, Gastroenterology, Emergency & Trauma Care, Knee replacement, Joint replacement, Hip replacement, Renal transplant and urology, General and bariatric surgery (minimal access), Dental and maxillofacial surgery, Plastic, aesthetic and reconstructive surgery, ENT, Head and neck surgery, Surgical Oncology, Obstetrics and gynecology, Ophthalmology
Fortis Escorts Heart Institute (FEHI), New Friends Colony, New Delhi	ICD Clinic, Pacemaker Clinic, Heart Failure Clinic, One Stop Shop for Counseling, Admission and Discharge, Overnight Attendant Lounge, ATM, Parking, Valet Parking, Pharmacy, Emerald Lounge, International Services Desk, Corporate Desk, Business Centre, etc.	Cardiac Bypass Surgery, Minimally Invasive Surgery, Interventional Cardiology, Non-invasive Cardiology, Pediatric Cardiology, Pediatric Cardiac Surgery, Electrophysiology, and Preventive Cardiology, Heart Transplant, Kidney and Urology Institute, Bone and Joint Institute, Liver and Digestive Diseases Institute
Akshaya Apollo Hospital, Bhat GIDC Estate, Ahmedabad	Prevention, Treatment, Rehabilitation and health education for patients, their families and clients, Spiral CT scan, Electrophysiology, Gamma camera, Cell saver in CT OT and Lithotripter, Preventive Health Checks, Occupational Health Centre, On-site Doctor, Ambulance Service, Screening Camps, Training and Education, Awareness Lectures, Health and Wellness Workshops, Dependent Health Care Programs, Corporate Emergency Management Services	Cardiac Sciences, Neuro Sciences, Orthopaedics, Cancer, Emergency Medicine, and Solid Organ Transplants
Max Super Specialty Hospital, Saket	State-of-art 1.5 Tesla MRI machine and a 64 Slice CT Angio, Asia's first Brain SUITE- an advanced Neurosurgical operation theatre	Cardiac, Oncology (Medical, Surgical and Radiotherapy), Neurosciences, Obstetrics and Gynecology, Metabolic and Bariatric Surgery, Bone Marrow Transplant, Urology, Nephrology, Kidney Transplant, Aesthetics, and Reconstructive Surgery, and other ancillary services
Medanta, Gurugram, Haryana	Air Ambulance, Emergency & Trauma Care, Wards & Rooms, Critical Care Units, eClinic-Telemedicine Services, Patient, Support Services, Lab Tests & Diagnostics, Day Care	Bone and Joint Institute, Cancer Institute, Breast Services, Head and Neck Oncology, Institute of Critical Care and Anesthesiology, Institute of Digestive and Hepatobiliary Sciences, Gastroenterology, GI Surgery, GI Oncology and Bariatric Surgery, Heart Institute, Clinical and Preventive Cardiology, Electrophysiology and Pacing, Kidney and Urology Institute, Institute of Liver Transplantation and Regenerative Medicine, Ayurvedic Medicine, Respiratory and Sleep Medicine etc.
Continental Hospitals, Gachibowli, Hyderabad	Advanced Diagnostics- Molecular, Advanced Diagnostics- Flow Cytometry, Cobas Modular 6000- Immunoassay + Routine Chemistry, Roche E411 Analyzer, D10 Hemoglobin Testing System- BioRad, Hematology, Hemostasis & Coagulation Testing, Microbiology & Serology, Histopathology	Continental Institute of Cancer, Continental Institute of Orthopedics, Continental Institute of Neurosciences and Rehabilitation, Continental Institute of Cardiovascular Sciences, Continental Institute Of Gastroenterology & Liver Diseases, Continental Centre For Women And Child, Continental Institute of Emergency, Trauma Services & Critical Care
Lilavati Hospital & Research Centre, Mumbai, Maharashtra	Ambulance, Blood Bank, Critical Care, Day Care, Diagnostics, Dialysis Centre, Emergency/ Trauma, Health Check-Up, Interventional Neuroradiology, Interventional Radiology, OutPatient, Pharmacy/ Chemist, Physiotherapy, Social Initiatives, Visa Investigation	Anesthesiology, Audiology & Speech Therapy, Bariatric Surgery, Cardiology & Cardio Vascular Thoracic Surgery, Chest Medicine, Corneal Transplant, Colorectal Surgery, Dental, Dermo Cosmetology, Diabetology & Endocrinology, ENT, Head & Neck Surgery, Gastroenterology & Gastrointestinal Surgery, Hair Transplant, Headache & Migraine Clinic, Infectious Diseases, Liver Transplant, Minimally Invasive Surgery, Urology/ Andrology etc.

Source: Medical Tourism (2019)

The other major hospitals in the ranking of Tourmy India (2016), includes, Rockland Hospital – New Delhi, Primus Super Specialty Hospital – New Delhi, Columbia Asia Referral Hospital – Yeshwanthpur, Apollo Hospitals – Bangalore, Fortis Hospital – Cunningham Road – Bangalore, Narayana Institute of Cardiac Sciences (NICS) – Bangalore, Global Hospitals – Chennai, Sri Ramachandra Medical Centre (SRMC) – Chennai, Apollo Gleneagles Hospitals – Chennai, Fortis Hospitals – Mohali and Fortis Hospitals – Amritsar.

9.2 Health Tourism in India - A SWOT Analysis

The various aspects of SWOT Analysis of Health Tourism in India are analyzed and summarized in Table 10, based on data from various secondary sources (Vandna, 2013; KPMG 2018, Aparna, Srinivas & Pathi, 2015)

Table 10. Health Tourism in India - A SWOT Analysis

Strengths	**Weakness**
The credibility of Indian Doctors, Flexibility, Special Skills Voice of Experienced Medical Travelers / Customers about Brand Image (Low-Cost Destination) World-Class Medical technology, equipment, facilities and infrastructure English Speaking Employees / Service Providers Absence of racial discrimination Excellent Education System, Supplying Consistent and Qualified Medical and Paramedical personnel, meeting the International Expectations Unique *Indian Systems of Medicine including Ayurveda, Yoga and Naturopathy, Unani, Siddha, and Homoeopathy*	Lesser availability of NABH Accredited Hospitals to Cater to Increasing Demand Maximum Inbound Medical Tourists are from Non-English-Speaking Countries (West Asia, Africa, etc.) demand special training in language skills for the workforce. Allied Costs of Medical Tourists, namely Accommodation, Transport, etc. are comparatively higher than similar Competitive Destinations like Thailand, Philippines, etc.
Opportunities	**Threats**
Non – Availability of Low-cost treatment, Quality Medical Care in Western Countries as well as third world countries, is a big opportunity to be exploited. Medical Care Quality, Standards, are comparatively higher than South Asian Countries like Myanmar, Bangladesh, Srilanka, Afghanistan, Maldives, etc. Similarly, the patients from Africa and the Middle East prefer India due to lack of good medical facilities and expertise in home countries, as well as there is no racial discrimination in India. Compulsory Employee Health Insurance Coverage Policy of USA provides the big opportunity of availing it in low-cost destinations like India. Insurance companies charge lesser premiums for treatments at low-cost destinations. Huge waiting lists of patients for non-urgent medical care, in Public Health Care Systems of Western Countries.	Competitors like Singapore, Thailand have the edge over India, since Medical Tourists, prefer to bundle their medical treatment along with leisure travel in such destinations, where India is lacking. Increased Non-English-Speaking Medical Tourist flow, Infrastructure Issues (Road, Airports, etc.), Lengthier Visa Processing Time, etc. Even the medical visa recently implemented has doubled the cost to the concerned Local Foreigners Registration Office of tourist visa, immediate and automatic registration of patients with Medical visas within 14 days of their arrival.

9.3 Competitive Position Analysis Based on Porter's Diamond Model

The entire framework he calls' diamond' involves a dynamic system, according to Porter (1990), in which each of the components communicates and merge. Thee various components of Porter's Diamond Model are detailed in forthcoming section for understanding in explaining the competitive position of India in Medical Tourism.

1. Good plan, structure, and competitiveness (Focuses on the dynamic nature of World / Competitive Conditions, which has a direct impact on the organizations to increases their productivity and innovation).
2. Demand conditions (Due to Increased Customer demand, the competing firms are constantly pressurized to improve their competitiveness by means of innovative products and high quality, etc.).
3. Similar and supporting industries (closer downstream and upstream companies, it provides an advantage and easy and quick information exchange, facilitates the continuous and creative exchange of ideas).
4. Conditions of factor (contradictive to conventional wisdom, Porter argues the development and not inheritance of "primary" output factors (or specialized factors). Skilled labor, capital, and infrastructure are treated as specialized factors of production. Non-key" factors (Raw material, unskilled labor), on the contrary, provide minimal competitive advantage). In Porter's Diamond Model, The Government Role is considered to provide catalyst and encouragement for the firms to move towards higher levels of performance.

Context of Firms' Strategy and Rivalry in the Indian Medical Tourism Sector

One of Porter's main findings on national competitiveness is that there are still active industries in clusters. They are usually in close relation to other related and friendly sectors and benefit from competitive advantages. India's strategic strategy is to achieve association with a world-class institution, a growing move towards an understanding with the International Medical Schools and work institutions in India. In this case, an international healthcare organization has an extremely productive approach. The affiliations provide the Institute with a leading edge in the latest field research and therefore provide a good image for the organization.

Increased foreign investment across vertical lines, including medical facilities, health care, clinical services, pharmaceutical, and product development services, private hospitals, competitively dynamic healthcare standards, and 21 Joint

International Commissions (JCI) certified and the hospitals in India (Aparna, Srinivas & Pathi 2015).

Demand Conditions in India

India draws ever-growing tourists mainly from the Middle East, Iran, Pakistan, Afghanistan, Bangladesh, Turkey, Europe, and the United States in its detailed analysis of Sheik (2013). Andhra Pradesh, Karnataka, Tamil Nadu, Maharashtra, and New Delhi are the States which are quickly becoming India's best medical resorts.

The local and regional demand for medical tourism led to the rapid growth of medical capacity. India is a world leader of choice in providing top-quality medical specialists such as cardiac treatments. The rise in budget airline travel to South and South-East Asia has made local travel to be considerably more affordable and accessible, driven by the international healthcare demand.

The media have also been instrumental in supporting the tourist industry in medical science by publicizing recent advances in medicine and technology, price comparison information, and patient evidence, thereby increasing patient trust.

It is projected that the Indian economy will grow along with the population. For the coming four decades, Goldman Sachs expects an Indian economy that will expand at least 5 percent per annum and will be the most vigorous development of the only emerging economy. Economic growth creates a healthy middle class. Through rising buying power parity, more discretionary revenues will be made available over healthcare spending, thereby growing demand (Price Water House Coopers, 2007).

Indian Health Industry-related and Supporting Industries

In India, there have been several support industries that enable the medical tourism sector to expand. A large pharmaceutical industry is also a new example and a successful international generic drug exporter (PWC 2007). A strong market is also one of the fastest-growing drug markets worldwide. In making India an attractive market for medical tourism, transport played an important role. In developing new airports in the 2 Tier 2 cities and metro stations, the government has allowed 100 percent FDI. This design resulted in the successful completion in less than five years of a functional and world-class airport, thus increasing the air traffic handling capacity in all of India's major cities (IEBF) (Prakash 2011).

Factor Conditions in India

The conditions of factors are divided into two categories: source and use factors. Historical, economic, mineral, agricultural and forest assets have origins in their nature-derived factors. These are commonly found in nature. Variables based on use are variables that are then manually determined. These factors include the number of qualified employees in the country's medical tourism sector, work hours and work ethics, infrastructure, accommodation facilities, the transport network, etc., particularly targeted at medical tourists and the use of skillful labor items. Competitiveness-related variables may be classified as human resources, physical resources, information resources, capital resources and investment in infrastructure (Porter, 1990).

India has a major advantage of a variety of climates, natural resources, and health tourists who come from the colder climate with source-based influences. The costs of care in India are not only lower under the definition of usage-based factors, but the waiting times are zero. On the one hand the decrease of access, an increase in medical treatment costs, and a decline of quality in the West, while on the other hand easy access, quality improvement, and low medical care costs in India are the primary drivers of growth in the Indian medical tourism industry. The medical services of India are primarily used for foreign purposes and include dental care, orthopedics and trauma, cardiac care including surgery, urology, neurosurgery, plastic and cosmetic procedures, laparoscopic surgery, gastroenterology, kidney transplanting, and knee / hip operations. Certain considerations of use are its personal knowledge and the diversity of medical disciplines in India.

The Role of Government and Chance

In the case of India, The Government has been instrumental in supporting the Medical Tourism Industry, especially in permitting private investments in Research and Development, Medical Technology, and Hospital Development. The Brand building activity of the Government using various IT tools has proven a success story in many sectors including Medical Tourism.

By chance, despite the many factors, India's strategic location has attracted Medical tourists not only from Asian countries like Bangladesh, Myanmar, Srilanka, etc., but also from Africa and Middle East. The Medical tourism industry is thriving not only by the International market but also due to the huge demand surge in local market also. This chance factor has led to developing India has top Medical tourist destination in terms of low pricing as well Quality Medical Care. The non-availability of low-cost treatment, increased waiting lists, in Western Countries, Opening of Financial sector of India, Easy FOREX transfer / Payment Methods can also be considered as a Chance factor for India.

Table 11 gives a classification of the services spectrum of medical tourism in India vis-à-vis its competitive countries.

Table 11. Classification of the services spectrum of medical tourism across the globe

Tourism Category	Wellness Tourism	Alternative Systems of Medicine	Cosmetic Surgery	Advanced and Life Savings Healthcare
Services offered	Spas, Stress relief, rejuvenation centers	Ayurveda's, Siddha treatment for diseases, e.g. (For Rheumatism Arthritis)	Fat reduction (Tummy reduction), Skin Care, Dental treatments, Plastic Surgery, Breast enhancement,	Open transplants, cardiovascular surgery, Eye treatment, Hip Replacement, In Vitro fertilization
Profit Margin	Low	Low	Medium	High
Key Competitors	Thailand, South Africa	No Competitors	South Africa, Cuba, Thailand	Singapore, Jordan, Thailand, and Malaysia
India's Strength	Low (Dominated by Thailand)	Kerala south is a leader in this product	Low (South African and Thailand are dominated)	High-India has a strong image in medical tourism

Source: Suman & Swati (2011)

The Federation of Indian Chambers of Commerce and Industry (FICCI) has made wide-ranging recommendations to capitalize on the available opportunities in medical tourism as detailed in the forthcoming section. (IMTJ, 2015).

- Simplified and relaxed medical visa regulations (Since The medical visa process for India is often a lengthy procedure taking 5 days to 2 months depending upon the country of visa application)
- Multiple entry medical visas to facilitate follow-up treatment. (Grant multiple-entry medical visas upon recommendation from healthcare provider)
- Promotion of medical tourism by all Indian embassies.
- Setting up of medical facilitation desk at Indian airports to eliminate the role of touts and middlemen and facilitate the smooth patient transition
- Faster immigration facilities at Indian airports. (Separate immigration counter for medical travelers)
- Checklist with every medical visa. (Involves instructions to carry all medical records, a copy of the visa invitation letter and their doctor's recommendations; Special checklist for patients traveling for high-end treatment (Transplants, Prior Legal approval); Advice to warn prospective patients about unreliable touts)
- Access to ambulance and stretchers at airports. (Especially that of Private hospitals)
- Fiscal laws to be relaxed for genuine foreign patients (Increase wire transfer limit for funds transfer to India; Sign treaties and agreements with foreign

countries to ease funds transfer to India for medical treatment; Hospital recommendation should be considered as proof for ease of funds transfer.)

- Specialist agencies to promote and improve Indian medical tourism (Regular meetings and updates; Multi-sector participative meetings)
- Single consultative platform representing all ministries involved in medical tourism, to endorse and encourage medical tourism at a national level.
- Nationally authenticated/recognized government medical tourism website
- Public Relations Campaign (On Indian medical tourism)
- Incorporate specialized training of nurses meeting International Quality requirements and expectations.
- Enable Indian Doctors working abroad with the latest experience, by way of easier procedural clearances.
- Improve infrastructure. (Roads, Airports)
- Promote NABH platform globally (NABH, the highest accreditation followed in India, is as internationally authorized as JCI.)

10. CONCLUSION

The chapter clarifies the fundamental differences in the various forms of health tourism and how medical tourism is unique and important to critically ill health travelers. The chapter also throws light on the growing trends in Medical Tourism, emerging destinations, promotion of Medical Tourism, Cost details, and comparison of Competitive destinations, drivers and challenges facing the medical tourism industry. With respect to the Quality standards, the chapter specifically elaborates the various components of JCI standards for better understanding of the Medical Tourism Industry stakeholders.

Current trends in medical tourism include foreign investment (private health centers and multi-specialty hospitals), expansion of Asia (technically equipped, cheaper), high standards of hotel accommodation, and the most advanced technology. And India is in the top position in terms of cost advantage in almost all types of medical procedures, led by Turkey, Malaysia, Thailand, and Singapore. Major medical tourism drivers include technology, brokers, insurance products, allies, service providers and country-level strategies. Globally, major challenges in medical tourism include the areas of safety (Food Preparation, Water, Environment), quality control (Staff Credentials, Actual Service Quality), accreditation (Standard Assessment / Monitor), follow-up care and the resolution of complications (Patient Consent / Policies and Procedures).

Even from the specific case of the Indian Medical Tourism Industry, rich insights are drawn into how Indians have developed into a world-class and low-cost medical tourist destination. The top cities and hospitals are identified in the context of the Indian Medical Tourism Industry. The pivotal role of Government support, FDI investments in Service industry, support from related industries (Finance sector, Easier payment methods, Transport infrastructure), Skilled personnel and Expert Physicians, Global Quality standards, Credibility, English speaking advantage, etc. are the major determining factors that promotes Brand India as one of the Top Medical Tourist Destinations.

REFERENCES

Adlung, R. (2009). *Trade in healthcare and health insurance services: The GATS as a supporting actor?* [Staff Working Paper ERSD-2009-15]. World Trade Organization Economic Research and Statistics Division.

Aircare1. (2017). *Medical Tourism Trends, Facts and Figures.* http://www.airambulanceone.com/2017-medical-tourism-trends-facts-figures/

Aparna S., Srinivas Rao P., Pathi S.N. (2015). Health Tourism and Its Impact on Economy. *IOSR Journal of Humanities and Social Science, 20*(3), 89-92.

Baker McArthur. (2015). *D. AlmaTourism – Journal of Tourism, Culture and Territorial Development. Medical Tourism Development, Challenges and Opportunities for Asia.*

Bowers, M. R., Swan, J. E., & Koehler, W. F. (1994). What attributes determine quality and satisfaction with health care delivery? *Health Care Management Review, 19*(4), 49–55. doi:10.1097/00004010-199401940-00006 PMID:7896552

Bushel, R., & Sheldon, P. J. (Eds.). (2009). *Wellness and Tourism: Mind, Body, Spirit, Place.* Cognizant Communication Corporation.

Carrera, P., & Lunt, N. (2010). A European perspective on medical tourism: The need for a knowledge base. *International Journal of Health Services, 40*(3), 469–484. doi:10.2190/HS.40.3.e PMID:20799671

Chandra, Sharma, Masih, Jamaluddin, & Sharma. (2013). *Medical Tourism in India: Perspectives and Marketing Challenges.* Academic Press.

Christopher, J. (2008). The biggest challenges facing medical tourism. *International Medical Travel Journal.* https://www.imtj.com/articles/christopher-jones-and-louis-keith-speak-biggest-challenges-facing-medical-tourism/

Cormany, D. (2008). Taking a pulse on potential medical tourism destinations: The hospitality and tourism industries. *Medical Tourism Magazine, 7*, 34–37.

Fernandes, J. V., & Fernandes, F. M. V. (2013). *Health and Wellness Tourism Today*. https://www.medicaltourismmag.com/health-and-wellness-tourism-today

Glinos, I.A., & Baeten, R. (2006, September). *A literature review of cross-border patient mobility in the European Union*. Brussels: Observatoire social européen.

Grönroos, C. (1990). *Service Management and Marketing*. Lexington Books.

Gupta, P., Pandey, B., Hussain, S., Kumar, A., & Sharma, R. (2015). Challenges and Strengths of Medical Tourism in Delhi NCR. *DU Journal of Undergraduate Research and Innovation*, *1*(2), 230–251.

Hesse-Biber, S. N., & Leavy, P. (2011). *The practice of qualitative research* (2nd ed.). Sage.

IBEF. (2018). *Health Tourism: Destination India*. https://www.ibef.org/download/Health-Tourism_091211.pdf

IEBF. (n.d.). *Upgrading India's Airport Infrastructure. Indo European business forum*. https://www.ibef.org/download/airport_upgradation.pdf

IHRC. (2018). *The International Healthcare Research Center - Medical Tourism Index*. https://www.healthcareresearchcenter.org/medical-tourism-index/

IMTJ. (2015). *16-point agenda to position India as a preferred medical tourism destination*. https://www.imtj.com/news/16-point-agenda-position-india-preferred-medical-tourism-destination/

IMTJ. (2017). *India medical tourism statistics released*. https://www.imtj.com/news/india-medical-tourism-statistics-released/

JCI. (2014). *Joint Commission International Standards for Hospitals*. https://www.jcrinc.com/assets/1/14/JCIH14_Sample_Pages.pdf

JCI. (2017). *Joint Commission International Accreditation Standards for Hospitals* (6th ed.). https://www.jointcommissioninternational.org/assets/3/7/JCI_Standards_Only_6th_Ed_Hospital.pdf

Kácha, O., Kovács, B. E., McCarthy, C., Schuurmans, A. A., Dobyns, C., Haller, E., Hinrichs, S., & Ruggeri, K. (2016). An Approach to Establishing International Quality Standards for Medical Travel. *Frontiers in Public Health*, *4*, 29. doi:10.3389/fpubh.2016.00029 PMID:26973825

KPMG. (2014). *Medical Value travel in India*. http://www.travelbizmonitor.com/images/kpmg_ficci_heal_sep_2014_271014.pdf

KPMG. (2018). *Medical Tourism - Industry focus, KPMG in Thailand.* https://assets.kpmg/content/dam/kpmg/th/pdf/2018/03/th-medical-tourism-industry-focus-secured.pdf

Leedy, P. D., & Ormrod, J. E. (2005). *Practical research: Planning and design* (8th ed.). Pearson Merrill Prentice Hall.

Lewis-Beck, M. S., Bryman, A. E., & Liao, T. F. (2004). Conceptualization, Operationalization, and Measurement. In *The SAGE Encyclopedia of Social Science Research Methods*. SAGE.

Linda, D. B., & Dianne, J. B. (2007). *Legal Issues - Traveling with Privacy Protection*. Available from: https://www.medicaltourismmag.com/issuearticle/legal-issues-traveling-with-privacy-protection.html

Lunt, N., & Carrera, P. (2010). Medical tourism: Assessing the evidence on treatment abroad. *Maturitas, 66*(1), 27–32. doi:10.1016/j.maturitas.2010.01.017 PMID:20185254

Lunt, N., Smith, R., Exworthy, M., Green, S., Horsfall, D., & Mannion, R. (2011). *Medical tourism: Treatments, markets and health system implications: A scoping review*. OECD. http://www.oecd.org/dataoecd/51/11/48723982.pdf

MacReady, N. (2007). Developing countries court medical tourists. *Lancet, 369*(9576), 1849–1850. doi:10.1016/S0140-6736(07)60833-2 PMID:17549816

McKercher, B. (2016). Towards a taxonomy of tourism products. *Tourism Management, 54*(June), 196–208. doi:10.1016/j.tourman.2015.11.008

Medhekar, A., & Haq, F. (2018). *Halal branding for medical tourism: Case of Indian hospitals. Digital Marketing and Consumer Engagement: Concepts, Methodologies, Tools, and Applications*. doi:10.4018/978-1-4666-6272-8.ch008

Medical Tourism. (2018). *Top 10 Hospitals for Medical Tourism in India.* https://www.medicalindiatourism.com/blog/top-hospitals-medical-tourism-india.html

Meštrovic, T. (2014). *What is Medical Tourism?* https://www.news-medical.net/health/What-is-Medical-Tourism.aspx

Mohanty, D., & Madhav, T. P. (2006). Medical Tourism: India's Competitive Advantage. *Health Tourism an Introduction, 73*.

MTA. (2019). *Medical Tourism Association*. https://medicaltourism.com/Forms/price-comparison.aspx

MTI. (2016). *2016 MTI Overview*. https://www.medicaltourismindex.com/overview/

Munro, J. W. (2012). What is Medical Tourism? *Best Practices in Medical Tourism*, *3*, 2–26.

NABH. (2019). *NABH Standards for Hospitals*. https://www.nabh.co/standard.aspx

Pankaj, M., Niyat, S., & Dilip, V. (2013). Medical tourism-destination India. *Commerce and Management*, *2*(3), 29–39.

Patil, C. V., Amrutkar, R. S., Bhavna, R. S., & Ramachandran, M. (2015). Emerging Trends and Future Prospects of Medical Tourism in India. *J. Pharm. Sci. & Res.*, *7*(5), 248–251.

Pollard, K. (2012). *How can we measure a destination's attractiveness?* https://www.imtj.com/blog/how-can-we-measure-destinations-attractiveness/

Porter, M. (1990). *E*. The Competitive Advantage of Nations.

PriceWaterHouse Coopers. (2007). *Healthcare in India Emerging market report 2007*. Author.

Pruthi, R. (2006). *Medical Tourism in India*. Arise Publishers and Distributors.

PTI. (2013). Retrieved on 1 Nov 2019 from economictimes.indiatimes.com/articleshow/19766120.cms?utm_source=contentofinterest&utm_medium=text&utm_campaign=cppst

L. Puczkó (Ed.). (2010). Health, Wellness and Tourism: healthy tourists, healthy business? *Proceedings of the Travel and Tourism Research Association Europe 2010, Annual Conference*.

Ramírez de Arellano, A. B. (2007). Patients without borders: The emergence of medical tourism. *International Journal of Health Services*, *37*(1), 193–198. doi:10.2190/4857-468G-2325-47UU PMID:17436992

Reddy, S., York, V. K., & Brannon, L. A. (2010). Travel for Treatment: Students' Perspective on Medical Tourism. *International Journal of Tourism Research*, *12*(5), 510–522. doi:10.1002/jtr.769

Reisman, D. (2010). *Health Tourism: Social Welfare Through International Trade*. Edward Elgar. doi:10.4337/9781849805537

Remya, V. (2015). Kerala: Health Tourism Hub for Ayurveda. *International Journal of Social Sciences and Management*, *2*(3), 222–227.

Shaikh, S. B. (2013). Medical and Wellness Tourism: Opportunities and Challenges-Marketing 'Brand India'. *Research Journal of Management Sciences*, *2*(1), 1–6.

Sharma, A. (2013). Medical tourism: Emerging challenges and future prospects. *International Journal of Business and Management Invention*, *2*(1), 21–29.

Shimazono, Y. (2007). The State of the International Organ Trade: A Provisional Picture Based on Integration of Available Information. *Bulletin of the World Health Organization*, *85*(12), 955–962. doi:10.2471/BLT.06.039370 PMID:18278256

Singh, N. (2013). Exploring the factors influencing the travel motivations of US medical tourists. *Current Issues in Tourism*, *16*(5), 436–454. doi:10.1080/13683500.2012.695341

Skyscanner. (2018). https://www.skyscanner.co.in/news/medical-tourism-spots-in-india

Smith, M., & Puczkó, L. (2008). Health and wellness tourism. Elsevier/Butterworth-Heinemann.

Smith, R., Chanda, R., & Tangcharoensathien, V. (2009). Trade in health-related services. *Lancet*, *373*(9663), 517–602. doi:10.1016/S0140-6736(08)61778-X PMID:19167053

Suman, K. D., & Swati, P. (2011). Medical Tourism in India: Issues, Opportunities and Designing Strategies for Growth and Development. *International Journal of Multidisciplinary Research.*, *1*(3), 188.

Turner, L. (2009). Commercial Organ Transplantation in the Philippines. *Cambridge Quarterly of Healthcare Ethics*, *8*(2), 192–196. doi:10.1017/S0963180109090318 PMID:19263601

Vandna, M. (2013). Health Tourism in India - A SWOT Analysis. *International Journal of Research and Development - A Management Review*, 2(1), 2319–5479. http://www.irdindia.in/journal_ijrdmr/pdf/vol2_iss1/12.pdf

Vivekanand, A. M., & Hundekar, S. G. (2017). Scope, Importance, Challenges and Problems of Medical Tourism in Northern Karnataka. *International Journal of Innovative Research in Science, Engineering and Technology*, *6*(10), 19924. doi:10.15680/IJIRSET.2017.0610133

Woodman, J. (2007). *Patients Beyond Borders – Everybody's Guide to Affordable, World-Class Medical Tourism*. Healthy Travel Media.

Chapter 4
Medical Travel and Public Health:
Definitions, Frameworks, and Future Research

Wafa K. Alnakhi
https://orcid.org/0000-0003-2875-4173
Johns Hopkins Bloomberg School of Public Health, Johns Hopkins University, USA

ABSTRACT

The medical travel market industry is growing as millions of people are crossing borders to seek healthcare services every year. Yet there is not sufficient empirical research around medical travel. People typically call all medical travelers "medical tourists," a practice that is not helpful. Therefore, from a public health perspective, it is important to understand the definition of medical travel, the motivations behind travel, and how to overcome public health challenges that may occur as a result of this practice. Since medical travel is an experience that does not finish with obtaining health services, it is important to gather medical travelers' profiles before and after they access healthcare services. This will allow healthcare professionals to follow medical travelers' outcomes and assess their health-related quality of life. A robust evidence base will promote better future decisions related to medical travel. Creating an evidence base for medical travel will support upstream policies and strategies aimed at regulating the medical travel market.

DOI: 10.4018/978-1-7998-3427-4.ch004

INTRODUCTION

Travelling internationally to obtain healthcare services is becoming an increasingly common phenomenon and is rapidly growing worldwide (Burkett, 2007; Chanda, 2002; Eissler & Casken, 2013; Forgione & Smith, 2007; J. N. Henson, Guy, B.S. and Dotson, M.J., 2015; Smith, 2007). Every year, the Dubai Health Authority (DHA), the government health entity that oversees healthcare facilities in the Emirate of Dubai in the United Arab Emirates (UAE), pays millions of dirhams to cover thousands of UAE national patients seeking healthcare overseas. Although the government in the UAE provides "free" healthcare services to UAE nationals, in order for nationals to access primary and tertiary healthcare facilities as per the government law, there are thousands of patients who travel seeking healthcare outside the UAE under the sponsorship of DHA and other different sponsorships (*Dubai Health Authority Annual Statistic Books*, 2016).

The UAE nationals seek some of their healthcare services overseas due to reasons such as unavailability of treatment and long waiting times in the UAE. People often mix the overseas treatment terminology with the term "medical tourism". The term "medical tourism" is not clearly defined in literature. Researchers tend to refer to all patients seeking healthcare overseas as "medical tourists", which is a practice that is not helpful. It is important to clarify the term medical tourism, since medical travel and medical tourism cannot be used interchangeably, especially given the fact that the government of Dubai has two separate strategies. On the one hand, "Overseas Treatment Strategy" sends patients overseas to receive treatments that are unavailable in the UAE. On the other hand, "Medical Tourism Strategy" is an initiative to attract foreigners to use the private healthcare sectors combined with tourism facilities in the emirate of Dubai (Balaban, 2010). Therefore, it is important to understand the definition of medical travel and its different components. However, there have been very few empirical studies to understand the motivational factors that lead to medical travel (Guy, Henson, & Dotson, 2015; J. N. Henson, Guy, & Dotson, 2015; Metin Kozak, 2002). Information about medical travel is important to understand the motivational factors underpinning it and help governments and others to better regulate and strategize the medical travel market. Having evidence around medical travel will aid in understanding how people obtain information, make decisions when seeking healthcare overseas and, most importantly, manage the follow-up care when patients return to their home country from the treatment destinations (Turner, 2011).

Another reason to understand and study the field of medical travel is the importance of understanding medical travelers differing motivational factors when choosing treatment destinations, healthcare facilities, healthcare practitioners, and the treatment procedures. These motivational factors will vary based medical travelers' circumstances, such as demographic characteristics, medical condition, previous experiences, medical coverage, risk aversion, reputation of the destination, and the quality of healthcare services offered abroad. This chapter will help readers understand definitions of medical travel, it will provide a framework to understand the motivational factors that lead to medical travel, and it will cover how to address problems that will emerge related to public health.

DEFINITION OF MEDICAL TRAVEL

According to the literature, there are five main components used to define the phenomena of seeking healthcare overseas (Cohen, 2014; Lunt & Carrera, 2010; Snyder et al., 2015). The five components are: *Patient Mobility, Legality, Payment Type, Complexity Level, Flow Directions*, as shown in Figure 1.

Patient Mobility in Medical Travel

Temporary Visitor

Patients who are vacationing away from their home country, may utilize the healthcare services of the country of destination due to illness or accidents. Some of these patients are covered by their health insurance, and some are not. If the temporary visitor does not have funding from their health insurance, the patient will pay out of pocket to cover the healthcare fees.

Long-Term Resident

Later life mobility, or retirement migration, is another route for people to use healthcare services overseas. Both lower costs, attractive destinations, and ease of travel, have given people the option to retire and live in a country that is different than their homeland. This phenomenon can be seen among Europe citizens due to open European Union borders. A retiree may be covered for treatment by the country of origin, country of residence, or a private insurance.

Common Border

Countries sharing common borders may collaborate in financing healthcare coverage. For example, this phenomenon can be seen between Belgium and neighboring countries in Europe. One the other hand, U.S. citizens utilize healthcare services in Mexico due to lower costs, and Gulf Cooperation Council countries' citizens in the Middle East are also crossing borders to seek certain procedures, hospitals, or certified physicians who are not found in their own country.

Refugees and Asylum Seekers

Refugees and asylum seekers are individuals who cross national borders due to political crisis or instability in their home country. These individuals, who are forcibly displaced outside their country or their healthcare, have needs are not met in their homeland. Some of these refugees will seek healthcare in countries with close proximity to their homeland. For example, Syrian refuges access healthcare in neighboring countries, such as Lebanon, Jordan, or Turkey, due to the political crisis and instability that has taken place in Syria since 2011. Other countries accept refugees and asylum seekers from countries that are not in close proximity. For example, the United States, Canada, and many European countries are major host countries to many Syrian refuges (Bhatia & Wallace, 2007; El-Khatib, Scales, Vearey, & Forsberg, 2013; Toar, O'Brien, & Fahey, 2009)

Outsourced Patients

Patients are sent overseas by healthcare agencies or authorities through cross-national agreements. Leisure and tourism are not necessarily supposed to be part of the agreement. These agreements are driven by long waiting times, unavailability of specific health services in the home country, and lack of the specialty or advanced technology. Some healthcare insurance providers seek to offer care overseas, and they have reported a significant savings from outsourcing patients to lower-cost destinations compared to their home country.(Boyd, McGrath, & Maa, 2011). On the other hand, some governments or agencies outsource their patients to high cost destinations compared to their home country due to lack of specialty treatment and advanced technology in their home country. Each year, for example, the Dubai Health Authority (DHA), the government health entity that oversees healthcare facilities in the Emirate of Dubai in the United Arab Emirates (UAE), covers the cost of thousands of UAE national patients seeking healthcare overseas. These outsourced patients seek an array of treatments ranging from preventive to complex. Most frequently, patients from the UAE who are sponsored by DHA travel overseas for orthopedic surgery, cancer, neurology and neurosurgery, ophthalmology, cardiology and general surgeries (Wafa K Alnakhi et al., 2019).

Medical Tourists

Patients who are mobile through their own volition and more likely to consider a leisure and tourism part of a package when seeking medical travel. For example, a number of medical tourists from different nationalities visit Bumrungrad Hospital in Thailand. These medical travelers visit the hospital for various reasons, such as joint replacement, coronary artery, by pass, new or repaired heart valve. As another example, the Emirate of Dubai has launched the Dubai Medical Tourism strategy in 2012 to promote medical tourism in the Emirate and offer healthcare services and elective treatments to foreigners. This strategy allows foreigners utilize the healthcare services in the private sector. As a result, thousands of medical tourists visit Dubai every year for elective treatments, such as ophthalmology, cosmetics, dentistry, orthopedic surgeries, wellness, and dermatology.

Ethical and Legal Issues in Medical Travel

Ethical and legal concerns are central for medical travel. Poor follow-up care, adverse outcomes, or even death may result following procedures performed overseas. There is little global regulation of medical travel, and in many countries, law is reactive rather than being proactive. There are number of stakeholders involved in the medical travel. The main stakeholders are payers, patients, and healthcare providers. Understanding the views of these stakeholders is essential in order to understand the landscape of the industry to overcome many barriers related to regulation (Cohen, 2012). From a regulatory and legal perspective, seeking healthcare services overseas can be divided into three legal categories: legal in both countries, illegal in one country, and illegal in both countries.

Legal in Both Countries

The healthcare service that is most often sought by medical travelers is legal in both patients' home countries and the treatment destinations. As explained earlier, medical travelers with common borders, those outsourced, and medical tourists travelling under their own volition are driven overseas for many reasons, such as to avoid long waiting time and to seek specialty treatments that are not available or at higher costs in the home country. Medical conditions that medical travelers seek treatment for range from organ transplantation to cosmetic surgeries.

Illegal in One Country

On some occasions, there are healthcare services that are illegal and not available inpatients' home country but are legal in other destinations. This phenomenon is known in literature as "circumvent tourism." Therefore, medical travelers may prefer travelling to these destinations that offer procedures such as surrogacy, euthanasia, experimental drug, and stem cell research or transplantation.

Illegal in Both Countries

Some medical travelers may prefer to receive illegal services overseas even though the services are illegal in both their home country and in the treatment destinations. Nevertheless, these services are less regulated in the destination of the treatment compared to the medical travelers' homeland. Organ purchase is an example that can be less regulated in some countries compared to others.

Sponsorship and Payment Types in Medical Travel

Payment type is an important component when defining medical travel, whether medical travelers pay from their own pockets or covered by insurance or their government.

Out-of-pocket Payment

Out-of-pocket payment occurs in some countries when patients are not covered or reimbursed for their healthcare services they have utilized. This could be due to patients being either uninsured or underinsured based on their healthcare plan. Out-of-pocket payments could also occur if patients seek services that are not within their healthcare plan. These patients would consider the option of seeking healthcare overseas, since it is a lower cost compared to healthcare services in their home country.

Insurance Coverage

In some countries, health insurance companies incentivize patients to obtain healthcare services overseas, where the insurance can obtain lower prices from the providers. Meeting patients' demands with lower costs inevitably reduces insurance losses. As a result, this increases the profitability and allow insurance companies to offer lower and more competitive health plan premiums.

Government Coverage

By law, all UAE nationals are provided healthcare services. Therefore, they have free access to primary and tertiary healthcare facilities in the UAE and overseas, if necessary. Three main government entities oversee healthcare in UAE: Department of Health Abu-Dhabi, Dubai Health Authority, and Ministry of Health. In addition, health authorities do not know with accuracy the total number of UAE nationals seeking healthcare overseas because there are many entities in the UAE that fund UAE nationals for their treatment overseas besides the government health authorities. However, each health authority creates their own reports about the annual number of patients covered by the government for overseas treatment.

Complexity of the Medical Conditions in the Medical Travel

Complexity level is based on the severity of the medical condition. The medical conditions that people travel for when seeking healthcare services overseas are classified into three categories:

Life Threatening Conditions

The primary condition can cause immediate death or eventual death in the person unless it is interrupted with a treatment. Examples such as organ transplants and heart surgery.

Serious but not Life-Threatening Conditions

The primary condition is not causing immediate or eventual death but may progress to a life threatening if left untreated. Examples such as hip replacement and gastric bypass.

Medically Optional Conditions and Wellness

Medically optional conditions are services that are not reasonable and necessary for the diagnosis or treatment of illness or injury or to improve the functioning of a malformed body member. Patients seek life-enhancing medical treatments or procedures when they travel for optional procedures. Examples of such procedures include cosmetic procedures, plastic surgeries, and wellness services.

Direction of Flow of Medical Travel

The direction of patient flow is another level of information to account for when trying to understand the definition of medical travel. There are four types for direction of patients flows: *from high-income country to high-income country; from high-income country to lower-middle and upper-middle income country; from low, lower-middle, and upper-middle income country to high-income country; and from low, lower-middle, and upper-middle income country to low, lower-middle, and upper-middle income country (Wafa K Alnakhi, 2018; Wafa K. Alnakhi, Segal, Frick, Ahmed, & Morlock, 2019; Cohen, 2014).*

From High-Income Country to High-Income Country

Individuals seek medical treatment from countries with high gross national income (GNI), in countries with similar GNI, as per the World Bank country classification. An example of patients' flow from high-income country to high-income country is patients within the Europe Union who cross their border to seek healthcare in a neighboring country. Another example is when patients from Canada cross the border to seek healthcare in the United States or when patients from the United States cross the border to seek healthcare in Canada. Waiting times could be a reason that drives patients to cross borders to seek healthcare since quality of care and cost are more or less the same in the two destinations.

When examining patients from the UAE who sought medical treatment overseas sponsored by the DHA during 2009-2016, one can see that patients considered countries such as Germany, the United Kingdom, and the United States as treatment destinations. The government of Dubai sends thousands of patients abroad every year for life-threatening and serious medical conditions since many of these medical conditions related to cancer, neurological and neurosurgical conditions, ophthalmological procedures, cardiology and cardio-surgery, and organ transplantations services are not available in the UAE. Instead, by traveling abroad, patients have the opportunity to receive medical services in leading health institutes worldwide.

From High Income Country to Lower-Middle and Upper-Middle Income Country

Individuals from countries with high GNI seek treatment from countries with lower-middle and upper-middle GNI. For example, these patients could be under government coverage or private health insurance coverage, or they could be uninsured patients and paying out-of-pocket. For example, the Health Authorities in the UAE refers patients for treatment overseas if the treatment is not available domestically. On the other hand, many UAE nationals pay out-of-pocket when they travel to upper-middle income countries to seek healthcare. However, we cannot pinpoint accurately how many UAE nationals travel every year overseas to seek treatment because there is no UAE national surveillance system that capture this data. As a result, many UAE nationals pay out-of-pocket rather than waiting for government approvals or when seeking medically optional procedures that are not covered by the government.

Patients with private health insurance coverage and who are uninsured (and thus paying out-of-pocket) may consider lower-middle and upper-middle income to avoid high costs and long waiting times in their home counties. Some private insurance companies may consider providing healthcare services in upper-middle income countries to perform certain medical procedures that will cost the health insurance more money in the home country compared to the cost of sending patients overseas. The cumulative cost from outsourcing a large number of patients overseas for medical procedures results in drastic cost-savings for health insurance companies. In the United States, people who are uninsured may find travelling overseas an option to care for their health if they cannot access healthcare or pay high domestic costs. These uninsured individuals may consider overseas treatment, especially for non-urgent care, an attractive choice for cost saving.

Dubai Health Authority and Dubai Statistic Center collaborated to conduct a survey to understand perceptions of medical travel among patients who experienced overseas treatment during the period 2009–2012 in the emirate of Dubai. The authors used non-probability sampling and included 336 families. Results showed that 79% of patients who experience treatment overseas reported being covered by the government, and 21% reported being covered by sources other than government, including out-of-pocket payment and private health insurance. Cost of treatment, waiting time, medical specialty, unavailability of treatment domestically were the main reasons that pushed patients away from the UAE to seek healthcare at the treatment destination. In the same study, patients considered Thailand, Republic of India, Egypt, and Philippines as lower-middle and upper-middle income countries that were treatment destinations.

From Low, Lower-Middle, and Upper-Middle Income Country to High-Income Country

Furthermore, individuals from low/low-middle, and upper-middle GNI seek treatment from countries with high GNI. Typically, wealthy patients from these countries do so to avoid long waiting times and to obtain high-quality or advanced medical technology for specialties that are not found in their home countries. Decades ago, this type of flow was the dominant direction of patient flow for medical tourism.

However, today, after understanding the different components in the phenomena of medical travel, this flow type becomes one part under the flow direction within the definition of medical travel given we now understand that there are different forms of the flow direction.

From Low, Lower-Middle, and Upper-Middle Income Country to Low, Lower-Middle, and Upper-Middle Income Country

Individuals from low and low-middle GNI countries also seek healthcare in countries with similar GNI . This flow involves patients within the same income group classification. These individuals mainly leave their countries to seek specialized care and are concerned about the quality of the care in their home countries. On the other hand, these individuals may seek services that are not available in their home country. These patients may not be able to afford travelling to high income countries. Instead, they may seek options that are available in countries with similar income group classifications.

Figure 1. Components of Medical Travel Definition

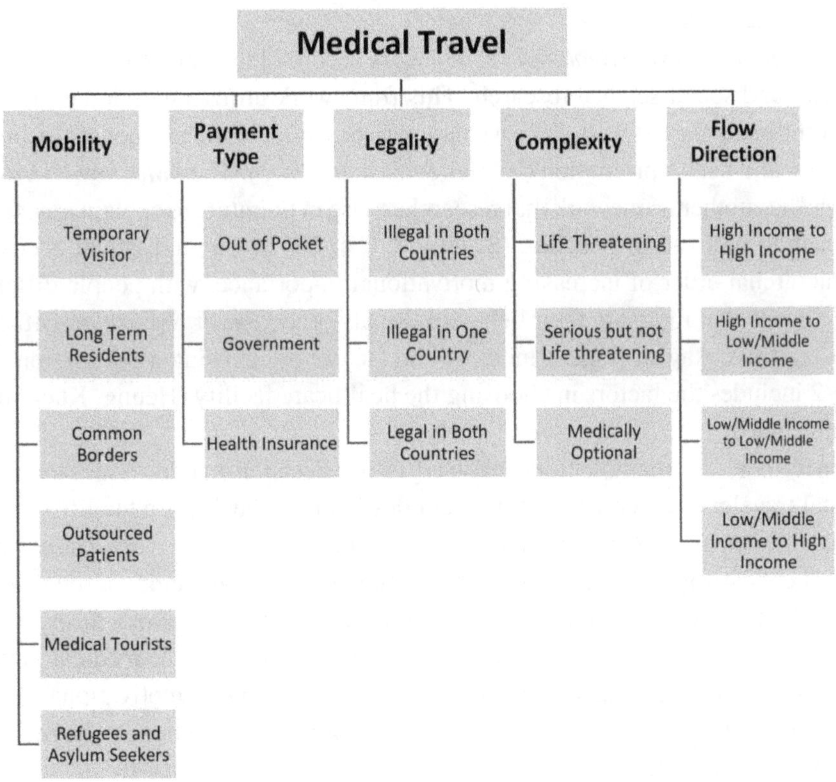

FRAMEWORKS IN MEDICAL TRAVEL

Researchers in the fields of sociology, anthropology and psychology have investigated the motivation to travel to seek medical care. For example, a qualitative study was conducted by the author to look at the motivational factors at different times: before, during, and after patient travel for healthcare. This study emphasized that the medical traveler's experience can be divided into three chronological stages: pre-travel, during travel, and post-travel. Understanding each of these stages is necessary to help meet medical travelers' needs at each stage(Eissler & Casken, 2013). Additionally, researchers use many frameworks, models, and theories to explain the phenomena of medical travel. Word of mouth, physician recommendation, waiting time, cost of treatment, quality of care, and availability of treatment in the home country appear to be the most important factors when making decisions related to medical travel. Several studies have sought to understand people's perceptions about choosing destinations. Some studies are focus on the tourism perspective, others focus on the medical tourism perspective, and some studies focus specifically on patients seeking healthcare abroad and tourism or leisure is not part of their experience. Moreover, some research studies have focused on the factors that influence choosing the destination, whereas other research studies have focused on factors influencing choice of facilities.

The *"Health Seeking Behaviors Framework"* is one of the frameworks that is used in health and social science research. This framework utilizes individual views of health and healthcare as well as other characteristics in explaining responses to illness, wellness, and health promotion (Eissler & Casken, 2013). The *"Maslow Hierarchy Theory"* is another framework that researchers use in literature to explain a systemic approach to motivation structure (S. Jang & Cai, 2002). The individual needs are in a hierarchal order of increasing motivational importance, with people differing on the needs that motivate their behavior. Finally, the *"Smith & Forgione Model"* consists of two stages: stage-1 includes the factors of choosing a destination, and stage-2 includes the factors in choosing the healthcare facility (Heung, Kucukusta, & Song, 2010).

Since there are many factors involved in the decision-making process for the medical traveler (e.g., choice of treatment destinations, healthcare facility, and the physician), *"Push and Pull Motivational Factors Framework"* is the frameworks that is the most applicable in understanding the motivational factors of the medical travelers. In other words, the *"Push and Pull Motivational Factors Framework"* can be viewed as an umbrella that covers most factors related to the medical traveler home country and the treatment destinations. Understanding the motivational factors influencing patients treated overseas is important for health planners, policymakers, and government officials in order to focus their work to rectify the factors that pushed the patient away from source in the home country. The Push and Pull Factors Theoretical Framework shown in Figure 2.

The push factors are defined as the factors that motivated the patients to choose overseas treatment destinations instead of having their treatment in the home country. On the other hand, the pull factors are defined as the factors that attracted patients to the country of destination, as they are perceived by the patient (Crooks, 2010; Hsu, 2009; S. a. C. Jang, L.A., 2002; M. Kozak, 2002; Moghimehfar, 2011; Mohammad, 2010). Push factors can include: *patients' characteristics, complexity of health conditions, financial issues, and health services in home countries.*

Patients' Characteristics

Age, gender marital status, educational level, income level, and other socio-demographic characteristics may contribute as push factors to treatment destinations. Some studies have suggested that medical traveler age plays a role in decisions related to medical travel. For example, younger people are more likely to be engaged with medical travel compared to older people (Gan & Frederick, 2013; J. N. Henson et al., 2015). Researchers conducted a cross-sectional survey in Korea by interviewing people at Jeju international airport. The study concluded that there were differences in the motivational factors among different ethnicity groups who visited the island. These differences were found to be statistically significant (Yu, 2012).

Complexity of Health Conditions

As noted earlier, medical travelers seek an array of treatments in the treatment destinations. These medical services range from preventive or medically optional to complex and life-threatening conditions. Some health insurance companies incentivize patients to obtain certain surgeries in low-middle income countries for lower costs when compared to the costs of the medical procedures in the home country (Boyd et al., 2011). On the other hand, other payers cover patients for medical specialties that are not available in their home country, whether or not the treatment is available to low-middle income countries or high-income countries, as long as the hospitals are accredited and the physicians are specialized and sufficiently trained to meet patients' needs. Besides, in travelling for medical procedures, many medical travelers from all over the world consider medical travel as an experience for maintenance, enhancement, and restoration of wellbeing of the mind and body, such as travelling to holistic health, spa, and wellness resorts.

Financial Issues

Self-coverage, health insurance or government coverage are factors that influence the medical traveler decision. Many studies report that financial cost plays a vital role in influencing decisions regarding medical travel (Culley et al., 2011; Noree, Hanefeld, & Smith, 2014; Ruggeri, 2015). As explained earlier in this chapter, there are different payment types considered as a part of medical travel. The type of financial coverage influences the medical traveler's final decision. Researchers consider healthcare services related to the home country, including long waiting time, low quality of care, and unavailability of treatment in the country of residence, as fundamental factors that push people to treatment destinations. Medical travelers seek quality facilities and specialized physicians that meet their needs. Therefore, it is important that destinations of treatment, facilities, and physicians who accept medical travelers ensure high quality treatment and a safe environment for medical travelers.

Health Services in Home Countries

Wish for patient privacy, long waiting time, unavailability of the treatment, low quality of care, and limited skills of medical and administrative staff in the healthcare facilities are factors that may push medical travelers to seek healthcare services overseas (Horowitz, Rosensweig, & Jones, 2007; Reed, 2008).

On the other hand, pull factors include: *patients previous experience, sources of information, information related to destination countries, and health services in destination countries.*

Patients' Previous Experience

Hospitals and physicians' reputations are important factors for medical travelers when they make decisions to seek treatment overseas. Researchers in the Netherlands have conducted studies to assess how patients make decisions when choosing hospitals when seeking surgical treatment - not medical travel *per se*. These studies illustrate predictors that influence patients' choice for hospitals. These studies conclude that patients' experience is equally important to hospital performance indicators that are available on the hospital website. Other factors influencing patients' decisions related to hospital choice are: travel time to the hospital, hospital quality rating publically available, waiting time, physicians' expertise and physician communication skills (Beukers, Kemp, & Varkevisser, 2014; De Groot et al., 2012; Varkevisser & van der Geest, 2007).

In terms of selecting a physician, patients consider physician characteristics, such as competence, expertise, training, and qualifications, as main criteria. Some studies demonstrate that physician demographic characteristics, such as age, gender, race, religion and marital status, are least important to patients when making choice about physicians compared to physicians' expertise. However, these findings cannot be generalized since some patients who come from certain cultures may have certain preferences related to demographic characteristics of the physician (Mavis, Vasilenko, Schnuth, Marshall, & Jeffs, 2005).Therefore, many factors may influence the medical traveler choice when making the decision to seek healthcare overseas.

Sources of Information

It is important to know the source of information and who the patient consulted to learn about the country of treatment, credentials of the physician, and characteristics of the facility. The patient may choose the country of destination based on the source of information. Internet, radio, TV, brochures, leaflets, medical travel agency, physician recommendations, and word of mouth from family and friends are all important factors to shape medical travelers' decisions to seek healthcare overseas. Researchers classify these sources as evidential sources, media sources, and word of mouth.

"Word of mouth" is one of the important factors that influences the medical travel decisions before patients make choices about the treatment destinations (Al-Hinai Al-Busaidi, 2011; Crooks, Kingsbury, Snyder, & Johnston, 2010; Henson, 2015; Lunt & Carrera, 2010; Yeoh, Khalifah Othman, & Halim Ahmad, 2013). Medical travelers use different sources of information to find out about the treatment destinations, physicians' credentials, and hospital reputations. Knowing the culture of the medical traveler provides a better understanding about the source of information most likely to be used (Heung, 2010; Lunt & Carrera, 2010). Some studies have indicated that the source of information is a proxy for the type of society. Patients who use recommendations from family, friends, relatives, or neighbors reflect that the patient comes from "a collective society", whereas patients who rely on the internet are more likely to be part of "an individualistic society" (Yu, 2012).

Information Related to Destination Countries

Economic and political stability, safety of the destination, destination attractiveness, geographic closeness, and countries' policies and regulations are all important factors that attract medical travelers to their treatment destinations. Researchers conducted a study on medical travelers referred to the Iran Fertility & Infertility Center. The author concluded that among the various factors that influenced the non-Iranian infertile couples' choice for choosing Isfahan as a treatment destination were cost, distance from home country, lack of expertise in the home country, tourist attractions, legal and moral restrictions for some treatments, and respect for patients' ethical and religion belief system (Moghimehfar, 2011).

Health Services in Destination Countries

Quality of care, physician qualifications and experience, availability of the treatment abroad, facility reputation, short waiting time, and skills of medical and administrative staff all attract medical travelers to their treatment destinations. Many destinations in the globe are competing to offer the most advanced medical, surgical, dental, wellness and spa services to medical travelers. These services attract medical travelers around the world to seek expertise and advanced technology in these leading centers since the services are either not available or more expensive in their home country.

Figure 2. Push and Pull Factors Theoretical Framework

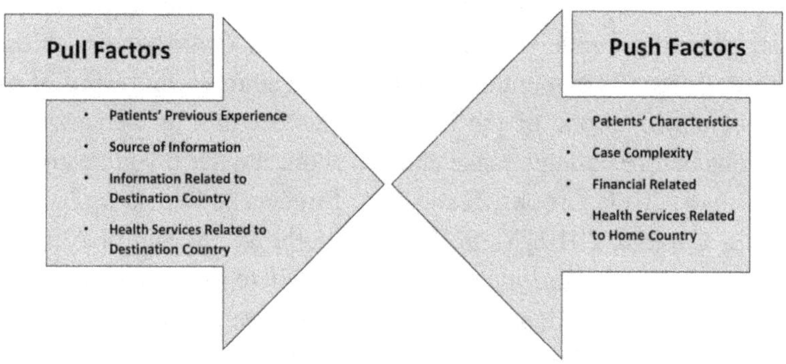

GAPS IN MEDICAL TRAVEL

Understanding patients' demographic characteristics, medical conditions, treatment destinations, and motivational factors are important aspects in medical travel. As mentioned earlier, this information will help the medical travel market and policy makers to create policies and strategies to support medical travelers. There is insufficient up-to-date information or empirical studies to reduce the risks and complications of follow-up care, following the medical travel experience. A system is required to be in place after medical travelers return home from international destinations in order to continue their appointments and treatment regimens recommended by the physicians in the treatment destinations.

Furthermore, different types of telemedicine can also be utilized in this field as substitutes to follow-up overseas trips for patients' assessments, monitoring, and reporting outcomes (Dickinson, 2014; Saliba et al., 2012). Telemedicine can help to reduce risks associated with obtaining medical treatment overseas. The follow-up care can be collaborative work between the treatment destination and the healthcare provider in the medical traveler home country. This follow up care for medical travelers will contribute to assessing medical travelers' health related quality of life. As a result, this will influence and promote better informed decision-making when choosing treatment destination, medical procedures, and the healthcare providers related to the medical traveler medical condition. Follow-up care and patients' outcome assessments will set the stage for "cost-effectiveness" and "comparative-effectiveness" studies.

FUTURE RESEARCH IN MEDICAL TRAVEL

Medical travel is growing internationally. Therefore, it is important to understand all the aspects related to this phenomenon. Currently, there have been very few empirical studies that rigorously explain medical travel. Therefore, it is essential to start building research around medical travel in order to have a better understanding of medical travelers' health outcomes, to contribute towards better policy, and ensure a better regulated market. Most of the studies that currently exist focus at a single point in time at medical travelers' lives (cross-sectional studies). Instead, it would be beneficial to look at certain medical travelers at multiple points in times and to follow medical travelers' quality of life over time to assess the change. Thus, patients reported outcome and health related quality of life tools play an important role in assessing patients' health status, especially before and after going through a medical procedure. There are several validated tools that have been translated into many languages and can be specific to patients' medical conditions. These tools will contribute to obtaining valid and reliable patients' outcome results. These measurements can be used to assess effectiveness of the treatment and medical services provided to medical travelers.(Gafni, 1991; Garcia et al., 2007)

Knowing medical travelers' characteristics, classifications of their medical conditions, and treatment destinations is vital to understand supply and demand in the medical travel market. Yet it is more important to understand medical travelers' perceptions, preferences, and willingness toward payments to better understand how medical travelers make decisions. Hence, economic studies can be helpful on this regard. Researchers can use qualitative and mixed method studies to better understand medical travelers' perceptions and attitudes towards the medical travel experience. For example, semi-structured qualitative interviews following quantitative studies would explain the results and help to understand processes, explanations, and concepts. Qualitative studies that focus on medical travelers' experiences at different time frames (i.e., pre-overseas treatment, during overseas treatment, and post overseas treatment) provide insight and help to develop hypotheses that address medical travelers' needs and perceptions (Jones, Nijman, Ross, Ashman, & Callaghan, 2014).

SUMMARY

Medical travel is not a new phenomenon. Rather, it dates back thousands of years. Today, travelling internationally to obtain healthcare services is becoming increasingly common, and medical tourism is a rapidly growing market. However, there has been little empirical research conducted to understand motivational factors and public health challenges related to medical travel. Using an appropriate definition and framework will help to create better robust research and contribute towards policies and strategies that improve medical travel market regulation and satisfaction of medical travelers. Medical travelers need to be monitored following treatment to minimize the risks and complications. Furthermore, creating international and domestic medical travel registration, establishing continuity of care to the medical travelers, and assessing health related quality of life for medical travelers are all important. Together, these actions would ensure that health professionals capture relevant information, influence future decisions, and deliver medical travelers' satisfaction and outcomes.

ACKNOWLEDGMENT

Our appreciation to Neil Lunt PhD, from Social Policy and Social Work at University of York for giving suggestions and feedback.

REFERENCES

Alnakhi, W. K., Segal, J. B., Frick, K. D., Ahmed, S., & Morlock, L. (2018). *Patients from the United Arab Emirates Seeking Healthcare Services Overseas During 2009–2016: Characteristics, Motivational Factors and Preferences*. Johns Hopkins University.

Alnakhi, W. K., Segal, J. B., Frick, K. D., Ahmed, S., & Morlock, L. (2019). Motivational factors for choosing treatment destinations among the patients treated overseas from the United Arab Emirates: Results from the knowledge, attitudes and perceptions survey 2012. Tropical Diseases [PubMed]. *Travel Medicine and Vaccines*, *5*(1), 18. doi:10.118640794-019-0093-9

Alnakhi, W. K., Segal, J. B., Frick, K. D., Hussin, A., Ahmed, S., & Morlock, L. (2019). Treatment destinations and visit frequencies for patients seeking medical treatment overseas from the United Arab Emirates: Results from Dubai Health Authority reporting during 2009–2016. *Tropical Diseases, Travel Medicine and Vaccines*, *5*(1), 10. doi:10.118640794-019-0086-8 PMID:31308954

Balaban, V. M., & Marano, C. (2010). Medical tourism research: A systematic review. *International Journal of Infectious Diseases*, *14*, 135. doi:10.1016/j.ijid.2010.02.1784

Beukers, P. D., Kemp, R. G., & Varkevisser, M. (2014). Patient hospital choice for hip replacement: Empirical evidence from the Netherlands. *The European Journal of Health Economics*, *15*(9), 927–936. doi:10.100710198-013-0535-7 PMID:24158316

Bhatia, R., & Wallace, P. (2007). Experiences of refugees and asylum seekers in general practice: A qualitative study. *BMC Family Practice*, *8*(1), 48. doi:10.1186/1471-2296-8-48 PMID:17711587

Boyd, J. B., McGrath, M. H., & Maa, J. (2011). Emerging trends in the outsourcing of medical and surgical care. *Archives of Surgery*, *146*(1), 107–112. doi:10.1001/archsurg.2010.308 PMID:21242454

Burkett, L. (2007). Medical tourism. Concerns, benefits, and the American legal perspective. *Journal of Legal Medicine*, *28*(2), 223–245. doi:10.1080/01947640701357763 PMID:17558794

Chanda, R. (Ed.). (2002). Trade in health services (Vol. 80). Academic Press.

Cohen, I. G. (2012). How to regulate medical tourism (and why it matters for bioethics). *Developing World Bioethics*, *12*(1), 9–20. doi:10.1111/j.1471-8847.2012.00317.x PMID:22420448

Cohen, I. G. (2014). *Patients with passports: medical tourism, law, and ethics*. Oxford University Press. doi:10.1093/acprof:oso/9780199975099.001.0001

Crooks, V. A., Kingsbury, P., Snyder, J., & Johnston, R. (2010). What is known about the patient's experience of medical tourism? A scoping review. *BMC Health Services Research*, *10*(1), 266. doi:10.1186/1472-6963-10-266 PMID:20825667

Culley, L., Hudson, N., Rapport, F., Blyth, E., Norton, W., & Pacey, A. A. (2011). Crossing borders for fertility treatment: Motivations, destinations and outcomes of UK fertility travellers. *Human Reproduction (Oxford, England)*, *26*(9), 2373–2381. doi:10.1093/humrep/der191 PMID:21715450

De Groot, I., Otten, W., Dijs-Elsinga, J., Smeets, H., Kievit, J., & Marang-van de Mheen, P. (2012). Choosing between hospitals: The influence of the experiences of other patients. *Medical Decision Making*, *32*(6), 764–778. doi:10.1177/0272989X12443416 PMID:22546750

Dickinson, R., Hall, S., Sinclair, J. E., Bond, C., & Murchie, P. (2014). Using technology to deliver cancer follow-up: A systematic review. *BMC Cancer*, *14*(1), 311. doi:10.1186/1471-2407-14-311 PMID:24885758

Dubai Health Authority Annual Statistic Books. (2016). Dubai, UAE: Dubae Health Authority.

Eissler, L. A., & Casken, J. (2013). Seeking health care through international medical tourism. *Journal of Nursing Scholarship*, *45*(2), 177–184. doi:10.1111/jnu.12014 PMID:23489601

El-Khatib, Z., Scales, D., Vearey, J., & Forsberg, B. C. (2013). Syrian refugees, between rocky crisis in Syria and hard inaccessibility to healthcare services in Lebanon and Jordan. *Conflict and Health*, *7*(1), 18. doi:10.1186/1752-1505-7-18 PMID:24004474

Forgione, D. A., & Smith, P. C. (2007). Medical tourism and its impact on the US health care system. *Journal of Health Care Finance*, *34*(1), 27–35. PMID:18972983

Gafni, A. (1991). Willingness-to-pay as a measure of benefits: Relevant questions in the context of public decisionmaking about health care programs. *Medical Care*, *29*(12), 1246–1252. doi:10.1097/00005650-199112000-00007 PMID:1745082

Gan, L. L., & Frederick, J. R. (2013). Medical tourists: Who goes and what motivates them? *Health Marketing Quarterly*, *30*(2), 177–194. doi:10.1080/07359683.2013.787894 PMID:23697856

Garcia, S. F., Cella, D., Clauser, S. B., Flynn, K. E., Lad, T., Lai, J.-S., Reeve, B. B., Wilder Smith, A., Stone, A. A., & Weinfurt, K. (2007). Standardizing patient-reported outcomes assessment in cancer clinical trials: A patient-reported outcomes measurement information system initiative. *Journal of Clinical Oncology*, *25*(32), 5106–5112. doi:10.1200/JCO.2007.12.2341 PMID:17991929

Guy, B. S., Henson, J. L. N., & Dotson, M. J. (2015). Characteristics of consumers likely and unlikely to participate in medical tourism. *International Journal of Healthcare Management*, *8*(2), 68–76. doi:10.1179/2047971914Y.0000000076

Henson, J. N., Guy, B. S., & Dotson, M. J. (2015). Should I stay or should I go? Motivators, decision factors, and information sources influencing those predisposed to medical tourism. *International Journal of Healthcare Management*, *8*(1), 4–14. doi:10.1179/2047971914Y.0000000083

Heung, V. C., Kucukusta, D., & Song, H. (2010). A conceptual model of medical tourism: Implications for future research. *Journal of Travel & Tourism Marketing*, *27*(3), 236–251. doi:10.1080/10548401003744677

Horowitz, M. D., Rosensweig, J. A., & Jones, C. A. (2007). Medical tourism: Globalization of the healthcare marketplace. *MedGenMed: Medscape General Medicine*, *9*(4), 33. PMID:18311383

Hsu, T. K., Tsai, Y. F., & Wu, H. H. (2009). The preference analysis for tourist choice of destination: A case study of Taiwan. *Tourism Management*, *30*(2), 288–297. doi:10.1016/j.tourman.2008.07.011

Jang, S., & Cai, L. A. (2002). Travel motivations and destination choice: A study of British outbound market. *Journal of Travel & Tourism Marketing*, *13*(3), 111–133. doi:10.1300/J073v13n03_06

Jang, S. C. (2002). Travel motivations and destination choice: A study of British outbound market. *Journal of Travel & Tourism Marketing*, *13*(3), 111–133. doi:10.1300/J073v13n03_06

Jones, J., Nijman, H., Ross, J., Ashman, N., & Callaghan, P. (2014). Aggression on haemodialysis units: A mixed method study. *Journal of Renal Care*, *40*(3), 180–193. doi:10.1111/jorc.12068 PMID:25042357

Kozak, M. (2002). Comparative analysis of tourist motivations by nationality and destinations. *Tourism Management*, *23*(3), 221–232. doi:10.1016/S0261-5177(01)00090-5

Lunt, N., & Carrera, P. (2010). Medical tourism: Assessing the evidence on treatment abroad. *Maturitas*, *66*(1), 27–32. doi:10.1016/j.maturitas.2010.01.017 PMID:20185254

Mavis, B., Vasilenko, P., Schnuth, R., Marshall, J., & Jeffs, M. C. (2005). Female patients' preferences related to interpersonal communications, clinical competence, and gender when selecting a physician. *Academic Medicine*, *80*(12), 1159–1165. doi:10.1097/00001888-200512000-00022 PMID:16306294

Moghimehfar, F. N.-E., & Nasr-Esfahani, M. H. (2011). Decisive factors in medical tourism destination choice: A case study of Isfahan, Iran and fertility treatments. *Tourism Management*, *32*(6), 1431–1434. doi:10.1016/j.tourman.2011.01.005

Mohammad, B. A. M. A. H. a. S., A.P.M. (2010). An analysis of push and pull travel motivations of foreign tourists to Jordan. *International Journal of Business and Management*, *5*(12), 41.

Noree, T., Hanefeld, J., & Smith, R. (2014). UK medical tourists in Thailand: They are not who you think they are. *Globalization and Health*, *10*(1), 29. doi:10.1186/1744-8603-10-29 PMID:24885204

Reed, C. M. (2008). Medical tourism. *The Medical Clinics of North America*, *92*(6), 1433–1446. doi:10.1016/j.mcna.2008.08.001 PMID:19061760

RuggeriK.. (2015). Evidence on global medical travel. from Bulletin of the World Health Organization doi:10.2471/BLT.14.146027

Saliba, V., Legido-Quigley, H., Hallik, R., Aaviksoo, A., Car, J., & McKee, M. (2012). Telemedicine across borders: A systematic review of factors that hinder or support implementation. *International Journal of Medical Informatics*, *81*(12), 793–809. doi:10.1016/j.ijmedinf.2012.08.003 PMID:22975018

Smith, P. C. F., & Forgione, D. A. (2007). Global outsourcing of healthcare: A medical tourism decision model. *Journal of Information Technology Case and Application Research*, *9*(3), 19–30. doi:10.1080/15228053.2007.10856117

Snyder, J., Adams, K., Chen, Y. Y., Birch, D., Caulfield, T., Cohen, I. G., . . . Zarzeczny, A. (2015). Navigating physicians' ethical and legal duties to patients seeking unproven interventions abroad. *Can Fam Physician, 61*(7), 584-586.

Toar, M., O'Brien, K. K., & Fahey, T. (2009). Comparison of self-reported health & healthcare utilisation between asylum seekers and refugees: An observational study. *BMC Public Health*, *9*(1), 214. doi:10.1186/1471-2458-9-214 PMID:19566954

Turner, L. G. (2011). Quality in health care and globalization of health services: Accreditation and regulatory oversight of medical tourism companies. *International Journal for Quality in Health Care*, *23*(1), 1–7. doi:10.1093/intqhc/mzq078 PMID:21148210

Varkevisser, M., & van der Geest, S. A. (2007). Why do patients bypass the nearest hospital? An empirical analysis for orthopaedic care and neurosurgery in the Netherlands. *The European Journal of Health Economics*, *8*(3), 287–295. doi:10.100710198-006-0035-0 PMID:17256180

Chapter 5
Dynamics of Medical Tourism Brand of India and Understanding Its Political and Economic Structures

Mitrajit Biswas
O. P. Jindal Global University, India

ABSTRACT

This chapter is about understanding the dynamics of medical tourism in a country like India. What drives the whole industry of medical tourism in India? To drive the brand of India as a medical tourism destination, the perspective India presents through its economic and political perspective holistically has been explored. Therefore, the idea of the chapter is to understand medical tourism and its impact on the Indian socio-economy.

DRIVING THE IDEA OF BRANDING INDIA THROUGH MEDICAL TOURISM

The idea of branding in India has been traversed with the idea of people, poverty, pollution, population & moral preaching. An idea of India coming up as a modern nation state with the flow of time post-independence supposedly from colonial regime had definitely turned a new leaf in the chapter of an old civilization such as India. India as a country supposedly is a very new nation state suffering from typical problems of a newly formed country under nation state system which we generally term as Third Worldism. A country founded on principles of unique constitution

DOI: 10.4018/978-1-7998-3427-4.ch005

however in a country which has diverse complexity (Fernandes, 2004.)However, the idea of the third world is so reductionist in approach and so clichédly discussed that personally this chapter related to medical tourism does not want to fall into the same trap. This chapter is about understanding what defines India if it has its own spirit. A country founded on principles of unique constitution however in a country which has diverse complexity. To add on to that illiteracy, broken education system as well as accountability of politicians towards citizens are the burning issues of our country. However, it is not as if we do not what the problems are. The onus is on understanding the bright spot and is the society of India ready to accept its responsibility to do so. The idea of cheap medical tourism in the world's largest democracy by population surely raised a lot of questions but despite all the questions and challenges it has survived. However, what about the parameters of the quality of medical treatment, the expectation of the billion plus people looking for a society free of corruption as well as the new idea of a truly unique medical practise not necessarily conforming to western standards may be the real deal for the people of India 70 years down the line after independence. The father of Indian constitution who had drafted the pillars of Indian democracy had a foresight that what India needed. Related to the equation of bringing in equity first into the society for true independence the idea of reservation was brought in. The same scenario has catapulted into the idea of vote bank politics although the demographics and the reach of the benefit of reservation is yet to be fully understood or answered from a very scholastic point of view. The pain of partition, the idea of diversity and the issue of an Indian independence which really touches all the people is what drives the idea of power and politics in India. Added alongside of the keywords is the dynamics of the people of India. However, the chapter deals in branding India through medical tourism. A question of unfathomable poverty vis a vis to be removed through democracy which is also sadly intertwined with corruption. Amidst all of this India despite having challenges in its health system has come up as the destination which also paradoxically has some of the best medical centre in the world at much cheaper cost than the west. The preaching of India's moral upstanding has been resonated only when the dynamics of the country is really resonating with the expectation of the people. Not the same old stories of potholes, pollution as well as the corrupt public bodies. That again brings into the equation the dynamics of accountability and the idea of its unique standing through medical tourism. India has been harnessing its strength through unique medical practises as well its talented medical pool in the private health sector mostly against all of its impediment which had been growing with the policy related to medical tourism including health infrastructure, law and social care based on an idea of ever-changing expectation of dynamic nature of our times. India's demographic dividend can be a serious problem unless that is turned into a proper workforce (Khodabakhshi, 2011).

MEDICAL TOURISM ECONOMY IN INDIA

The idea of India which is working on the shoulders of so many unknown, unappreciated and unsung heroes who are all around. When it comes to the understanding of the Indian power projection let us first start with the trade. The idea of trade is most important to understand and what it holds for the political economy of a country. India today ranks in the top 7 GDP ranked countries sliding between 5 to 7 and aims to come in top 3 by 2025-2030. However, the most important question is where India needs to project its economic strength and how has it been able to do it. On the question of Indian lobbying in international forums it is no more a secret but rather a very established fact that Prime Minister, Modi had been there in the international forums amidst his heavy campaigning for India to make it the investment decision. India had achieved the world's fastest growing economy but the main question of India's trade actually chugging the economy is the most important. India's medical tourism dividend can be a serious potent that is turned into a proper workforce. However, the focus should be on India trying to garner its image as a holistic country of skilled resources and not just mere labour in the form of some other economies (Harish, 2010). The political situation in India which is now trying to focus on the enactment of new laws in India related to reinforcing political economy. That includes the newly introduced Bankruptcy code, labour law reforms which will try to break the shackles of the age old Indian economic deficiencies. However, it is very important for the Indian economy to have farsightedness which needs to involve skilling the medical tourism industry of the country. Speaking about medical tourism in India, India receives the greatest number of patients from neighbouring countries such as Bangladesh, Srilanka and even western countries such as from England. India has unfortunately built on an education which is commercialized and uses education as a gateway to escape poverty. India has a huge pool of engineers and scientists but is the quality and research work necessary for global standards of medicine is also being reached. This brings us to the question of Multinational Corporations in India which have been investing in India apart from homegrown corporate houses but where. Research based innovative centres have come up with the likes of Airbus in Bangalore, Chinese companies like [VIVO, OPPO etc.] and many others. However, the focus should be on India trying to garner its image as a holistic country of skilled resources and not just mere labour in the form of some other economies. Medical tourism in areas especially Kerala with its Ayurveda has reached all over the world. Football stars such as Neymar Jr. also came to Kerala for treatment after his life-threatening injury in FIFA world cup. The idea of India as a mere assembling and labour pools is also important but if only supplemented with the use of modern industrial revolution known as Industrial Revolution 4.0. The engines of growth coming in from developing world had been driven by Asia starting from East, moving into South East Asia and of course China and India as the two giants. However, India is unique in the sense that its service-oriented economy has driven the country and projected itself as a growing economy but how long? The politics of India is still suffering from caste divide which is nevertheless a socio-economic phenomenon of so many years and would probably take a lot of time in aligning the internal policies of the domestic oriented process where the politics and the battle of power is related to development (Mooij, 1998). This is where India has suffered from cyclical economic slowdown which is natural but the investment cycle neds to come in. In this scenario the micro trade units in India which is a part of Small, Micro, Medium enterprises should be the focus of large-scale investment. However not only that medical tourism as an industry which can fit into a huge investment sector cannot be overlooked. Especially for branding of India as a major investment destination. That is happening through Amazon, Uber etc focusing on investing in research units as it is also very important for India's economic aspirations. India needs to work on the idea of the nation branding to be pushed ahead but that is not possible where there are several loopholes already existing. The economic growth needs to seep down to the bottom and the quality of life. The question here is the power projection in terms of its politics and policies. As the chapter is related to Medical tourism therefore understanding its dynamics is important and multidimensional. The politics of India is still suffering from caste divide which is nevertheless a socio-economic phenomenon of so many years and would probably take a lot of time in aligning the internal policies of the domestic oriented process where the politics and the battle of power is related to development. It has been seen from the perspective of India's trade policy including investment that it has been protective of its domestic industries but at the same time not making them competitive for global markets except for I.T., Pharmaceuticals etc. The situation of garments and textile industry in India is a clear testimony to the fact where the politics of the small and medium sector appeasement has taken over the understanding of a larger picture of the modernisation of export-oriented policies. It is therefore very important for the Indian policy making in terms of its political economy to be in line with the global aspirations. Not only is the economy of India ever adaptive with several complexities and challenges the idea of the politics in India still seem to be rural and more regressive in nature. The idea of skills development, usage of artificial intelligence as well as the development of the economic parameters in India is more of a policy-oriented politics in India. It may be the time to understand that mere rhetoric of the government or the figure head will not turn out to be that great for India. It may be the time to understand that mere rhetoric of the government or the figure head will not turn out to be that great for India (Brass, 2004). The political economy of India has been gradually moving from a rural to a more urban approach. However, there have been some leaps which may seem quantum in nature but may have left deeper gaps which can turn out to be deadly in the coming future. Therefore, the idea of the political economy of India probably lies in the brand image of India that is created from Indian politics needs to change. The politics of certain states such as West Bengal and Kerala had a very agrarian based model along with the onset of the socio-economic parameters. However, these are the same states which gets a lot of medical patients from Bangladesh and Gulf respectively. Whereas Karnataka, Maharashtra, Punjab, Haryana, Rajasthan and Gujarat have an industrial belt surrounded by agrarian as well as caste politics which is even more tricky. However, these places have also developed world class private medical institutions. Therefore, the idea of political economy of India is varied where the respective states have their own agenda. It just gets complicated in the overall sense of a national power projection and to create a universal idea of medical tourism branding policy in India. The question from the time of independence to the present day is based on the understanding that how can a uniformity through uniqueness in diversity. Poverty in India has been there from centuries from a materialistic concept but India's political economy now has a hybrid form of take (Varshney, 2000). Indian elections are a classic example of how root of politics and power originates for the economy of India. That brings us to the question doing round for Indian political circle which is chest thumping on growth of Indian economy as its own story but can be connected to the niche medical tourism growing in India in time.

THE QUESTION OF THE GROWTH SUSTAINABILITY IN INDIA

In India the biggest question is that there is a huge disparity in the wealth distribution of India and that definitely creates a big question on the understanding of growth. A growth in India over the last 70 years despite the constitutional welfare and the idea of poverty politics in India has still not managed to hit at the core of chronic poverty. It does not mean that India did not pull people out of poverty but those people are meagre in numbers and also form the chunk of the much-hyped India "typical middle class" segment and not the high-end people including upper middle class. Poverty in India has been there from centuries from a materialistic concept but India's political economy now has a hybrid form of take. Overburdened cities with the urban poverty in slums have been the fight of politics which also brings in the concept of marginalisation, ghettoization as well as caste prejudices (Aghion and Bolton,1997). One is the politics of urban poverty where the people who have moved in from rural areas and economically deprived areas of India. The challenge is here as it keeps on growing over a period of time. Overburdened cities with the urban poverty in slums have been the fight of politics which also brings in the concept of marginalisation, ghettoization as well as caste prejudices. This is where the idea of growth in India probably needs to convert into development of the human lives amidst the challenges of Indian economy and the political angles related to it. However as already mentioned India has a hybrid structure. Then comes the question of the urban challenges in itself related to the aspiration for a quality life style. Indian cities have been always at the forefront of fires due to lack of safety precaution, rain floods due to problems in drainage and most importantly the notorious Indian traffic and congestion in cities. Similarly, world class facilities such as Dr. Devi Shetty's Narayana Hrudalaya have changed the dynamics of affordable world class medical care. The issues of medical affordability not only in India but globally have been picking up but not in the mainstream politics of India yet. However, these are the very important quality parameters to make the mark as a seriously improving country in terms of quality and development standards. The system of British Raj colonial times has changed more into an Oriental-Occidental Hybridisation for India and in its system of political economy (Tilak,2007). The feudal mindset of the majority of Indian politics need to change more quickly it can be put. The politics of poverty though remaining constant has changed in meaning and aspiration from Roti, Kapda aur Makaan (Food, Clothes and Shelter) to Education, skills development and as well as most importantly the question of employment in India which is the key focus now. The politics of India and its aspiration for global power however is incomplete without the bigger picture of rural economy. A country which is urbanising fast but still has an agrarian economy and the people in the rural areas are still cut with the deep root issues of caste, low quality of life (not excepting minimalistic or even improving consumerism) but includes the access to basic facets for quality life such as health, electricity and education. Indian economy is now trying to move into a new direction which included the politics and policies of remonetizing India through demonetization as well as digitalisation of Indian economy. Most importantly even though critiqued the idea of bank accounts access to the entire population is a great step as well. Indian economy has come a long way when it comes to the understanding of the achievement of the welfare state as enshrined in the Indian constitution. There are of course a lot of numerous challenges related to the last mile distribution of public services which is marred by corruption and power structures which are still feudal in nature. The system of British Raj colonial times has changed more into an Oriental-Occidental Hybridisation for India and in its system of political economy. The caste system and the idea of India's one size fits all with the centre being in power of finance despite having state council needs to be corrected. India may be aspiring for global role however some of its indicators in several states are dismal even in comparison to Sub Saharan Africa. The idea for these states to be integrated into the centre as well as provide them with autonomy and accountability of their public finance is very important. States like Bihar, Uttar-

Pradesh have severe power lobbies coming in from the caste strata where basic amenities and human dignity for the lower caste is still questionable. India despite remaining relatively calm after having huge disparity of income is really a surprise probably because of the fact that a democratic safety valve is still considered crucial (Demetriades and Luintel,1996). However, speaking about political economy of India and marginalized section of India socio-economic problem of Naxalism, regionalism related to economic prosperity and control on inter-state migration in India are some of the very severe challenges. India's politics revolves around these issues to a screening level hardly reaching national level politics. On the national front over the last few years agricultural policy rehauling, industrial and labour laws reform, tax compliance and non-performing assets reduction and defence budgeting have taken the limelight of Indian politics. This very well are the core elements of a country's domestic economic policy building from both micro and macro perspectives. However, the deep-rooted problems of education, skills development, health care infrastructure and public amenities improvement seem to be chaotic in the mix of all these factors. India has very low GDP spent on Education and Health even amongst its BRICS peers which is a shame despite having shown improvements in certain health indicators but still lagging behind in many others areas of health (Bosworth and Collins,2008). Lack of doctors, children mortality rate etc never seem to hog the limelight of Indian mainstream politics which are only stuck at sub state and may only be carried forward to the state level. India's political vision related to its economy for this century and coming times needs to be based on structural reforms which will be next covered in the chapter. It would be to understand the vision and mission of Indian economy for the near future through medical tourism.

POLITICS AND POWER RELATED TO MEDICAL TOURISM

The idea of the political structure in India is important for the understanding of the system related to power structures. As the paper title already suggests that the idea of medical tourism in India is interrelated to the power structures and politics. India's global aspirations lies in the global acceptance of its democratic fabric and power projection however that has been put to several questions on several areas as mentioned above. The idea of politics in India has a direct linkage to the question of marginalisation and the hierarchical power structures in India still dominating the political machinery (Bose and Jalal, 2009).The idea of politics in India has a direct linkage to the question of marginalisation and the hierarchical power structures in India still dominating the political machinery. The idea of politics in India seems to be a mix of the hybridization of the oriental as well as the occidental with neither of it properly coming into shape. The concept of the British Raj economics resulting in a strange political economic scenario of India has kept on even today with the feudal system of pre-British Raj in India morphing into a western -Indian adapted kind of political system. The problem of religion, caste divisions that have been the bedrock of the Indian politics have a lot of power structures which have been taking forward the Indian society in terms of its politics and that's how the image of India has come up over the period of time. It's true that the Indian politics has been constituted based on the democracy but the permeation of politics in India derives itself from the structures of caste, religion. The power and politics in India also drive the idea of business. Business in India have been mostly family based with certain first-time entrepreneurs who have been broken down the barriers of political system of India. Off late it is true that the nexus of politics and bureaucracy in India which is the most potent power structure in India seems to be the central focal point of the politics in India. India is an idea which has several political points with the dynamics of secularism not being with compatible with the main reality where India's historical traditions have been built over a period for two millennia. It is indeed true that India now has been portraying an image of a country as per western traditions which has been imposed and adopted for last 70 years. The idea of India has evolved and so has its politics over a period. However, the basic tenets of the politics have been functioning around regionalism as well as the caste and the religion. The latest of such have just metamorphized in the form of NRC (National Registry of Citizens) away from the age-old politics of Ayodhya or Muslim sectarianism. Off late it is true that the nexus of politics and bureaucracy in India which is the most potent power structure in India seems to be the central focal point of the politics in India (Jenkins, Kennedy and Mukhopadhyay 2012). Not to mention the marginalized turned violent revolt of Naxals in the red belt of India stretching from Central to East part of the country as well as the movements of secession in Kashmir and even North East complete the politics of India on a larger canvas. Now this is what drives the politics of India and carries forward the power structure of India related to economics and as well as the social framework of India till date. Similarly, for medical tourism a nexus of politics and power structure function which is related to middle men/ touts for admission to hospitals, blood bank access and till very recently an ancillary form of medical tourism in the form of surrogate motherhood. That is why the entire chapter has not focused on the core dynamics of medical tourism. The chapter has moved on from a lot of perspectives bypassing the core idea of medical tourism and its idea of nation branding of India. That is because India is one of the only countries which has access to world class health infrastructure but as already explained that the idea of accessing quality medical care has a lot of core power structures and politics involved. India has been using medical tourism as a soft power projection and also to brand its nation. An idea of political, economic as well as social factors have been covered to bring in the perspective of medical tourism and its overall ancillary factors that leads to it in India. As idea of associating medical tourism in India and its branding equity is determined holistically. The mission of 70 years plus of branding India has been largely derived from the cacophony of Indian politics (Mukerjee, 2007)

REFERENCES

Aghion, P., & Bolton, P. (1997). A Theory of Trickle-Down Growth and Development. *The Review of Economic Studies*, *64*(2), 151. doi:10.2307/2971707

Bose, S., & Jalal, A. (2009). *Nationalism, democracy and development*. Oxford Univ. Press.

Bosworth, B., & Collins, S. (2008). Accounting for Growth: Comparing China and India. *The Journal of Economic Perspectives*, *22*(1), 45–66. doi:10.1257/jep.22.1.45

Brass, P. (2004). Elite interests, popular passions, and social power in the language politics of India. *Ethnic and Racial Studies*, *27*(3), 353–375. doi:10.1080/014919 87042000189187

Demetriades, P., & Luintel, K. (1996). Financial Development, Economic Growth and Banking Sector Controls: Evidence from India. *Economic Journal (London)*, *106*(435), 359. doi:10.2307/2235252

Fernandes, L. (2004). The Politics of Forgetting: Class Politics, State Power and the Restructuring of Urban Space in India. *Urban Studies (Edinburgh, Scotland)*, *41*(12), 2415–2430. doi:10.1080/0042098042000294574

Harish, R. (2010). Brand architecture in tourism branding: the way forward for India. *Journal of Indian Business Research*. Available at: https://www.emerald.com/insight/content/doi/10.1108/17554191011069442/full/html

Jenkins, R., Kennedy, L., & Mukhopadhyay, P. (n.d.). *Power, policy, and protest*. Academic Press.

Khodabakhshi, A. (2011). *Relationship between GDP and Human Development Indices in India*. SSRN Electronic Journal.

Mooij, J. (1998). Food policy and politics: The political economy of the public distribution system in India. *The Journal of Peasant Studies*, *25*(2), 77–101. doi:10.1080/03066159808438667

Mukerjee, R. (2007). *India's economic transition*. Oxford University Press.

Nation branding: A study of India's brand equity and capabilities in comparison to two other South Asian countries. (2009). *The Journal of Management Awareness*, *12*(2), 51–71.

Tilak, J. (2007). Post-elementary education, poverty and development in India. *International Journal of Educational Development*, *27*(4), 435–445. doi:10.1016/j.ijedudev.2006.09.018

Varshney, A. (2000). Is India Becoming More Democratic? *The Journal of Asian Studies*, *59*(1), 3–25. doi:10.2307/2658582

Chapter 6
Host Community Role in Medical Tourism Development

G. G. Saxena
Total Synergy Consulting Pvt Ltd, India

Ambuj Saxena
GMS Hospitality Services Pvt Ltd, India

ABSTRACT

Today, healthcare is one of the most prominent factors in man's life, and man will continue to explore ways to find remedy from any illness. In the present time, distance is no hurdle, and therefore, man will cross all boundaries in quest of getting rid of imminent fatalities or for other healthcare problems. The study shows that there are four important reasons due to which a patient will travel to another country to seek medical care: (1) destination for medical care should be affordable, (2) waiting time for getting treatment should be minimum, (3) medical care and support system is better in foreign country than home country, and lastly, (4) such treatment is not available or not up to the mark in home country.

WHO ARE MEDICAL TOURISTS?

Before host community role is defined in medical tourism development, it is logical to understand as to who are medical tourists with reference to ecosystem of host community. When a consumer elects to travel across international borders with the intention of receiving some form of medical treatment, he is called a medical tourist. This treatment may span full range of medical services, but most commonly includes dental care, cosmetic surgery, elective surgery, and fertility treatment. Within this

DOI: 10.4018/978-1-7998-3427-4.ch006

range of treatments, not all would be included within health trade. Cosmetic surgery for aesthetic rather than reconstructive reasons, for example, would be considered outside the health boundary' (OECD, 2010). However, with the word 'tourism' prefixed with 'medical (treatment hidden), this will solely depend upon the host nation, ecosystem and community.

Medical tourism can be understood as a subset of the wider notion of patient mobility which itself may be sub-divided on the basis of comprehensive research by OECD Countries as follows:

- ***'Temporary visitors abroad*:** These include those individuals holidaying abroad who use health services as a result of an accident or a sudden illness. These would not be considered as 'medical tourists', more just 'unfortunate tourists '.
- ***Outsourced patients***: Those patients who are sent abroad by health agencies using cross-national purchasing agreements. Typically, such agreements are driven by long waiting lists, high cost of medical treatment and a lack of available specialists and specialist equipment in the home country. These patients often travel relatively short distances and contracted services (both public and private) are more likely to be subject to robust safety audits and quality assurance *(***Lowson*et al., 2002*, Glinos*et al., 2006***). These individuals could be described as collective medical tourists, albeit they remain state or agency-sponsored rather than acting as individual consumers in the traditional sense. There may be a future market in developing countries from some developed countries where medical bills are sky-rocketing. In such cases, the medical tourist and accompanying attendant intend to visit nearby tourist places out of saved expenses or expected medical treatment required to be incurred in patient's country. Patterns of travel between source and destination countries are well-established, particularly related to those in Europe. However, more accurate data are required about patient flows between different countries and continents. It would appear that geographical proximity is an important, but not a decisive factor in shaping individual decisions to travel to specific destinations for treatment (**Exworthy and Peckham, 2006**). Though there is inadequate research material available for inbound medical tourism trends in all popular medical destinations like India, general outcomes of OECD and other Organisations are found applicable in such cases including in India, too.

As per interpretation of World Tourism Organization (WTO), the word "Tourism" comprises of "the activities of persons travelling to and staying in place outside their usual environment for leisure, business and other purposes." Medical Tourism, which is essentially the activities of persons travelling to places for getting treatment simply means 'cost effective' personal healthcare treatment with the association of the tourism industry for patients needing surgical as well as other specialized treatments.

Goodrich & Goodrich (1987) defined health-care tourism as "the attempt on the part of a tourist facility (for example a hotel) or destination to attract tourists by deliberately promoting its health-care services and facilities, in addition to its regular tourist amenities".

Connell (2006) defined medical tourism as a popular mass culture "where people travel often-long distances to overseas destinations like India, Thailand, and Malaysia to obtain medical, dental and surgical care while simultaneously being holidaymakers, in a more conventional sense."

Carrera and Bridges (2006) defined medical tourism as "the organised travel outside one's natural healthcare jurisdiction for the enhancement or restoration of the individual's health through medical intervention".The authors define medical tourism as a subset of Health Tourism, whose broader definition involves "the organized travel outside one's local environment for the maintenance, enhancement or restoration of the individual's wellbeing in mind and body".

According to Anil Khare, "The Medical Tourism is an action wherein patients of treatable disease have to opt to travel overseas with predominating purpose and confidence of receiving quality assured treatment with safety, in a comfortable authentic health-care institute facilitating services by and under experienced qualified Medical experts pertaining to patient's ailment and skilled to apply approved manoeuvre. Tourism in the sense of visiting the other attractions in destination country may or may not be a supplementary choice". Bookman & Bookman (2007) have defined medical tourism as travel with the aim of improving one's health, and also an economic activity that entails trade in services and represents two sectors: medicine and tourism.

So, according to this interpretation and other similar interpretations, it may be seen that the role of the host community does not carry much importance. If a medical tourist-cum-patient arranges his itinerary himself without the help of a travel agent or a tour operator, there is hardly any significance of host community except medical treatment per se.

As per the traditional model, the patient travels from developing country to developed country for advanced treatment. On the other hand, modern trend is aptly put by Horowitz and Rosensweig(2008) that medical tourism is a rapidly evolving trend wherein patients from industrialized nations seek health care in less developed countries, bypassing services offered in their own communities. Although the term medical tourism is sometimes used in reference to all travel for medical care, it is believed that this phenomenon is meaningfully different from the traditional pattern of international medical travel. Travelling from under-developed countries to developed countries for life-saving surgeries when ultra-modern treatments were not available in travellers' country, used to be excluded from the dictionary of medical tourism with the simple logic that there is hardly a concept of "tourism" involved in it. Such patients, with limited budgets only focus on their advance and high-level treatment, generally confined to the hospitals and its associated wards rather than having any outside contact. However, with the popularity of term 'medical tourism' even the advanced countries like USA and Europe are working on attracting medical tourists to visit places in host countries so that there are good earnings of members of host community under the umbrella of 'medical tourism'.

Medical Tourists as Consumers: So, medical tourism more commonly refers to patients who are mobile through their own volition and this type of 'patient mobility and its effect on host community' is the focus of this Chapter. Such medical tourists may choose to pay *out of pocket*, if they come to a developing country for treatment and therefore are better casted as consumers.

DEFINING COMMUNITY FOR MEDICAL TOURISM

Medical Tourism takes a top-bottom approach when it comes to defining the community and the respective roles of the community members.

- *Decision Makers:* Policymakers and Bureaucracy
- *Facilitators:* Tourism consultation agencies, Semi-Government organisations, Tour and travel related organisations, Tourism Research organisations, Tourism Accreditation agencies.
- *Service Providers:* Hotels, Bed and Breakfast accommodations, Restaurants, Cafes, Quick Service Restaurants, Tourism souvenirs etc.
- *Civil Society groups:* These consist of all above plus common man directly or indirectly related to tourism.

In this analysis, the first layer of Medical tourism community is the Decision makers' layer which comprises of Policy makers and high-level bureaucracy. A case of general 'tourism development' is cited here when the Government of India launched its 'Incredible India' campaign in year 2002 to promote India as a tourist destination. It had propelled number of foreign tourists' arrival in the forthcoming years. Such campaigns are planned at higher level by the policy makers and bureaucrats. These campaigns brand a nation at the global level and result in a positive brand recall for such nations. The Facilitators' layer of the community helps in providing the research led affirmation of such a campaign. The facilitators would include Tourism consultancies, Research agencies, and Tourism development membership-led agencies. Inbound tourists formulate their opinion and travel plans based on the research and insights provided by the facilitators. The Service providers play a vital role in forging a positive picture of similar campaigns as mentioned above by providing the tourists a hassle-free stay. A well trained and hospitable service provider provides a positive experience to the traveller, which leads to the traveller spreading a positive word of mouth to the fellow countrymen. Finally, the ancillary tourism service providers forming part of the civil society groups also contribute to the *Aha* experience of the foreign tourists.

In the same vein, if a medical tourist plans to get a treatment outside the home country, the patient or the family members find out the branding of the prospective destination with respect to medical facilities and infrastructure. Next, a detailed study is done with accreditation agencies, research agencies and other sources to finalise a hospital where medical treatment shall be undertaken along with stay and other basic-cum-leisure activities in a planned manner. Finally, the destination is planned and with the help of service providers, the trip is undertaken and then the medical tourist and the caretaker enjoy the medical tourism experience at ground zero. Based on such experience exhibited by Tourism service providers and the ancillary service providers, the tourist and the companion form an opinion that is either positive or negative in nature. This completes the cycle of all constituents of host community with respect to medical tourism development.

HISTORY OF MEDICAL TOURISM VIS-A-VIS HOST COMMUNITY

The first kind of archaeological evidence on destination of medical tourism is from the Third Millennium BC in Syria, where ancient Mesopotamians travelled to the temple of a healing god or goddess at Tell Brak, seeking relief for eye problems. The Sumerians also commercialised health units by way of majestic elevated temples with flowing pools. The Mediterranean region became the centre of host countries for medical tourism for Greeks & Roman forms of spas and cult centres after a few thousand years from the above period. It is also believed that the world's first health centres were created by ancient Greeks who laid the foundation for medical tourism network in real sense. In fact, they provided services such as Gymnasium, a snake farm, a dream temple, thermal bath, temple spas etc. Thus, it became first host community to provide relief to the pilgrims who would seek solace for their ailments by sleeping and dreaming of "Asclepios" representative Greek God of Medicine... In their heydays, Romans became global leaders, introduced hot-water baths and springs called thermals, which became commercialised and served higher income people mainly from Europe, through social networking centres. With the popularity of yoga and Ayurveda medicine, the history of medical tourism in India slowly picked up

The Middle Ages

The fall of the Roman civilization saw Asia as the most important medical tourism host for medical travellers. Around 1248 AD, a Hospital named as 'Mansuri' was set up by a community of Cairo in such a professional manner that it provided OPD and in-wards patients unit which could accommodate about 8000 patients at one time and was perhaps the most advanced Hospital in the world at that time. The role of host community was very important because it provided healthcare destination for all irrespective of caste, creed and race.

The Renaissance Period

During the renaissance period of the 14th to 17th century also, medical tourism flourished. Subsequently, in the 16th century, the rich and the elite of Europe rediscovered Roman baths and flocked to tourist towns with spas like St Mortiz, Ville d' Eaux and Bath (England).

The Post Renaissance Period

In the 1720, the most noteworthy traveller in the history of medical tourism was Michael Eyquem de Montaigne, who documented the spa guide gait in medical tourism history. It is worth noting that during 1600's, with the discovery of 'New World', the medical tourists were able to explore destinations and welcoming communities. In fact, elite and resourceful medical travellers from Europe had discovered large number of countries and communities as destinations to find the cure of even tuberculosis through spas and health retreats.

Medical Tourism History From the 1900s to 1997

During this time, USA and Europe were the centres of the healthcare world. American Board of Medical Specialties (ABMS) came into existence in 1933 and started playing the role of an umbrella organization for the medical specialist boards in the United States. In 1958, the European Union of Medical specialties (UEMS) was formed. With the cost of healthcare rising in the 1980s and 1990s, American patients started considering offshore options and it opened the floodgates of medical tourism in Asia, South America and Europe.

World Economic Forum, World Bank, UNWTO, UNWTC, and a large number of international, national and local organisations are in the process of evolving the methods for bringing more prosperity through tourism. The goal of every country is to connect community with tourism benefits by way of prosperity and employment generation.

Today, development of tourism is based on various factors like source of origin of incoming tourist, mode of arrival, destination and effect on environment at destination etc. The composite study of all such cutting-edge factors is a burning topic of research called, 'Contemporary Tourism'

Taking a cue from the abovementioned four dimensions of Contemporary Tourism', a fifth dimension of "Contemporary tourism" may be added as 'community at place of destination' because prosperity of community is not yet given adequate importance in most of the developing countries including in India. As per general understanding, 'environment' interpreted herein does not address human aspect adequately which is as important as 'environment' itself.

World Bank is working on contemporary tourism products in India (Buddhism circuits), Nepal (Lumbini's local community especially women) and Bhutan (in assisting the country to create and regulate "cultural landscape"). All the three projects relate to Inclusive development of community, i.e., the fifth dimension of 'Contemporary Tourism'.

As regards destination experience, hotels are generally treated as the only "accommodation resources". The authors have worked on "Disruptor in the accommodation industry" by way of popularizing homestays/Bed and Breakfast and other experiential accommodation beyond boundaries of hotel. (Book Reference: "Indian BnBs: An emerging disruptor in the hospitality sector" (Saxena et al.,2018). In this context, the hosted accommodation is a different kind of immersive experience as the Preamble of "Incredible India Bed and Breakfast Scheme" reads:

"The basic idea is to provide a clean and affordable place for foreigners and domestic tourists alike including an opportunity for foreign tourists to stay with an Indian family to experience Indian customs and traditions and relish authentic Indian cuisine."

A number of governments in Asian Countries including that in India are promoting their health facilities and emerging consumer markets are stimulated by brokers, websites and trade-fairs. For some medical tourist destinations, attempts are being made by stakeholders to promote their destinations as a cultural, heritage and recreational hub for incoming medical tourists and their attendants. In order to attract diaspora living in rich nations, the countries resort to similar traditions, culture and practices for example, Korean health care services relate to those settled or the second-generation within the United States, Australia and New Zealand. On the same lines, India addresses '*Pravasi Bhartiyas*' settled in UK and USA.

ESTABLISHED AND EMERGING MEDICAL TOURISM MARKETS

As per release of PRNewswire (Dublin, 21st, May 2019) the global medical market will grow at a CAGR of 16.1% during the forecast period 2019 – 2025. Most of the outbound tourists from USA and Europe get treatment away in developing countries due to high cost of treatment, surgery and long-term care in developed countries. On the other hand, the package of medical tourists is quite cheaper for medical treatment and aftercare in regions like LATAM and Asia-Pacific. Industry partnerships with global medical travel agents, suppliers, hotels, alternative accommodation providers and hospitals have facilitated packages studded with various amenities clubbed with significant support from host governments. For example, Apollo has collaborated with American international medical University for treatment and tourism plans in the region like Bahamas and Saint Lucia.

In regard to the medical tourism market, it was observed in 2018 that significant share of the Asia-Pacific region (APAC) comes from India, Thailand, Singapore and Malaysia due to availability of high-quality healthcare facilities at a lower cost. Of late, Philippines, South American and Eastern European countries are also making a dent in the Medical tourism market share. It may be seen from study on medical tourism development that state-of-the-art facilities in hospitals in general and niche treatment in particular find priority in selection of host community. In 2017, around 2.4 million individuals availed low-cost and decent quality of medical facilities in Thailand. In India, Apollo Hospitals and Bumrungrad International hospital in Thailand are the top medical service providers.

To make a country more attractive for medical tourists, apart from its medical facilities, other medical facilities taken into consideration are:

1. Ease of medical record transfer issues
2. Lesser complication in services and less possibility of epidemic outbreak, i.e., post operational service ecosystem
3. Support from government agencies and service providers,
4. Strategic marketing by all stakeholders including host nations.

There are agencies which analyse medical facilities at host countries and provide rating which serve as a guide for medical tourists to choose among the best host destinations. JCI-accredited hospitals are preferred by medical tourists who search such for facilitators online to ensure good treatment, satisfactory amenities and suitable atmosphere during post-surgery observation and convalescence Americans are constantly in search of cheaper, comfortable, hygienic and quality healthcare outside USA due to very high cost of treatment in home country. So, they prefer to see benchmarking of various host nations through JCI. Since 1999, JCI is considered a trusted agency to provide all information about facilities available elsewhere. Even international hospitals seek JCI accreditations to attract medical tourists from USA and even Europe.

Trent International Accreditation Scheme is another source of information for choice of host nations in the U.K and Hong Kong. Benchmarking depends upon various factors available in the host nation, like skill, quality, size facilities after operation, hygienic conditions, overall environment related to care and hospitality in caring for the patient and accompanying attendant. Deloitte Consulting had worked on these issues and published a forecast in 2008 regarding medical tourism for standard of accreditation by JCI, Society for International Accreditation (SOFIHA), ISQUA and Trent. There are some free-to-join groups which are interactive in nature and provide a platform for discussion and for sharing of ideas and good practices by providers of international healthcare accreditation in a chosen host nation. AUSA based NGO called HealthCare Tourism International gives authentic information about non-clinical aspects of health tourism, such as language issues, business environment, and misleading and luring publicity by host stakeholders.

The United Kingdom Accreditation Forum (UKAF) and International Medical Travel Association (IMTA) are another establishments which have innovated other, hitherto untouched aspects which help the medical tourists to make a better choice of host nation for treatment. These organisations play major role in assisting to identify quality standards, pricing, legal liability, and continuity-of-care issues. Though various aspects related to host nation are covered, the issue of hospitality for patient and accompanying attendant by host community is not given requisite importance. Hardly any literature or survey is available which goes deep into the emotional aspect of patient and the attendant in host destination.

Authors would like to draw attention of readers to popular Indian home stays, BnBs and other hosted accommodations available in main Indian cities like Delhi, Jaipur, Mumbai, Pune, Chennai, Bangalore etc. which are emerging as the choicest destinations for medical tourists. There are specific reasons for ever increasing potential of medical tourism market in developing nations like India where 'after-surgery-stay' period is spent by the patient and the attendant in a very hospitable environment created by members of the host community. The tourists who come for treatment in the hospitals of Indian cities, invariably come with one or two attendants who are generally family members of the patients. They all generally stay for a substantial period of time for the purpose of treatment of the patient and then for convalescence which may continue for a longer period of time. The tariff in regular hotels for patient and one or two attendants is generally too high which compels such patients to search for a low budget accommodation with support of suitable cultural background.

It is interesting to note that medical tourists and their relatives who need long term medical treatment outside their countries spend a great deal of time on the Internet. On the other hand the community members particularly those having homes near hospitals like Apollo, Escort, Fortis, Max etc. in major Indian cities where medical tourists get treatment have excellent opportunities to accommodate medical tourists and their attendants. In fact, a good number of community members own residential properties in the vicinity of such hospitals. They are already taking advantage of this opportunity and making reasonable earnings by converting their residential properties into home stays.. For this purpose the owners publicize their properties on websites, take help of various on-line agencies and arrange online accommodation with reservation and cancellation facilities. Such accommodations owned by members of community exist in residential areas which helps medical tourists to get noise-free and relaxed environment for rest, convalescence, post-operative check-ups, monitoring, healing etc. as against noisy and not-so-familiar environment near hotels located in commercial areas.

A large number of medical tourists also show interest in visiting popular medical tourist destinations like India for its majestic monuments, vibrant culture, wellness, rejuvenation, preventive health and traditional & medicinal practices like Ayurveda, Yoga etc. The research article, published by the author on "Tapping Accessible and Medical Tourism by BnB Establishments of Delhi" **(Saxena, G.G., 2013)** describes the scenario of community involvement and home stays accommodation for use of incoming medical tourists which is an excellent example of the concept of "Shared Economy". Airbnb and bnbnation.com are good examples of this concept where some people rent out their residential properties while other people get it on rent for a fixed period through these online aggregators. In Croatia, almost all hotels are part of chain of multinational hotels owned by big corporate and therefore, all earnings of these hotels are flushed out of Croatia. Government and host community of this country promote and encourage home stays so that earnings through services of accommodation providers are shared by members of host community like 'shared economy'.

There is a vast potential for marketers belonging to the host community to meet huge demand of medicines and medical equipments as local chemists because medical tourists need it in bulk quantity for post-operative and long convalescence period either in host country or in their own country. In India, local chemists dealing in wholesale or large retail medicines hire services of language interpreters in mother tongue of patients to facilitate bulk sales to such patients.

While availability of above mentioned various facilities encourage medical tourists to get treatment in developing countries, there are some recommendations as 'Do's and Don'ts' for host community members lest such hospitality should not be perceived as hostility by medical tourists. It is therefore advisable that the community coming in contact with medical tourists should respect faith, traditions and sentiments of patients and should have positive attitude towards them. An impolite behaviour with use of derogatory words like racial or sexist remarks will create discomfort amongst patients and dissuade them from intermingling with host community.

There is hardly a comprehensive and deep study on 'role of host community for medical tourism development'. However, one such study was made by community leaders and tourism authorities in *Las Vegas USA* on this subject especially on 'impact of economy' due to promotion of medical tourism. Outcome was quite interesting as the study showed that community members were convinced that they will be willing to pay higher taxes and support for development of medical tourism if it improved their economy. The study was based on 'Social Exchange Theory', according to which a hypothesis was proved that economic development due to medical tourism will help them to have positive attitude towards medical tourism. It was based on various parameters like better healthcare facility and well-being of members of community due to increased opportunities etc. This Theory was evolved by George C. Homans and Peter Blau. Homans' (1958) and details were published in 'Social Behaviour as Exchange'. Authors found that institutionalized behaviour and elementary forms of behaviour were generally distinct. According to them elementary behaviour could sometimes 'crack the institutional crust,' forcing changes in the institutionalized ways of doing things (Cook, 2015)

The community representatives and tourism authorities in Las Vegas used the hypothesis of 'willingness to Pay' through random surveys of community members to find out whether they would be willing to pay higher taxes if their economy improves due to arrival of medical tourists and expenditure involved in their purchase of medicines, food, stay in local accommodations and visit of local sites. Since, general presumption is that individuals would not be ready to pay more taxes even if their income increases, an innovative methodology of questionnaire was evolved. Instead of directly asking a person to state 'willingness to pay', he was given a random 'dollar amount' and asked if he would vote for the policy if it would cost him that amount in higher taxes or increased costs for other goods. The response was in affirmative indicating that in view of ' Social Exchange Theory', members of host community were 'willing to pay more' if development of medical tourism enhanced their income. This inference could be extrapolated to overall picture of 'development of medical tourism' (Suess, C., Baloglu, S., & Busser, J. A. 2018).

MEDICAL TOURISM INDUSTRY

In 2018, international medical tourism market was valued around USD 16,760 million and by 2024 it is expected to reach around USD 27,250 million. Apart from direct economic factors discussed above, health insurance portability, and advertising and marketing of the medical tourism also play an important role in its economy.**(Wellness Tourism Markets-Growth, Trends and Forecast, 2019)

Role of Governments of Host Nations in Medical Tourism Development

India wants to make medical tourism a $9 billion industry by 2020 (Medical Tourism Market - Growth, Trends, and Forecast, 2019) As per report of Manveena Suri in CNN, dated February 15, 2019, India, which is one of the most potential competitors in this sector, is eyeing to achieve a growth of medical tourism industry at USD 9 billion by 2020 with 200% growth rate. India has a strong case in influencing arrival of medical tourists as it has competent physicians and specialists, state-of-the-art facilities and equipments in private sectors, low cost treatment, quality cuisines, five thousand years old system of Ayurveda, Yoga, culture and heritage, '*AtithiDevoBhav*' attitude and support of the Government in its development. In fact, Ministry of Tourism and Ministry of Ayush, Government of India are making an endeavour to promote medical tourism in 'Mission Mode'. India is trying to make it easier for people to visit for medical treatments. Former Tourism Minister Mr. K.J. Alphons said in a written response to a query in the Lower House of Parliament that "India can provide medical and health care of international standards at low costs

By 2017, the number of arrivals more than doubled to 495,056 as per Government figures. Other countries can take a leaf out of India's endeavour to promote medical tourism. A separate category is introduced for medical tourists in an Indian e-tourist visa with a longer duration of six months. Government of Mauritius has its unique policy to attract medical tourists on the theme of 'pleasure'. Mauritius's immigration policy encourages people from countries like India, China, and the US to visit as in most cases visas are issued on arrival. More than 36% of the medical tourists that arrived in 2016 were from France in Mexico, as French is widely spoken.

While there is cut throat competition for attracting medical tourists there are some serious issues which need to be addressed by host nations, as pointed by Dr Johanna Hanefeld, a well-known expert and academician on 'health policy' at the London School of Hygiene and Tropical Medicine. In case of wrong treatment or defect in service in medical care, non-redressal of grievance on defective medical service may dissuade medical tourists' arrival and it will bring down reputation of host nation. However, he has observed that low cost treatment not only attracts rich countries' but equally attracts lower middle-income countries' travel for treatment.

As regards overall earnings from medical care, nearly 10% of total revenue comes from foreign medical tourists.

Economic and Social Impact of Medical Tourism on Host Community

Case of Mexico

(Contreras, T. C. (2015)Mexico shares its border with USA and is seen as a destination for those who seek quality medical care at affordable prices. The desired facilities include high-level surgical services, primary healthcare and dental care. The medical patients from USA received high level of services and amenities in Mexico due to which Mexican export of health services in 2013 represents $4.1 billion. Mexico's rank is 23rd with respect to foreign exchange earnings while tourism contributes 9% to Mexican GDP. USA has a relatively newly introduced as compared to Europe. Europe boasts of three decades of experience with patients travelling from one EU Member State to another Member Stateto avail medical facilities. Furthermore, the southern part of United States has witnessed a shortage of doctors and nurses as compared to its northern counterparts.

Profile of Medical Tourists From USA

It has been observed that majority of the Medical tourists crossing the border from USA and into Mexico is Hispanic by origin. These medical tourists arrive from the states of Texas, Arizona and California that border Mexico.

Among the various cities of Mexico, the city of Chihuahua is the most prominent medical tourism destination. According to 2010 US census project, there are 40 million retired Americans and his number is expected to increase to 90 million by 2050. According to US-Mexico Chamber of Commerce study, there are 5 million American retirees that are settled abroad in the following geographies.

- 2.2 million American retirees in Western hemisphere in Mexico, Dominican Republic and Brazil with 800,000 residing in Mexico alone.
- 1.5 million American retirees live in Europe
- 8,50,000 American retirees reside in Asia.

Thus, a sizeable USA retired population residing in Mexico presents Mexico as an opportunity to become a medical tourism hub par excellence. In the same vein, Mexico can develop its medical infrastructure through construction of new hospitals with various specialisations. There is a need for Mexican government and other tourism stakeholders to increase the level of hospitality to the incoming medical tourists and assist them in every manner possible. These improvements shall help attract greater number of foreign patients and Mexican economy shall reap greater socio-economic benefits.

A study indicates that U.S. government spends4.3 times on healthcare as compared to national defence and boasts of the highest Organization for Economic Co-operation and Development (OECD) per capita spending on healthcare. Thus, the reasons for medical tourism can be summed up as follows:

- High costs of medical treatment in US
- Promptness of treatment obtained
- Number of treatments not available (or illegal) within home countries
- The desire for privacy
- The desire to combine various elements of tourism like hotels, climate, food, cultural visits with medical procedures is an important source of inspiration for medical tourists.

Caveats for Mexico as a Medical Tourism Destination

Like all medical tourism economies like India, Thailand, Singapore etc. Mexico faces an increased volume of tourists' influx that is bound to have adverse effects at the socio-economic level. Some of the basic amenities required are increased accommodation and better quality of basic infrastructure. However, there are a few issues that Mexico needs to take into consideration:

- Licensing standards
- Differences in standards of health care
- Different medical protocols
- Protectionism of territorial language barriers
- Prejudicial image and safety certification by the Hospital Joint Commission or their counterparts in Mexico

Impact on Host Community on Medical Tourism Development: Case of Thailand

There is a research study conducted by World Health Organisation (WHO) on Thailand's experience on revenue earnings on medical tourism by Anchana NaRanong and Viroj NaRanong published in Bulletin of the World Health Organization 2011; 89:336-344. doi: 10.2471/BLT.09.072249(WHO,2011).

Most countries including Thailand do not maintain separate data of incoming medical tourists and the foreigners who come to Thailand only for medical care. Both categories of patients have similar rights, needs and demands except that a medical tourist would spend more as his/her agenda includes visit of sites at destination, experiencing and interacting with locals and enjoying its heritage and culture. The study is divided into three parts. The first part estimates the effect of medical tourism on Thai economy with respect to the revenues from medical services and value added services gained from the activities of patients and their attendants before and after medical treatment.

Net earned revenue generated due to arrival of medical tourists can be arrived at by excluding revenue earned due to treatment of exclusively the foreign patients and the tourists who were not medical tourists but fell ill during the stay in Thailand. The researchers could collect consolidated revenue from either medical services or tourist activities' data of import of new drugs and medical equipments, value addition in medical services provided to all foreign tourists including hotel or other accommodation charges paid by all such foreign tourists.

In the Thailand case, the spending on accommodation is taken as 10% of the total spending by a medical tourist. It was inferred that the attendants spend more on accommodation than the medical tourist. On empirical estimates it was observed that out of total earnings from hotels, 60% was earned from foreign patients, 10% from tourists who fell sick during stay while remaining 30% earnings was due to medical tourists who come to Thailand exclusively as medical tourists and spend on accommodation and tourism. Such medical tourists spend about one third of their total spending on abovementioned non-medical expenses. Other assumptions based on Government data and interviews of representatives of the hospitals who are treating all medical tourist or foreign patients were that (a) only 75% foreign patients bring an attendant, (b) the attendant would spend twice as much on hotels and tourism as the patient spends. The estimates arrived after computing all earnings including value additions indicate that Thailand earned 46 to 52 billion baht (1US$ equal to 30 baht during period of study of 2008 data) towards medical services and about 12 billion baht from tourism related activities of the medical tourists. It was computed that the value added at 31 to 35 billion baht from medical services and 5.8 to 6.5 billion baht from related tourism. This amounts to a total value added of 36.8 to 41.6 billion baht or 0.45 of gross domestic product! So, it would be interesting to observe as to how the sub-sector of Medical tourism contributes to national GDP. In the case of Thailand, the contribution of Medical tourism to national GDP varied from 0.4% to 0.7%. It brings prosperity in medical services sector, the tourist services, raises income of host community, and it brings other intangible benefits.

Second part of the research work relates to human resources deployment in medical tourism industry. As a part of the qualitative analysis, an important area of concern is the Human Resources used for medical tourism which could be in the form of physicians, surgeons, paramedical staff like nurses etc. Some data are obtained from identified hospitals that treat the foreign medical tourists/patients.

As a negative consequence, the physicians of the public hospitals are lured by the private sector hospitals at sky high remuneration which leaves the domestic citizens, dependent on the public hospitals at a less advantageous situation.

Third part of research relates to negative impact in terms of economy for the host community which is required to pay more for health care in private hospitals while there would remain shortage of physicians and specialists in public hospitals.

The authors have discussed this research study under WHO in detail because it is an authentic analysis and can be extrapolated to all developing countries that are competing with each other in attracting more medical tourists.

The researchers have given references of other studies wherein similar problems related to Medical tourism such as shortage of specialists, nurses' other para-medical staff and high cost of health care for host community have surfaced. India is no exception. It is indicated by researchers that development of medical tourists does not always result into a "win-win situation". Host nations need to take care of negative effects as host communities would expect higher budget and subsidy on healthcare by its respective governments as the host government has moral responsibility to keep a balance between extra revenue generated by promoting medical tourism vis-a-vis welfare of the host community. Since medical tourists have high purchasing power, they may reduce the burden of tax payers of the host community in return of getting cheap and quality health care in the host country. Such governments have logical ground for levying a tax on medical tourists, who, unlike the host community taxpayers and expatriates residing in host country, reap benefits without contributing to taxes. The tax money, thus earned, supports extra budget on human resources shortage and related medical tourism infrastructure. The earnings from such taxes could set off all negative economic aspects of the host community.

Top Asian Countries Leading in Medical Tourism Development

As mentioned elsewhere in the chapter, Medical tourism has been on the rise globally. While the budding tourism sector involves 50 countries across continents, a few Asian countries are leading the pack as Medical tourism destinations (Asia top five Medical Tourism destinations, 2012). Prominent among Asian countries are India, Singapore and Thailand that comprise approximately 90% of medical tourism market share in Asia.

Asia is a leader in medical tourism industry mainly because of affordable medical care, state-of-the-art medical infrastructure and surgical equipments, well qualified specialists and easily accessible patient care with lesser waiting time. Issues related to respective government policies of leading nations in this field were discussed above. However, the medical tourism industry and private sectors of the following five Asian countries are equally responsible for significant growth of medical tourism development:

Thailand

Thailand tops the list among other Asian nations with more than 1.2 million medical tourists visiting in 2013.However, ten years ago Singapore used to be considered as hub for this industry in Southeast Asia. World Health Organization has rated its medical care facilities as "world class". The credit goes to the government which has hand-held its development. Medical tourists are assured about safety and professionalism through Joint Commission International: a global group has set high standards for all health care centres which meet multiple quality benchmarks, and have very safe record system with legal remedies readily available. Besides being cheap in providing health care, Thailand is an aviation hub with very cheap flights options available at Bangkok Airport. A detailed WHO case study is also discussed in this Chapter as a representative booming economy model for this industry.

India

Singapore, Thailand and India together have a lion share of 90 percent of Asia's medical tourism industry, India attracts more foreign investments which helps it in procuring state-of-the-art infrastructure and equipments in the private sector. In human resources availability, no other Asian nation out of top five giants in this sector can match in talent and qualification with a command on English language. With respect to price too, India offers cheapest healthcare which can save up to 85 percent on surgical procedures. In coming years, India will be a world leader in this industry with strong support from its Government, which is driving this industry in mission mode. Indian stakeholders are making concerted efforts to popularize health tourism with ease in visa regime, preparation of itineraries and comfort for attendants, sightseeing attractions including hosted accommodation and Ayurveda and Yoga as additional alternatives. This industry needs to give more attention to hygiene and clean after-surgery care.

Singapore

It is surprising to notice that medical tourists prefer this country for healthcare despite the fact that it is one of the most expensive cities in the world with the cost of living more than 30 percent than a costly American city. Surgery here is more expensive than in Malaysia and Thailand. Nevertheless, overall healthcare cost is surprisingly cheap with additional advantage of availability of other ultra-modern facilities in all

15 specialised hospitals meant for medical tourists. English is widely spoken and the modern and orderly infrastructure makes medical tourists feel more comfortable.

South Korea

This country is more popular for cosmetic and plastic surgery particularly with innovative 'Tip Plastry' for nose shaping. Though it is a costly country for accommodation, food and sightseeing, it has unique features to attract medical tourists due to availability of 'real time' computerized record maintenance. South Korea is also excelling in the field of robotic surgery, which may attract more tourists to avail the facility of ultra-modern techniques.

Malaysia

Malaysian Government and stakeholders are promoting medical tourism industry with both Eastern and Western Systems of medicine. It provides treatment through acupuncture, herbology, and other forms of traditional Chinese and Southeast Asian systems. Arrival of medical tourists in this country has doubled since 2010. Malaysian physicians and surgeons are well versed in Muslim customs and this fact, alone is responsible to attract Muslim medical tourists seeking a medical care experience with familiar traditions and practices like availability of Halal meat and prayer rooms. This destination is fast developing as a hub for Muslim medical tourists.

CONCLUSION

Today, health care is one of the most prominent factors in man's life and man will continue to explore ways to find remedy from any illness. In present time, distance is no hurdle and, therefore, man will cross all boundaries in quest of getting rid of imminent fatalities or for other healthcare problems (Medical Tourism magazine, 2019). Study shows that there are four important reasons due to which a patient will travel to another country to seek medical care, i.e.,

1. Destination for medical care should be affordable,
2. Waiting time for getting treatment should be minimum
3. Medical care and support system is better in foreign country than home country and lastly,
4. Such treatment is not available or not up to the mark in home country.

Impact on Global Healthcare

Positive Impact

Social Impact

The World Economic Forum has conducted an in-depth analysis on tourism sector through the Travel and Tourism competitiveness Index (TTCI) of 136 economies across the world. TTCI measures "the set of factors and policies that enable the sustainable development of the travel and tourism sector, which in turn, contributes to the development and competitiveness of a country". The TTCI enables tourists and other stakeholders to identify nations having higher ranking amongst other nations on the basis of TTC Indices which may attract more tourists' arrival for various reasons, like, visiting cultural places, overall cheaper travelling or high price competitive Index, affordable health care, and comfort etc. The authors had presented a research paper titled "Tourism prospects in South Asia" in an International Tourism Conference organised by UET Italy and ITHC in Palermo, Italy in December, 2018 wherein it was shown that South Asian nations have very high ranking in Price Competitiveness Index as compared to developed nations which is one of the factors that attracts tourists to South Asian nations (Saxena et al.2018)Medical tourists prefer to select a country for medical treatment where they find treatment as well as cost of living cheaper. Top Asian nations in medical tourism industry, with exception of Singapore and South Korea are able to promote medical tourism in their country on these factors only. Other social factor is that tourists are welcomed by host community as tourism has 'multiplier effect' in bringing prosperity and employment generation amongst members of the community. On the other hand, as per the latest trend, developed countries have started discouraging arrival of tourists as economic and employment issues are irrelevant for these countries..

Financial Impact

As tourism is an engine for growth with its multiplier effect on various other sectors like transport, manufacturing, foreign investments, exports, consumer products, aviation, entertainment information technology services, etc., its contribution to any nation's Gross Domestic Products (GDP) is about 9% which is very significant. At present, share of medical tourism is approximately 5% to 10% of total foreign tourist arrivals, its year to year growth is more than double, i.e., around 20% to 25% (India has 10-11% tourism arrival growth as against 28% year to year growth in medical tourism though its present market share is at 5%. Therefore, it is going to bring significant prosperity and generate employment opportunities in the host community. As per official figures of Ministry of Tourism in India, an investment of about US$ 15000 creates maximum jobs i.e., around 78 as against 45 and 18 jobs are created if same investment is made in manufacturing and agriculture sectors respectively. In view of such huge advantages, medical tourism is likely to play a significant role in the upliftment of the host community in terms of financial and employment generation.

Impact on Other Sectors

- As mentioned above, growth of medical tourism will have great impact on Pharmaceutical, tourism services, cottage and living industries, food, amusement, ICT, aviation and transport sectors, etc. All medical tourists tend to invest the amount they save from healthcare in sight-seeing, entertainment, shopping, eateries etc. Which earn significant revenue through the tourism industry. Most of the medical tourists seek help from travel agents, international agencies of hospitals, concierge service providers and newly created agencies staffed by a team of professionals who are equipped to offer a seamless assistance including 'through a single window system'. Both public and private sectors contribute to overall infrastructure and associated processes like permitting medical visa, clearing foreign passports, facilitating foreign exchange, ensuring comfort & hospitality as well as state-of-the-art equipments, healthcare facilities and human resources in medical profession. There is tremendous scope of developing public-private partnerships to build infrastructure and share profits.
- There are many intangible benefits for the host community in terms of checking 'Brain-Drain' which would rather tend to convert into 'Brain-Grain' due to lucrative offers of huge financial packages for native specialists working in other countries to join back mother country. Development of medical tourism will also forge deep relationship between political leaders of countries from where these tourists are coming and leaders of host countries as there are important issues related to patients' medical record system, visa related issues, legal and medical remedies etc. Leaders of Governments of Afghanistan, Nigeria, and Bangladesh etc. are having frequent meetings with their counterparts in Indian Government on various issues which crop up due to medical complexities.

Negative Impact

Healthcare Impact

Some of the top Asian countries including India are facing criticism on unhygienic conditions and infection 'after-surgery' convalescence. Recent superbug research has already alerted the medical fraternity and patients. With transfer of patient to his or her home country, significant risk of corresponding bacterial travel cannot be ruled out. Danger lurks due to negative impact of communicable diseases too. Hence, all such issues are to be addressed and good strategies need to be developed by all stakeholders and respective governments to take care of negative impact on the development of medical tourism.

Environmental Impact

It is a fact that every tourism activity is associated with an adverse impact on environment of the host country. More infrastructures will be at the cost of natural greenery and forest coverage. All hospitals cause continuous discharge of polluted air, toxic medical waste besides creation of huge solid waste and faeces problems related to sewage disposal. The host community is deprived of its due share of power, food stock and other natural and manmade resources resulting into high prices payable by the members of the host community. Medical tourists and attendants generally misuse the rare and non-replenish-able commodity like water in their hotel rooms and private ward rooms. As discussed in the case study of 'Thailand Experience' under aegis of WHO, inaccessibility of physicians, specialists, para-medical staff and high cost of treatment for members of the host community are other significant negative impacts of development of medical tourists. Other negative economic impact too, is discussed in abovementioned case study of Thailand and a proposal of levying a separate tax on medical tourists is made therein.

Ethical and Legal Impact

There are instances that some private sector medical tourism hospitals have resorted to unethical practices to lure international patients, by way of organ transplants, restricted regional treatments or illegal practices of arranging birth through surrogate mother by exploiting poor families. There is urgent need of legislation in host countries for redressal of grievances of medical tourists. These pros and cons in medical tourism industry create opportunities as well as challenges for all stakeholders in the industry and require a balanced approach by all concerned, particularly by policy makers.

REFERENCES

Allen, L. R., Long, P. T., Perdue, R. R., & Kieselbach, S. (1988). The impact of tourism development on residents' perceptions of community life. *Journal of Travel Research, 27*(1), 16–21. doi:10.1177/004728758802700104

Bansal, S. P., Kulshreshtha, S., & Gautam, P. (n.d.). *Tourism Towards New Horizons – Status*. Academic Press.

Bookman, M. (2007). *Medical tourism in developing countries*. Springer.

Carrera, P. M., & Bridges, J. F. (2006). Globalization and healthcare: Understanding health and medical tourism. *Expert Review of Pharmacoeconomics & Outcomes Research, 6*(4), 447–454. doi:10.1586/14737167.6.4.447 PMID:20528514

Connell, J. (2006). Medical tourism: Sea, sun, sand and... surgery. *Tourism Management, 27*(6), 1093–1100. doi:10.1016/j.tourman.2005.11.005

Cook, K. S. (2015). *Exchange: Social*. Academic Press.

Erdeli, G., Dincă, A. I., Gheorghilaş, A., & Surugiu, C. (2011). Romanian spa tourism: A communist paradigm in a post communist era. *Human Geographies--Journal of Studies & Research in Human Geography, 5*(2).

Exworthy, M., & Peckham, S. (2006). Access, choice and travel: Implications for health policy. *Social Policy and Administration, 40*(3), 267–287. doi:10.1111/j.1467-9515.2006.00489.x

Exworthy, M., & Peckham, S.Establishments in Delhi. (2006). Access, choice and travel: Implications for health policy. *Social Policy and Administration, 40*(3), 267–287. doi:10.1111/j.1467-9515.2006.00489.x

Glinos, I. A., Boffin, N., & Baeten, R. (2005). Contracting cross-border care in belgian Hospitals: An analysis of Belgian, Dutch and English Stakeholder Perspectives. *Observatoire Social Européen*.

Goodrich, J. N., & Goodrich, G. E. (1987). Health-care tourism—An exploratory study. *Tourism Management, 8*(3), 217–222. doi:10.1016/0261-5177(87)90053-7

Horowitz, M. D. (2007). Medical tourism-health care in the global economy. *Physician Executive, 33*(6), 24. PMID:18092615

Issues & Perspectives. (2013). *Tapping Accessible & Medical Tourism by B&B*. Academic Press.

Lowson, K., West, P., Chaplin, S., & O'Reilly, J. (2002). *Department of Health: Evaluation of Treating Patients Overseas—Final Report. University of York, UK.* York Health Economics Consortium.

OECD. (2010). *Medical Tourism: Treatments, Markets and Health System Implications: A scoping review*. OECD.

Reddy, S. G. (2013). *Medical tourism in India: an exploratory study* (Doctoral dissertation). Kansas State University.

Reinhardt, U. E., Hussey, P. S., & Anderson, G. F. (2002). Cross-national comparisons of health systems using OECD data, 1999. *Health Affairs*, *21*(3), 169–181. doi:10.1377/hlthaff.21.3.169 PMID:12025981

Saxena, G. G., Saxena, A., & Saxena, A. (2018). Indian BnBs: An emerging disruptor in the hospitality sector. Delhi, India: Pragun Publication.

Suess, C., Baloglu, S., & Busser, J. A. (2018). Perceived impacts of medical tourism development on community wellbeing. *Tourism Management*, *69*, 232–245. doi:10.1016/j.tourman.2018.06.006

Chapter 7
Domestic Medical Tourism to Study the Expectations of Domestic Medical Tourists

Sukanya Roy
Indian School of Business, Mohali, India

ABSTRACT

The objective of the study was to document the features of the medical tourism sector in the state and analyse its possible implications on domestic healthcare in Jaipur, Rajasthan. In the present study, in-depth interviews were conducted with the key stakeholders in the state. The major finding that emerged from the study was that although there will be an improvement in the overall quality and availability of advanced healthcare services, accessibility to the services will be affected particularly for poorer sections due to increased cost of care. Policymakers believed the gradual growth of the private sector in healthcare and the decline of the public health sector will lead to the exclusion of a section of the domestic population from access to quality healthcare.

INTRODUCTION

In present era nation witness new type of rise in Indian hospital which is known as a medical tourism. Medical tourism is most important segment in health care segment. India has a unique combination of advanced facilities of skilled doctors with low cost of treatment which considered nation as most popular hub of medical tourism. Past studies report showed that India is growing as the most preferred destination of "medical tourist." and added a value of around US$6 billion dollar(IBEF Report).

DOI: 10.4018/978-1-7998-3427-4.ch007

Health tourism is a multibillion-dollar industry which is promoted by the Indian Govt and nourished by the corporate boom in medical care. Medical tourism is an economic activity that entails trade in services and represents the mixing of two of the largest world industries: medicine and tourism.

Reasons for the rise of Domestic Healthcare tourism:

Unique trio combination of high-quality medical facilities, Proficient Regional-speaking medical professionals and low cost effective

Medical tourism is generally categorised into two section (a) Global Tourism and (b) Domestic tourism. The present chapter mainly focused on the issue face by a domestic's tourist. Domestic medical tourism is the practise of travelling from one city to another or within the country to able better medical treatment. Several past studies found that Domestic medical tourism is preferably found in rural India as compared to Urban areas. The main reason behind the medical tourism in rural India is due to improper medical facilities and poor health infrastructure.

IMPORTANCE OF RESEARCH TOPIC

Several studies in the global health tourism captured on the economic benefits which is created by the overseas tourist, but few studies have explored that domestic tourism. According to Ji Sook Han, 2017, highlights the demands for health tourism in domestic tourists. According to Simon Hudson And Xiang, 2012 highlights the consumers attitudes and beliefs towards the domestic medical tourism. The present research paper mainly identifies a) the pain points of the domestic tourist especially the patients from rural India who are in hope to get a better medical facility in Urban medical hospital and secondly it identify the "medical tourist" expectations choosing urban hospital as medical tourism destinations.

OBJECTIVES OF THE STUDY

1. To identify the major health care treatment methods adopted by domestic tourist patients
2. To understand the opinion of domestic tourist patients regarding the influencing factors like cost of treatment, doctors, staff of hospital and other legal and technical procedure.
3. To understand the factors which directly affect the decision of domestic tourists related to taking health care treatment in Indian hospitals.
4. To identify the reason or the expectations why domestic tourist prefer urban health tourism.

5. To develop a conceptual model of domestic medical tourists.

LITERATURE REVIEW

Reviewing the research on medical tourism, there are several studies found on International medical tourism. Few studies mentioned in domestic medical tourism (Hudson et al,2012). Hudson was the first who introduced the concept of Domestic medical tourism. To gain more insight into domestic medical tourism, the authors provide a detailed explanation on domestic medical tourism literature.

Domestic medical tourism is a recent concept in medical tourism industry, main previous studies mainly focused on international tourism, very few works have been done in the domestic medical tourism. Domestic medical tourism is the practice of travelling from one city to another or one state to another within one's country for treatment. According to **Goodrich & Goodrich (1987)**, medical tourism is the attempt to attract tourists by deliberately promoting its health-care services and facilities, in addition to its regular tourist amenities.

INTERRELATIONSHIP BETWEEN TOURISM AND HEALTH

In ancient era, the links between travel and health is about taking of waters at minerals and hot springs (Lowenthal,1962). But with the evolve of technology, change in socioeconomic factors leads to drastic change in the relation of health and tourism sector. Health tourism, as defined by IUOTO,1973 is "the provision of health facilities utilizing the natural resources of the country, especially mineral and water". According to Tejeida et al,2006 proposed that health-tourism system impact the social well-being and economic development. A fundamental aspect of the health-tourism system is its impact in the health of the inhabitants of the cities.

MEDICAL TOURISM

"Medical tourism is the term to explain the phenomenon of people travelling outside their home country primarily for the purpose of seeking medical treatment" Gaines, J & Lee,C.V, 2019. Many past studies have found that there are numerous factors for the purpose of seeking medical treatment outside their home country. The primary factors of this study were low cost and good medical treatment.

Health tourism data showed that the most common categories has drawn attention to tourist found that cosmetic surgery, cardiac surgery, orthopedic surgery and dentist surgery. According to Hamid Beladi et al, 2019 research it has been found that medical tourism has a positive influence on economic growth on host country economic growth. Medical tourism creates major economic growth on developing countries (Milica & Karla,2007). According to the report by Dr.Chi Kin, 2007 the prime reasons for the health care tourism in developing countries are as follows

1. "Large price differentials for health procedures in developing countries"
2. "Overburdened public healthcare system in developed countries leads to influence medical tourism"
3. Best medical facilities with low cost is the prime factors that promote the healthcare tourism in developing countries.

Health Tourism in India

India is the most favored destination of medical tourist, it is promoted by Government and fueled by corporate hospitals like (Max, Narayan Hridalaya, Fortis etc etc). Medical tourism is a multibillion industry promoted by government after the clearance of National Health Policy, 2002 it widely supports the medical tourism.

The unique selling points of the "Indian medical tourism" Gupta, A. S. (2008) are as follows:

1. High quality medical facilities
2. Cost effectives: Nominal cost, the cost differential is huge Open-heart surgery cost $70,000 in Britain, $15,000 in USA and India cost vary from $3000 to $10,000. Medical tourist generally ger a package deal that comprises of flights, hotels, treatment and post-operative vacation.
3. Easy access to language: English speaking medical professionals
4. India is a tourist centered destination.

Health tourism is broadly categorized in two sections a) International medical tourism & b) domestic medical tourism. In the present research study, the focus is on domestic medical tourism.

Domestic Medical Tourism

Domestic medical tourism broadly refers to domestic travel for medical tourism purpose. According to Ajay Bakshi & A.k.Verma, 2012 study showed that individual's travelled from his homeland to another city within the country to avail the better medical treatment in less cost in addition there study also found that individuals from the rural cities were more frequent to travel urban cities to avail the best medical treatment. Simon Hudson & Xiang Li, 2012 they have focused on the literature on medical tourism which studies about the international medical tourism, where people fly to acquire best health care services, both the researchers gave more importance on both foreign and domestic patients, in addition there study also showed that there is an increasing numbers of domestic patients who fly for health care services inside their own country. Muralidar Trivedi, 2003 proposed that growing numbers of Naturopathy, Yoga and AyurVaid centers have drawn attention to the numbers of rural patients which directly impact on domestic medical tourist.

Expectation of Domestic Medical Tourism

Expectations, with reference to healthcare relate to the belief about the healthcare system and doctors. It a mental picture that captured by the patients during the process of interaction with the healthcare system. Fatima Lateef, 2011 explained patient expectations and categorized into two elements a) Value based care and b) patient-centered care. Sadd Ahmed Javed, 2017 examined the five services quality ("empathy", "responsiveness", "tangibility", "reliability" and "assurance") on Pakistani expectations and the study found that patient's satisfaction is strongly associated with empathy in public sector and responsiveness in private sector. Adugnaw, Berhane & Fikre,2016 proposed that post consultation expectation have a major influenced on patient satisfaction.

Several studies in the global health tourism captured on economic benefits as well as the expectations of the global patients but few studies highlights on the on the expectations of the domestics medical tourist. So present study mainly focused on the expectation of domestic medical tourist

BRIEF DESCRIPTION OF RESEARCH METHODOLOGY

Materials and Methods

The present study design was a qualitative investigation, that involve face to face and telephonic interview with the patients who frequently visit Jaipur for treatment.

Participant Recruitment

Patients were enrolled through a multi-specialty hospitals in Jaipur, as a large proportion of registered patients had already self-identified as a "rural domestic patients". Purposive sampling was carried out in the present research. Cresswell,2003 purposive sampling seeks participants and help to understand the research problems

According to Participants were included if they were over 18yrs of age and self-identified as "Domestic Rural Patients"

In total, 14 patients were enrolled between "August to 1st week of October, 2019". Enrolment along side of data collection and ended when researchers found that data saturation had been achieved.

Data Collection

Interviews were carried out by the researchers at Jaipur multi-speciality hospitals. Interviews were recorded for transcription later. The audio recordings of the interviews were transcribed verbatim and then checked thrice to ensure accuracy by the researchers but were not returned to respondents for checking. Each interview lasted for 30-40mins

Selection Factors

All products have a series of qualitative specifications which have difference combinations of the attributes that represent a different variety of the products.

1. **Independent Variables:** Price, Availability of specialist doctor, Accommodation and Healthcare quality (Kaijun Yu et al,2018)

Research Context

The study mainly conducts in the capital city of Jaipur, Rajasthan where numbers of rural tourist from the adjacent villages, Tier 2 and Tier 3 cities visit Jaipur for Health check-ups.

The prime hospital of Jaipur city which draw attention for the domestic tourist

1. SMS Hospital
2. Fortis
3. Manipal Hospital
4. Dunlopji
5. Tongiya Hospital
6. Mahatma Gandhi Hospital
7. Bhagwan Mahaveer Cancer Hospital

Selection Factors

The selection factors of the respondents on the socio-demographic factors like age, sex. Marital status.

RESULTS

Sample Analysis

Study included in-depth interview of 14 respondents shown in Table 1.

Table 1. Detailed explanation of participants.

Acceptance Nos.	Sex	Age	Marital Status	Occupation	Financial Support	Medical Tourism Product
1.	M	7	NA	NA	Self-Finance	Paediatrician
2.	F	25	Married	Homemaker	Self-Finance	Gynaecologist
3.	M	60	Married	Family business	Govt sponsored (Bhamasah Card)	Cardiologist
4.	M	6	NA	NA	Self finance	Naturopathy
5.	F	65	Married	Homemaker	Govt sponsored (Bhamasah Card)	AyurVaid
6.	F	53	Married	Homemaker	Govt sponsored (Bhamasah Card)	Cardiologist
7.	F	27	Married	Homemaker	Self finance	Infertility Issue
8.	F	29	Married	Homemaker	Self-finance	Oncologist
9.	M	30	Unmarried	Govt Employee	Insurance	ENT
10.	F	32	Married	Pvt employee	Insurance	Gynaecologist
11.	F	38	Married	Homemaker	Self finance	MD
12.	M	30	Married	Pvt Employee	Insurance	Orthopaedic
13.	M	75	Married	Family Business	Govt sponsored (Bhamasah Card)	Accidental Case
14.	F	32	Married	Homemaker	Self finance	Gynaecologist

Gender Distribution

Sample included 57% females and 43% of males (Table 2).

Table 2.

Row Labels	Count of Sex
F	8
M	6
Grand Total	**14**

Marital Status

Sample includes 9- Married respondents, 3-Unmarried respondents, 2-Kids (Table 3).

Table 3.

Row Labels	Count of Marital Status
Married	9
Unmarried	3
Kids	2
Grand Total	**14**

Occupation

Occupation is one of the most important demographic markers. Sample includes in the Table 4.

Table 4.

Row Labels	Count of Occupation
Family business	2
Govt Employee	1
Homemaker	7
NA	2
Pvt employee	2
Grand Total	**14**

Medical Tourism Product

Cardiac treatment is the most popular product of Indian medical tourism, which is followed by Gynaecologist, Orthopaedic. Oncologist. All details are provided in Table 5.

Table 5.

Row Labels	Count of Medical Tourism Product
Accidental Case	1
AyurVaid	1
Cardiologist	3
ENT	1
Gynecologist	2
Infertility Issue	1
MD	1
Naturopathy	1
Oncologist	1
Orthopedic	1
Pediatrician	1
Grand Total	**14**

Source of Financial Support

From the qualitative data it has been found that Jaipur is the domestic medical tourism destination for the nearby tier 2/tier 3 cities, data has revealed that more that fifty percentage of patients have to support their own medical treatment, followed by Govt sponsored (Bhamasah Card) and Private health insurance (Table 6).

Table 6.

Row Labels	Count of Financial Support
Govt sponsored (Bhamasah Card)	4
Insurance	3
Self finance	7
Grand Total	**14**

DATA ANALYSIS

The "Thematic framework" method of analysis was applied. The whole analysis was occurred in six steps

1. "Familiarization with the raw data, achieved by rereading the transcripts and field notes".
2. "Identification of the thematic framework, which entailed identifying recurring subthemes".
3. "Indexing the transcripts according to the subthemes identified".
4. "Charting and rearranging the data into the area of the thematic framework to which they related".
5. "Mapping and interpreting the data; this involved the interpretation and categorization of the charts of data collected in order to create broader themes from the subthemes".

Analysis began soon after the completion of the entire interview. By carrying out data collection and analysis concurrently, it was possible to employ an iterative approach to the investigation, such than findings were used to shape the discussion in a subsequent interview. As the data interviews were progressed data were analysed and new themes added were necessary

Figures 1-3 provide a detailed explanation of coding tree represent how the themes and subthemes were formed from the initial categories found an analysis of the data.

THEMES

Sixe core themes were identified, each with their own subthemes (1.2)

Theme 1: Attitudes Towards Domestic Medical Tourism

This theme addresses how participants conceptualized medical tourism, what they understood about medical tourism and why they prefer domestic medical tourism.

Subtheme 1a: "Lack of Facilities Leads to Move Jaipur Hospital"

All respondents stated that due to lack of specialist doctor and poor medical infrastructure facilities is the prime cause to able the treatment from Jaipur Hospitals.

Figure 1.

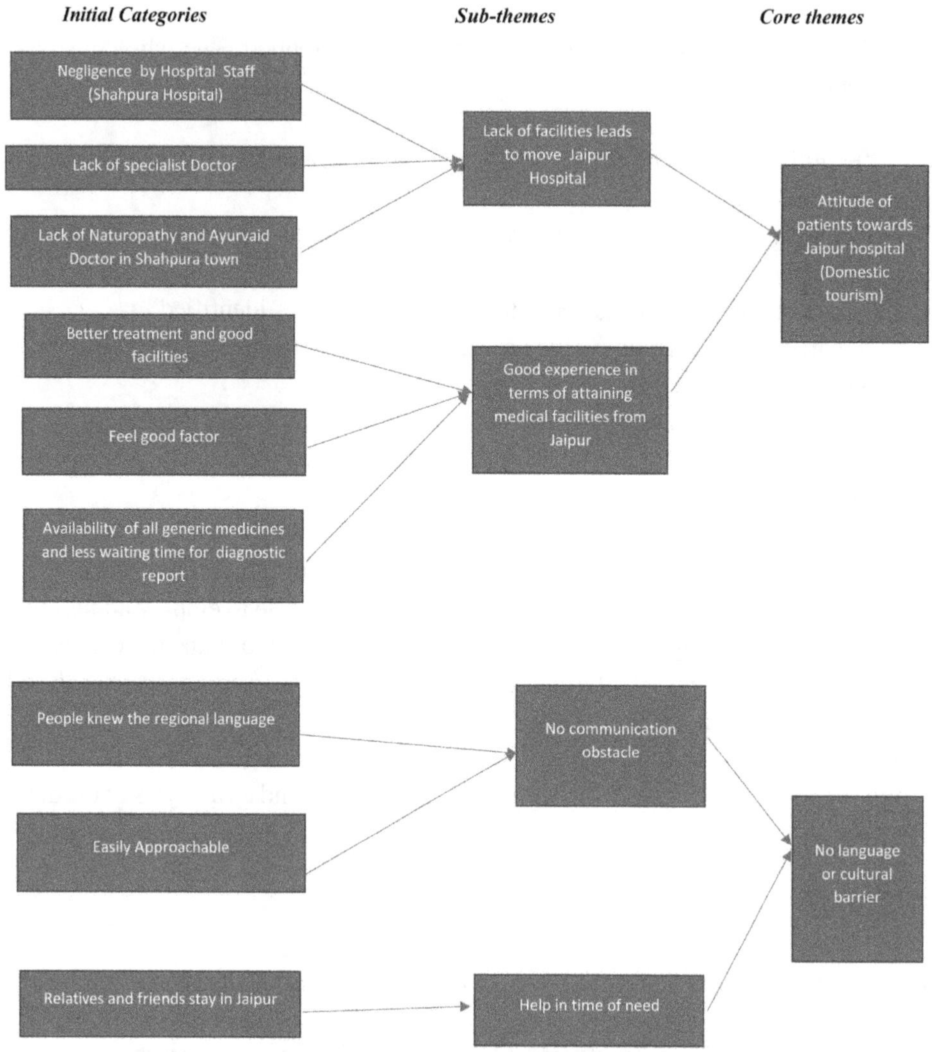

"I am sixty years old heart patient, already suffer from minor heart attack. in my area there is no heart specialist from whom I can able treatment for that reason I have to travel Jaipur in the interval of every thirty to get the treatment from Tongya hospital Jaipur" 3M,60yrs

Figure 2.

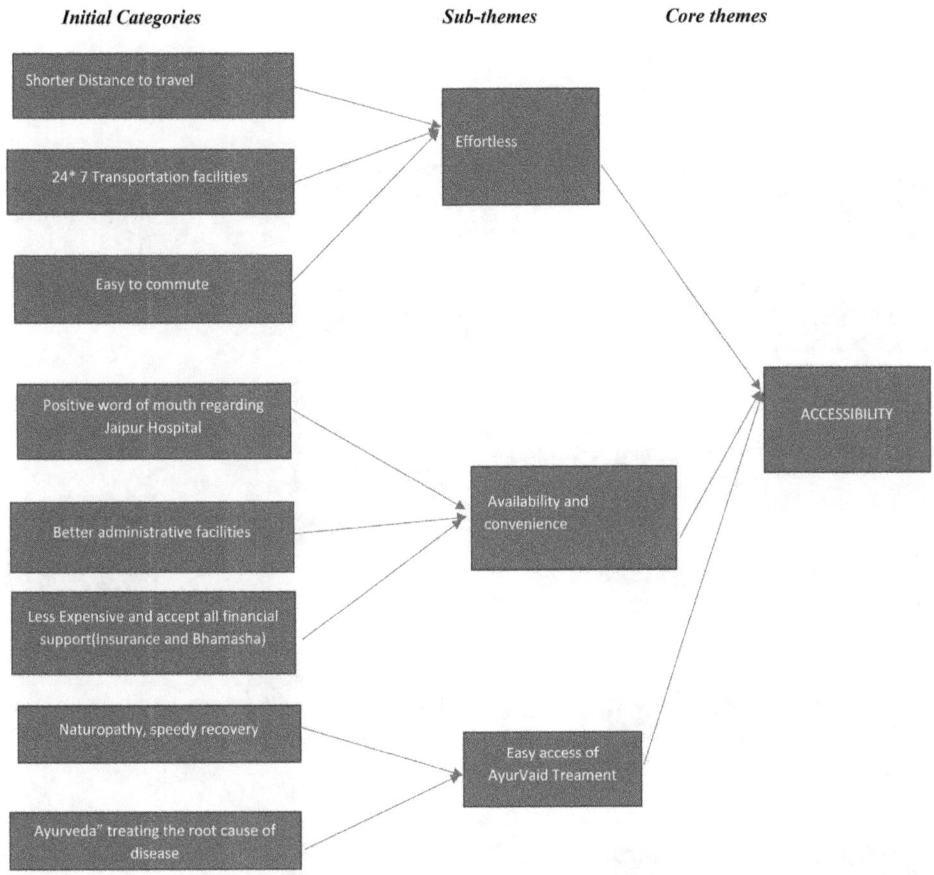

Subtheme 1b: "Good Experience in Terms of Hospital Facilities"

The domestic medical tourism perceived as easy and patients have to suffer less while getting treatment from the Jaipur hospital.

"During my child treatment from J.K.Loan hospital, doctors diagnose my son with great care and prescribe less medicine and that also generic medicine, where I have to spend less amount on medicines, and I able a generic medicine in stores too" 1M,7yrs

Figure 3.

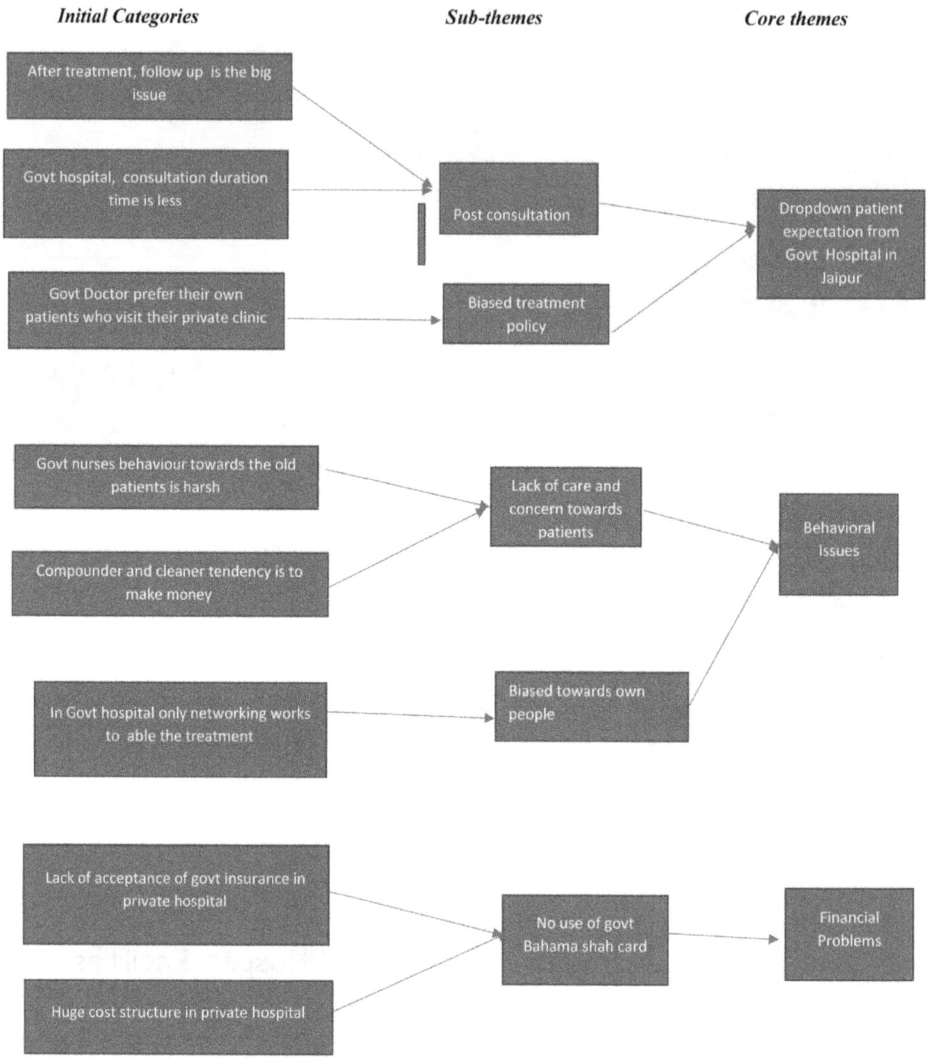

Theme 2: "No Culture and Language Barrier"

This theme explored the respondent's views on how the language directly influence the domestic tourism.

Subtheme 2a: "No Communication Obstacle"

Among participants who identified the language helps them to prefer Jaipur hospital because, people are aware of the regional language for which they can easily communicate with the doctors and other staff attending the hospitals and apart from that we respondents found the same food habit (vegetarians) in Jaipur.

"I am 75yrs old person, while getting treatment from Jaipur hospital I share my health issues with the doctors in my language and I find more comfortable"

Subtheme 2b: "Help in Time of Need"

Several respondents found that presence of relatives in Jaipur city, helps them lots while getting treatment, attendent can stay in time

"While I met with accident, those days my wife has to take care of me, In hospital there is no facilities to stay attendant, in those days my wife stay in my brother's place"

Theme 3

Subtheme 3a "Accessibility: Where Patients Can Easily Acquire and Use the Service"

- **Effortless:** Getting medical treatment in Jaipur perceived as easy and convenient, which acted as stimulant and encouragement for the Jaipur hospital to provide better medical treatment for the domestic patients.

*"Jaipur is hardly 60km away from my place easily, 24*7 transportation is available. So for heart treatment I prefer to visit Jaipur Hospital" m,60*

Subtheme 3b: "Availability & Convenience"

Domestic medical tourism is in high demand in Jaipur hospital, most of the respondents found that for emergency treatment they prefer Jaipur hospital, because of the better medical facilities, availability of doctors and less waiting time leads Jaipur hospital more convenient.

"Once I met with a severe accident, without delay my son prefer Jaipur Fortis hospital, I have get a best medical treatment"

Theme 4: "Dropdown Patients' Expectation From Jaipur Govt Hospitals"

Subthemes 4a: "Post Consultation"

This subtheme addresses how participants expectations has dropdown towards the Govt Hospitals, participants share their pain points while seeking treatments from "SMS" & "Janana Hospital".

"after my operations the follow up procedure is not at all good, I suffer lots after operations" f, 63

Subtheme 4b: "Biased Treatment Process"

This subtheme addresses how participants have to suffer while getting treatment from SMS Doctors, Govt doctors mainly prefer their own patients first who visit their clinic.

"in my queue one of my patients share his doctor prefer his own patients who get the consultation from his own clinic" f,28

Theme 5: "Behavioral Issues"

Subtheme 5a: "Lack of Care and Concern Towards Patients Especially Old Patients"

This subtheme addresses that how respondents suffer from the several factors like the harsh behaviors of hospital employees and unskilled people are always looking for making money.

"I was strange when I was discharged from hospital the compounder came and charge money from me"m,75

Subtheme 5b "Biased Towards Own People/ Networking Matters for Getting Treatment"

This subtheme address how participants to get the treatment from Govt hospital, networking play a vital role in getting the treatment.

"I have to call ruling party member for seeking the hospital facilities in SMS"

"Theme 6: Financial Problems/Not Acceptance of Bhamashah Card"

Subtheme 6a "Less Use of Bhamashah Card in Private Hospital"

This subtheme address how patients have to face problems while paying the high bills in private hospital, because large sections of the private hospital don't accept the Bhamasha Card.

"While seeking my treatment from one of the private nursing home in Jaipur, I have to borrow money from lenders as they don't accept my Bhamashah card and the hospital bills is too high that I can't afford" f,63

DISCUSSION OF RESULTS

Respondents have a practical view regarding the function and expectation domestic medical tourism; from the study it has been found that instead of allopathy domestic medical tourist adopted the Naturopathy and Ayurvaid treatment. The study found that good medical infrastructure, specialist doctor, same language and culture and easily access to local resources are the important elements which determine the domestic tourist from Tier1/Tier2/village to travel Jaipur hospital for better treatment.

In the present study the main purpose of the study is to find the expectations of the domestic medical tourist who travelled from their hometown to bog cities to able the better medical treatment. The study reported that the exceptions of the patients towards govt hospital has been declined and the major determinants are a) lack of post consultation by the doctors, b) biased treatment policy (where govt doctor prefer those patients who get a checkup from their own clinic), and c) lack of care and concern towards the patients especially old age people. In additional study also found that "Behavioral issues" are the major factors that mainly effect the domestic medical tourist to able the Govt hospital treatment and the major factors are a) Networking in the govt hospital play a major role to able the treatment from Hospital b)) lack of care and concern towards the patients especially old age patients and the last factors where patients suffers lots is the less usage of "Bhamashah Card" or govt supported financial insurance are largely not accepted by the private hospital.

CONCLUSION

According to Ehrbeck et al, 2008 medical travel is most relevant, and it has a direct impact on the economic growth for the country, but for some reason medical tourism studies didn't covered much about the domestic medical tourism (Reddy etal,2010). Hudson et al,2012 first introduced the framework of domestic medical tourism and his impact on regional economies in the United states. Bowling et al, 2012 proposed and developed a questionnaire which capture the patient's expectation in the health domain. Adugnaw et el, 2016 examined a study on patient expectation in the context of public health sector, but for some reason domestic medical tourism studies has not covered much especially about the expectation and the patients satisfaction about the domestic medical tourist. In this paper, researched concluded about the expectation about the medical tourist who travelled from their own city to another to able the best medical care.

The present study concluded that there is a positive attitude towards domestic medical tourism, however present study uncovered several determinants (accessibility in the Jaipur hospital, good medical infrastructure, friendly staff behavior, and patients are more aware of the Jaipur city). In additional it also concluded that in the recent era the expectations of the domestic medical tourist towards government hospital has been declined and it covered several factors(lack of care and concern towards old patients, post-consultation were not followed up properly, Biased treatment process followed by doctor.

On the basis of our finding's researchers recommended that, each and every hospital strictly follow the post-consultation steps towards the patients who travelled to different city to able the best medical facilities. The present study is limited in terms of participants and future research with a large sample size can help in presenting more robust findings.

REFERENCES

Baksi, A., & Verma, A. K. (2013). Domestic medical tourism in India: Some facets. *Journal of Hospitality Management and Tourism*, *4*(2), 29–58. doi:10.5897/JHMT11.019

Baksi, A., & Verma, A. K. (2013). Domestic medical tourism in India: Some facets. *Journal of Hospitality Management and Tourism*, *4*(2), 29–58. doi:10.5897/JHMT11.019

Beladi, H., Chao, C. C., Ee, M. S., & Hollas, D. (2019). Does medical tourism promote economic growth? A cross-country analysis. *Journal of Travel Research, 58*(1), 121–135. doi:10.1177/0047287517735909

Berhane, A., & Enquselassie, F. (2016). Patient expectations and their satisfaction in the context of public hospitals. *Patient Preference and Adherence, 10*, 1919–1928. doi:10.2147/PPA.S109982 PMID:27703337

Bowling, A., Rowe, G., Lambert, N., Waddington, M., Mahtani, K. R., Kenten, C., Howe, A., & Francis, S. A. (2012). The measurement of patients' expectations for health care: A review and psychometric testing of a measure of patients' expectations. *Health Technology Assessment, 16*(30). Advance online publication. doi:10.3310/hta16300 PMID:22747798

De Arellano, A. B. R. (2007). Patients without borders: The emergence of medical tourism. *International Journal of Health Services, 37*(1), 193–198. doi:10.2190/4857-468G-2325-47UU PMID:17436992

Ehrbeck, T., Guevara, C., & Mango, P. D. (2008). Mapping the market for medical travel. *The McKinsey Quarterly*, 11.

Gaines, J., & Lee, C. V. (2019). Medical Tourism. In *Travel Medicine* (pp. 371–375). Elsevier. doi:10.1016/B978-0-323-54696-6.00039-2

Gupta, A. S. (2008). Medical tourism in India: Winners and losers. *Indian Journal of Medical Ethics, 5*(1), 4–5. doi:10.20529/IJME.2008.002 PMID:18630244

Han, J. S., Lee, T. J., & Ryu, K. (2018). The promotion of health tourism products for domestic tourists. *International Journal of Tourism Research, 20*(2), 137–146. doi:10.1002/jtr.2161

Health Tourism. (n.d.). *Destination of India*. https://www.ibef.org/download/Health-Tourism_091211.pdf

Hudson, S., & Li, X. (2012). Domestic medical tourism: A neglected dimension of medical tourism research. *Journal of Hospitality Marketing & Management, 21*(3), 227–246. doi:10.1080/19368623.2011.615018

Javed, S. A., & Ilyas, F. (2018). Service quality and satisfaction in healthcare sector of Pakistan—The patients' expectations. *International Journal of Health Care Quality Assurance, 31*(6), 489–501. doi:10.1108/IJHCQA-08-2016-0110 PMID:29954278

Kaur, M. (2014). Medical Tourism in India. *Indian J Res, 3*(1), 64–66.

Lateef, F. (2011). Patient expectations and the paradigm shift of care in emergency medicine. *Journal of Emergencies, Trauma and Shock*, *4*(2), 163. doi:10.4103/0974-2700.82199 PMID:21769199

Mishra, S. (2014). Prospects in medical tourism–India. *Journal of Tourism: A Contemporary Perspective, 1*(1), 13-17.

Reddy, S. G., York, V. K., & Brannon, L. A. (2010). Travel for treatment: Students' perspective on medical tourism. *International Journal of Tourism Research*, *12*(5), 510–522. doi:10.1002/jtr.769

Saravanan, M. (2013). Medical tourism–The new face of tourism. *Global Journal for Research Analysis*, *2*(2), 153–156.

Singh, L. (2014). An evaluation of medical tourism in India. *African Journal of Hospitality, Tourism and Leisure*, *3*(1), 1–11.

Suess, C., Baloglu, S., & Busser, J. A. (2018). Perceived impacts of medical tourism development on community wellbeing. *Tourism Management*, *69*, 232–245. doi:10.1016/j.tourman.2018.06.006

Tejeida, R., Pino, J., Morales, O., & Santos, J. (2006, June). Systemic Analysis of the Tourism and Health Relationship. *Proceedings of the 50th Annual Meeting of the ISSS-2006*.

Yu, K., Gong, R., Xu, F., Jiang, C., & Luo, Y. (2018). Key Success Factors in Healthcare Ecology Integrated Tourism Development. *Ekoloji*, *27*(106), 351–355.

Yu, K., Gong, R., Xu, F., Jiang, C., & Luo, Y. (2018). Key Success Factors in Healthcare Ecology Integrated Tourism Development. *Ekoloji*, *27*(106), 351–355.

Chapter 8
Yoga Tourism as a Quest for Mental and Physical Wellbeing:
A Case of Rishikesh, India

Nikhil Singh Charak
Ambedkar University, India

Priyanka Sharma
University of Jammu, India

Rajesh Singh Chib
University of Jammu, India

ABSTRACT

Yoga tourism has become an important part of the 'travel to feel well' trend. Yoga tourism can also be seen as a subset of wellness tourism. Yoga means the amalgamation of body, mind, and spirit. Yoga is widely believed as a source to diminish stress, improve breathing, strength, and improvement in flexibility. The data has been collected through primary and secondary sources (journals, articles, and newspapers). The current study is focusing on the linkages between wellness, spirituality, and yoga tourism through an examination of the motivations of tourists visiting Rishikesh, India. Present research is exploratory in nature conducted in 2019 in Rishikesh, India. The current study tried to explore this under-researched segment by interviewing and surveying yoga travellers visiting Rishikesh, India. Current research emphasized the effect of yoga tourism on the physical and mental healing of tourists at Himalayan destinations as well as the motivational characteristics of yoga tourists.

DOI: 10.4018/978-1-7998-3427-4.ch008

INTRODUCTION

Tourism is an ever-growing service industry with hidden vast growth potential and has, therefore, become one of the critical concerns of not only the nations but also of the international community as a whole. It has come up like an important link in gearing up the speed of socio-economic development globally. Therefore, tourism is generally inspected and addressed for its prospective to grant changes within the economic, biological, communal and hierarchy of a nation. Tourism is travel for happiness also the theory and practice of touring, the business of attracting, accommodating, and entertaining tourists, and the business of working tours. Tourism may be worldwide or within the traveller's country.

Yoga tourism which is a subset of Wellness tourism is popular all over the world. In 1948 The World Health Organization (WHO) originally suggest that "health is not the mere absence of diseases but a state of wellbeing "(2014). People are inclined towards yoga, spa, meditation, and Ayurveda, etc as it relaxes the mind, soul, and body. Concept of yoga originated in India several years ago. The literal meaning of the Sanskrit word yoga is to yoke, its founders were great saints and sages. People have changed their lifestyle through yoga. Yoga techniques have now been changing to need and lifestyles. Meditation being one of the important subsets of Yoga tourism is a very unique universal phenomenon integrating all religions, traditions, languages, cultures, irrespective of caste, creed, colour, and nation. Every aspect of day to day human living involves one or the other form of meditation. In all religions, namely Hindu, Muslim, Christian, Sikh, Jain, Buddhist, meditation appears to be an integral part of prayer. Eminent sages have described meditation in different ways, depending evidently on their own experiences. This goes to confirm the Vedic saying ''truth is one, but the wise interpret indifferently.

Yoga Tourism and Its Significance

Meditation and yoga can sharpen your mind confirming what yogis have claimed for long, new research has found that meditation and breath-focused practices such as pranayama can work as a fertilizer for the brain focused on the task. Many types of research in the past have shown that breathing- a key element of meditation and mindfulness practices directly affects the levels of a natural chemical messenger in the brain called noradrenaline. The way we breathe, in other words, directly affects the chemistry of our brains in a way that can enhance our attention and improve our brain health.

Wellness: A Subset of Yoga Tourism

Wellness tourism is an important element for Majority of the tourists seeking peace of mind, body and soul as well as performing Yoga. The word 'Wellness' refers to the position of being well and fit mentally, physically and emotionally. Wellness is the merger of spiritual, mental peace, relief, and leisure. (Parmar, 2016). Wellness is an energetic process of becoming conscious of and making choices toward a healthy and fulfilling life. Wellness is more than being free from illness. It is a dynamic process of change and growth.

DIMENSIONS OF WELLNESS

- **Emotional wellness:** Emotional wellness relates to understanding your feelings. From experiences and ponder you can nurture your inner soul and it's essential for relaxation and self-care.
- **Environmental wellness:** Environmental wellness inspires us to live a lifestyle that is respectful of our surroundings. To secure the Earth various activities are taking place like to live with harmony. Ecological health promotes dealings with nature in your environment.
- **Financial wellness:** Financial Wellness involves the process of learning how to successfully manage financial expenses. Today financial issues and stress are many it is effecting our lives, not only for working people or but for college students also and it is affecting their health as well as intellectual performance.
- **Intellectual wellness:** Intellectual wellness involves having an open mind when you meet with new ideas and continuing to expand your knowledge. It encourages active participation in academic, cultural and community activities.
- **Occupational wellness:** Occupational wellness is about optimistic towards work and should have to know the balance between work and relaxation, keep yourself motivated and feel good about your work. Increased your skills and capacities for further growth.
- **Physical wellness:** Physical wellness is the ability to maintain the good health of your body. It's very important to be healthy in this polluted area we live, you can achieve physical fitness through yoga, exercises, proper nutrition, strong mind, and proper sleep. It's very essential to nurture your body in top priorities.

- **Social wellness:** Social wellness helps you perform social roles effectively and comfortably, and create a support network. It's very vital to maintain social relationships it can support us during difficulties. People should know the balance between professional lives, personal lives and social lives it will develop the comfort level. Having good social relations is important in building emotional flexibility.
- **Spiritual wellness:** Spiritual wellness allows you to develop a set of values that help you seek meaning and purpose. Spirituality can be represented in many ways, for example, through relaxation or religion. Spiritual does teach one should enjoy life to the full, there is no sense of possession. Everything belongs to God and humanity, god knowledge is that the serious and genuine practitioners of religion are helped to graduate into spirituality.

Figure 1.

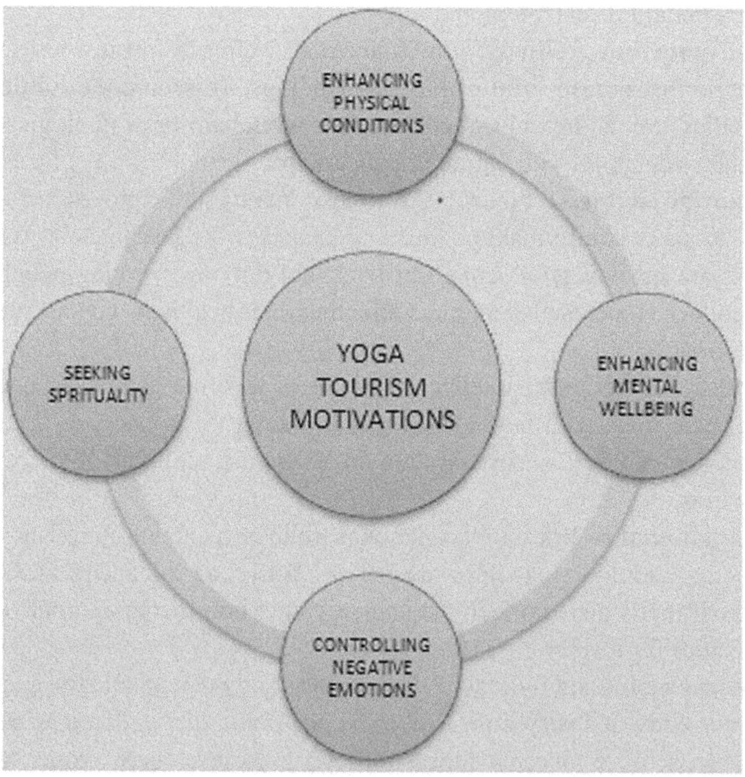

Figure 2.

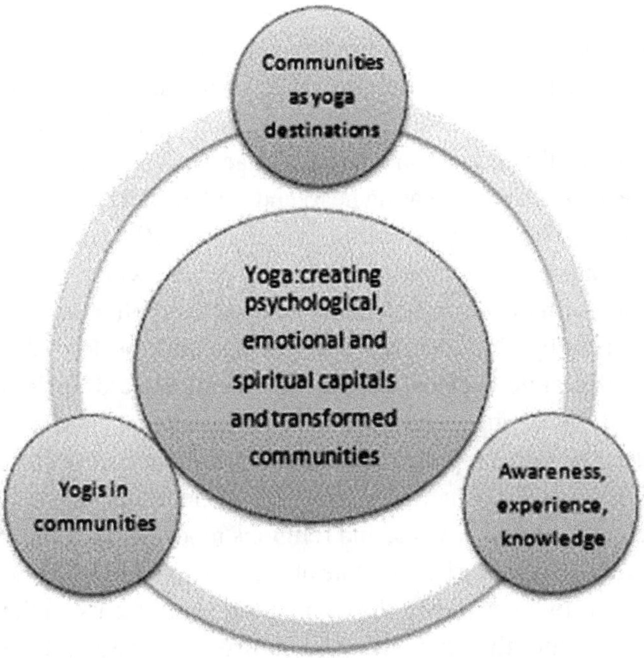

CONCEPTUAL MODEL OF THE TRANSFORMATIVE POWER OF YOGA TOURISM (SOURCE: PONDER AND HOLLADAY, 2013)

Wellness and Yoga Tourism- An India Perspective

The prospective of wellness systems, developed through centuries of knowledge of this early civilization would be fully tapped. This is being done by positioning India as a centre of Ayurveda, Yoga, Sidha, Naturopathy, etc. Ministry of Tourism has drafted instruction for wellness tourism. These strategies address issues regarding making available quality advertising material, training and facility building for the service providers, participation in international & domestic Wellness related events, etc. Growth of wellness centres in the country has given rise to the anxiety for quality service. The Guideline for authorization of wellness centres has been developed by the National Board for Accreditation of Hospitals & Healthcare Services (NABH) in consultation with AYUSH. Presently the wellness centres attributed by State Tourism Departments are also eligible for the authorization. After the authorization guidelines of NABH is in place, all wellness centres seeking authorization would be asked to be as close to the accreditation guidelines of NABH as possible and it has been motivated by the ministry of tourism.

Retreat With Yoga in Rishikesh

Rishikesh is a famous hill station in the Uttarakhand state of India and one of the most popular destinations in the religious map of India. Uttarakhand is popularly known as 'Adobe of the Gods (Devbhumi)'. Rishikesh apart from its high elevation natural beauties of Himalayas and spiritual legacy offers great stay facility with yoga practice. Rishikesh is the beating heart and soul of India and also term as Yoga destination of India. There are many services available in Rishikesh like yoga teacher training courses, ashrams, meditation healing, reiki, etc which cause soothing for a person. To start with the term "Rishikesh" is usually applied somewhat droopily. What visitors mean by The Laxman Jhula Bridge and the Ram Jhula Bridge is energetically the emerald Ganges. People are moving towards India from all over the world for Ayurveda, yoga, and meditation in Rishikesh, Uttarakhand, which is practised for decades. India rapidly turns out as a health tourism destination because of them. India is a secular is nature so, from the ancient time this sort of practices has been done via spirituality, yoga, and religious mode. In ancient time Yoga was famous as a practice to get everlasting state of peace in mind. Earlier India was called the gate of heaven. India is known throughout the world for its ancient restorative practices and substitute therapies. It is no surprise that people from around the world turn to the Indian subcontinent for the course towards the further spiritually pleasing way of life.

In Rishikesh, there are huge numbers of Yoga Teacher Training Center which is offering fusion yoga teacher's training course to provide a traditional style of yoga, comprehensive and genuine information of philosophy, yogic life, asana-pranayama, anatomy, meditation-breathing techniques, mantra-chanting, spiritual life, and much more. You will learn from enthusiastic yoga teachers who have studied yoga, meditation, and spiritual techniques from yoga universities (Gurukulam) since their childhood. The peaceful vibrations of soft Himalaya make Rishikesh, especially for yoga study. In Rishikesh wellness, yoga centres their goal to teach traditional and ancient knowledge of yoga.

Yoga is not just about doing some postures or doing asana or pranayama its more than that we need to learn about life through the yoga, how we can live the life how we can leave the life. Life is not just about living it's about leading and through yoga we can do that thing. In postures and asana we don't just improve our flexibilities or strength we also improve our concentration, we decrease the frustration we improve the patient's power through the postures that's what we need to do, we need to focus on our breath we need to focus on the postures and we need to concentrate.

Yoga is the union of body, mind, and soul. In this universe everyone is curious about that question that who am I, yoga teaches us the reality of life ourselves why I am here. When the waves of the mind are still, the oneness that already exists is realized, we become established in our wholeness. The significance of attention and absorption, a practice that facilitates to still the mind, and the peak of meditation known as *Samadhi*.

International Day of Yoga

29th International yoga festival was held in Rishikesh from 01 to 07 March 2018 which is organized by Parmarth Niketan, they host this festival every year since 1999, 21 yoga asanas were performed by 84 nations. This was recorded in two Guinness world records the one was it featured 35,985 people and second was 84 nations that are having the highest number of participating. Now the international day of yoga is well known in across the globe. About 2,000 attendees come from 100 countries and many yoga gurus from the globe. People come across the globe to enjoy the event, you can get the pleasure of many things like yoga classes, lectures, cultural program, etc. you realize there that yoga is not a physical activity but it's done by soul and you feel connected to almighty which is beyond everything. You feel your inner peace, self-realization and you imbibe power and positivity through yoga.

THE RATIONALE OF THE STUDY

Although there have been few studies conducted related to the role of traditional Indian therapies and wellness in promoted India as a favoured wellness tourists destination. Yoga, in general, has recently become an important research topic in the areas of social and economic life and a new measurement to the tourism industry is added, yoga refers to a process increasingly definitive liberty of the bonds of karma and rebirth. Rishikesh is one of the first choices of tourists coming to India for Ayurveda, yoga, and meditation. While yoga and meditation are practised and taught in ashrams on riverbanks, there are reputed universities here where Ayurveda is taught. It is a proper subject, is measured as a branch of science and regular researches are conducted in the field. According to a report by Dixit (2005), tourists visiting Uttarakhand can be categorized into three major categories. These tourist classes are: (i) Pilgrims / Religious tourists, (ii) Pleasure tourists / Holiday Makers, (iii) Special interest tourist / Adventure and Nature Lovers. Husain (2007) analyzed the Promotional aspects of the marketing strategy of the tourism industry in a tourist-rich state, Uttarakhand in India. The study reveals that the tourists are significantly influenced by the package incentives offered by tour operators. Aggarwal et al. (2008) developed various marketing strategies to boost tourism in Rishikesh, India. The work highlights the role of yoga and spirituality in Indian tourism. The authors also attempted to bring out the motives of foreign tourists behind visiting ashrams.

Karar (2010) discussed the importance of Haridwar as a potential spot for attracting tourists to the state. Karar further analyzed at length the historical and mythical aspects related to Haridwar and why the place is being considered as a sacred city.

Wellness and Yoga Tourism can enhance our well being and quality of life especially if we do it regularly enough, and we may even experience moments of joy because it is more about visiting natural palaces where there are different ecosystem and environmental condition they're they provide this kind of services. There is an incredible amount of ancient and useful knowledge within yoga philosophy (on breathing techniques, meditation, curing disease, benefits of different asana, a theory of reality and existence, way to manage stress and social behaviour, anatomy and so much more!). yoga is similar to other Eastern philosophies in that it is practical, realistic and asks one to ask respondents for their actions. Like some other religion in the east, the final goal is enlightenment. In this case, the state is called Samadhi, the blissful state where you are in perfect health as a whole (mind, body, soul). Yoga means to have complete perfection in your action, complete focus and to be in the moment. It is realizing your true reality is an expression of the entire universe and not just the ego and name that you identify with daily. So yoga can happen anywhere to anyone. Their objective is to be able to give tourist and environment which is kind of the whole in itself, in which they not only just practice but also spend time on certain ideas and certain concepts which can be new to them in some aspects because of differences in the lifestyles and then with that relational what they will get is a way to implement those elements in their life that how they can give them space accommodate them but we talk about self-sustainability in terms of health or the ability to self heal and to ability to keep yourself on the right track so you do not fall into the trap of being sick, diseases whether its physical or mental.

OBJECTIVES OF THE STUDY

- To assess the effect of Yoga tourism on the physical and mental healing of tourists at Himalayan Destinations
- To analyze the role of wellness centres in promoting Yoga tourism in Rishikesh

RESEARCH METHODOLOGY

The present study is empirical and descriptive and is based on the data collected from primary and secondary sources. Primary data has been collected from the tourists visited wellness centres in Rishikesh.

- **Area of Study:** Data was collected from the tourists visiting wellness retreats in Rishikesh, Uttrakhand (India).
- **Sampling Design:** Convenience sampling was used due to time constraints.
- **Tool Used:** Self-Structured questionnaires used based on secondary data as well as after consulting the Yoga practitioners and Yoga tourism travel writer.

DATA ANALYSIS AND INTERPRETATION

Data was collected from the 90 yoga tourists visiting Rishikesh only 50 questionnaires were found useful for analysis:

SD: Strongly Disagree
D: Disagree
N: Neither Agree nor Disagree
A: Agree
SA: Strongly Agree

Table 1. Q1: Yoga tourism will help in Weight loss. Inner peace. Boost Immunity?

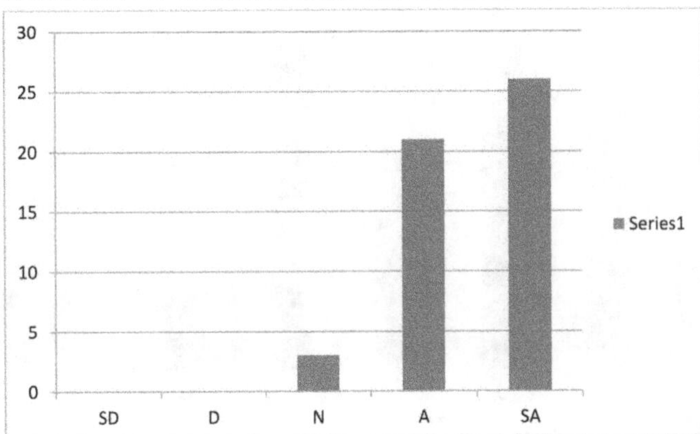

SD	D	N	A	SA
00	00	03	21	26

INTERPRETATION: It is clear from the above chart that 52% of the respondents in Rishikesh strongly agree and 42% agrees that yoga tourism will help in weight loss. Inner peace. Boost Immunity.

Table 2. Q2: Yoga Tourism would help to Maintains your nervous system?

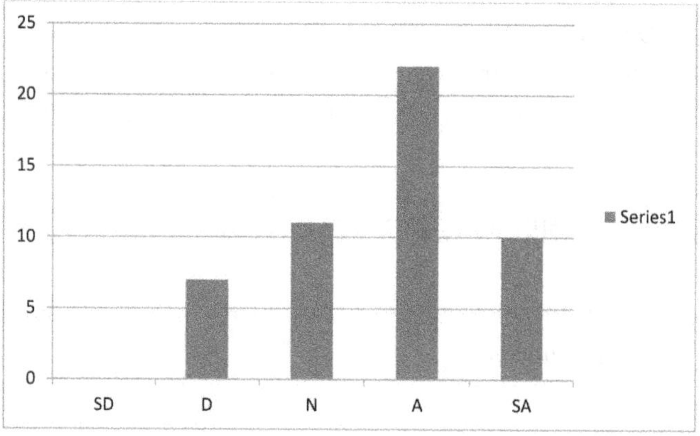

SD	D	N	A	SA
00	07	11	22	10

INTERPRETATION: The above chart depicts that 20% of the total population in Rishikesh strongly agrees that yoga tourism would help in maintains your nervous system.

Table 3. Q3: Is there any issue related to yoga tourism in Rishikesh?

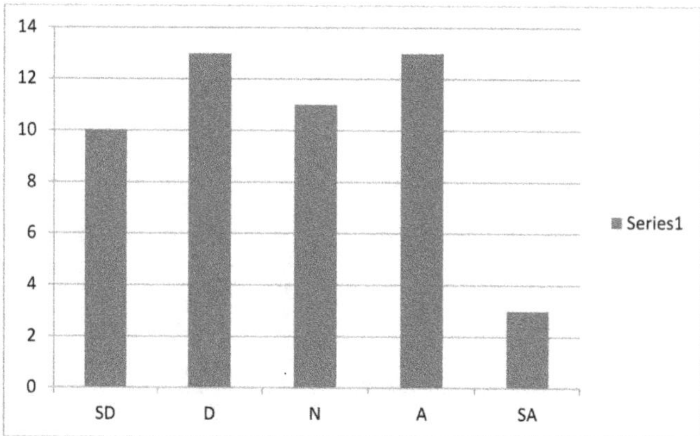

SD	D	N	A	SA
10	13	11	13	03

INTERPRETATION: the above graph reveals that about only 06% of the population strongly agrees that there is an issue related to yoga tourism Rishikesh 26% agrees with the statement. 22% of the population is neutral, 26% & 20% are Disagree and Strongly Disagree with that statement.

Table 4. Q4: Yoga Tourism would help in Maintains your Control blood sugar & blood pressure level?

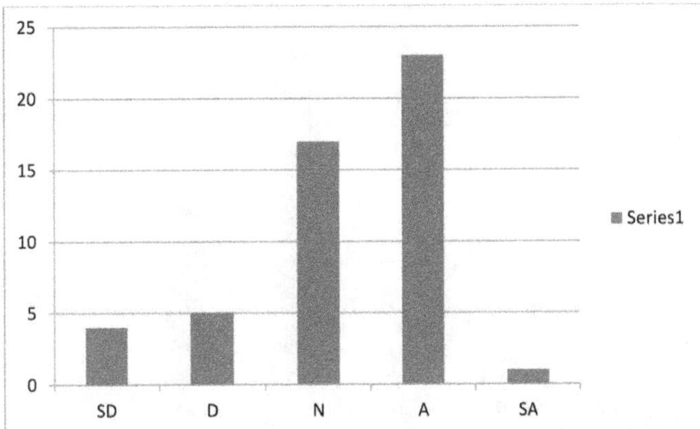

SD	D	N	A	SA
04	05	17	23	1

INTERPRETATION: The above chart reveals that 46% of the respondents agree that yoga tourism would help in maintaining your control of blood sugar and blood pressure level. whereas 38% are neutral to it and 2% strongly agrees with it.

Table 5. Q5: yoga tourism would help in keeping you drug free?

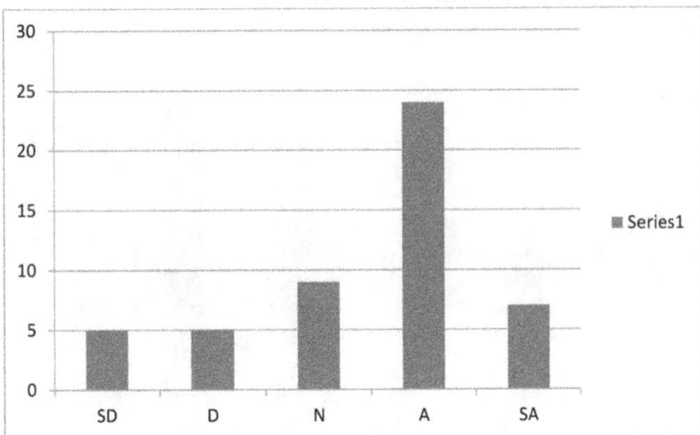

SD	D	N	A	SA
05	05	09	24	07

INTERPRETATION: The above chart reveals that 48% of the respondents agree that yoga tourism would help in keeping you drug-free whereas 18 are neutral to it and 14% strongly agrees with it.

Table 6. Q6: Yoga tourism would help in Increases your blood flow. Helps you serve others. Relaxes you & helps you to sleep properly?

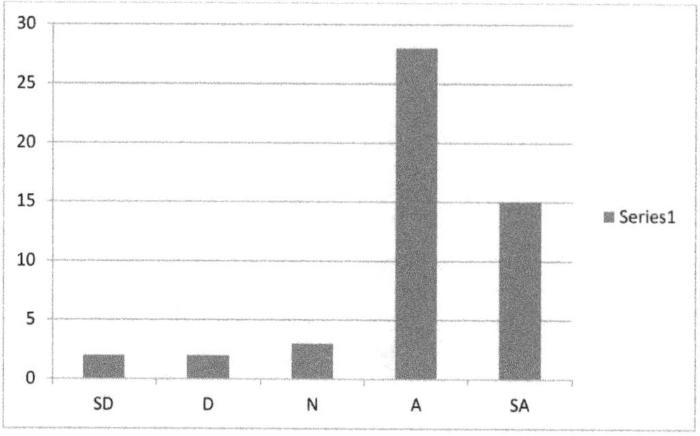

SD	D	N	A	SA
02	02	03	28	15

INTERPRETATION: The above chart depicts that 56% of the population believes that Yoga tourism would help in Increases your blood flow. Helps you serve others. Relaxes you & helps you to sleep properly

Table 7. Q7: Yoga tourism would Help you in meditation. Improves your flexibility & Posture?

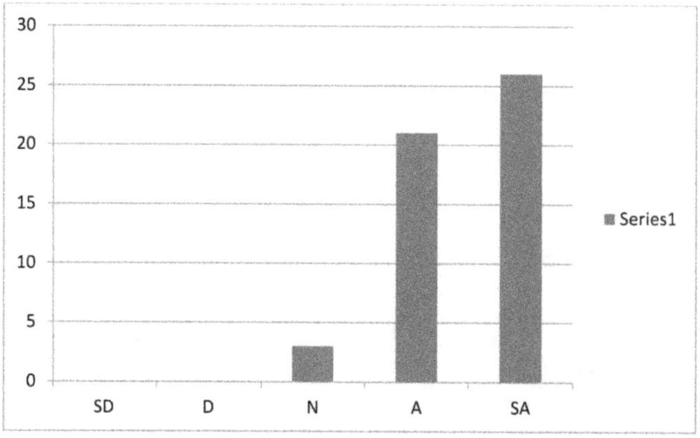

SD	D	N	A	SA
00	00	03	21	26

INTERPRETATION: It is clear from the above chart that 52% of the respondents strongly agrees and 42% are agree that Yoga tourism would help in Helps you in meditation and improves your flexibility & Posture

Table 8. Q8: Yoga tourism would help in Betters your bone health. Massaging of all Organs of the Body?

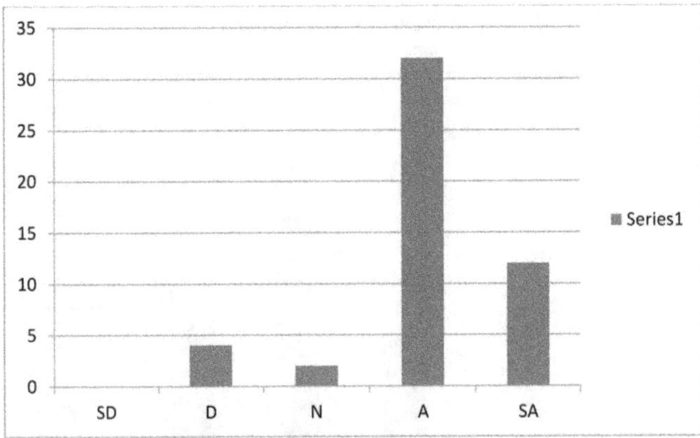

SD	D	N	A	SA
00	04	02	32	12

INTERPRETATION: The above chart depicts that 64% of the population Agree that Yoga tourism would help in Betters your bone health and massaging of all Organs of the Body.

Table 9. Q9: Yoga tourism will help in Complete Detoxification?

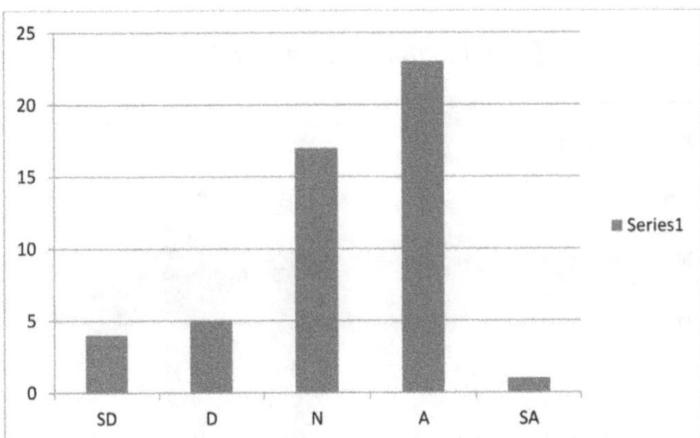

SD	D	N	A	SA
04	05	17	23	1

INTERPRETATION: The above chart reveals that 46% of the respondents agree that Yoga tourism will help in Complete Detoxification whereas 38 are neutral to it and 2% strongly agrees with it.

Motives Behind the Tourists Visiting the Wellness Centre

Table 10. Q1: Provision of fitness exercise guidance?

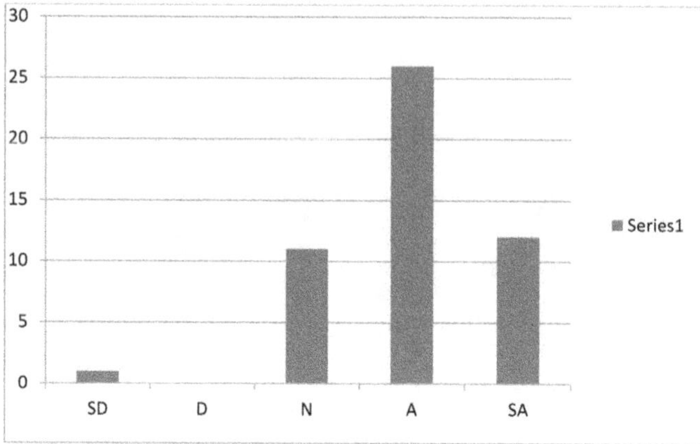

SD	D	N	A	SA
01	00	11	26	12

INTERPRETATION: the above graph reveals that about 24% of the population strongly agrees that they are attaining proper fitness guidance whereas 52% agrees with the statement. 22% of the population is neutral & 2% are Strongly Disagree with that statement.

Table 11. Q2: Provision of weight control guidance?

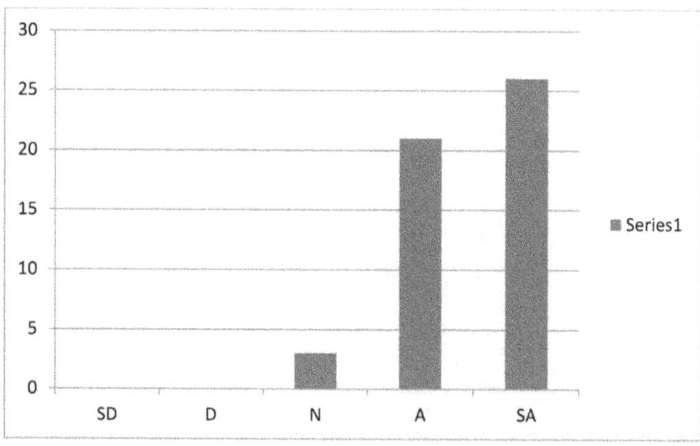

SD	D	N	A	SA
00	00	03	21	26

INTERPRETATION: It is clear from the above chart that 52% of the respondents strongly agrees and 42% are agree that tourist attaining proper weight control guidance in Rishikesh.

Table 12. Q3: Provision of hot spring therapy guidance?

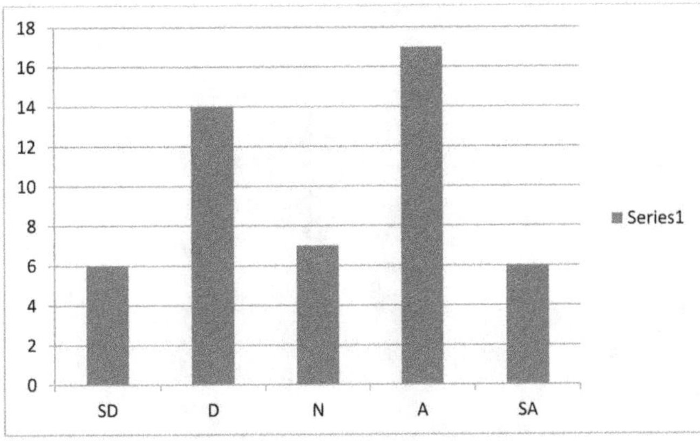

SD	D	N	A	SA
06	14	07	17	06

INTERPRETATION: The above chart depicts that 34% of the respondents agree that they would like to avail hot spring therapy where as 28% disagreed.

Table 13. Q4: Provision of medication consultation?

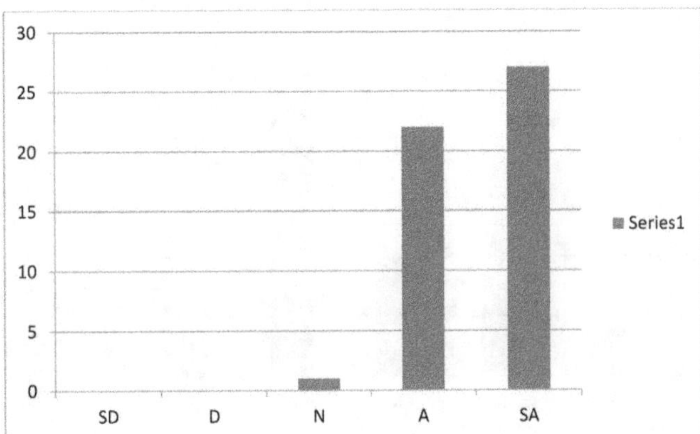

SD	D	N	A	SA
00	00	1	22	27

INTERPRETATION: The above chart clearly depicts that 54% of the respondents strongly agrees whereas 44% agree with the statement.

Table 14. Q5: Provision of Indian traditional healing?

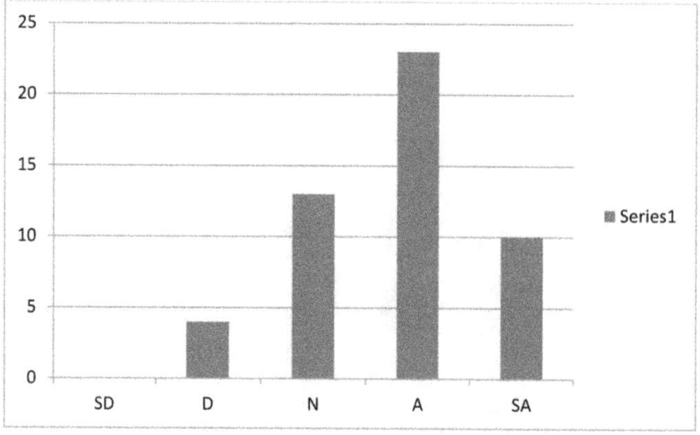

SD	D	N	A	SA
00	04	13	23	10

INTERPRETATION: above chart depict that 10% of the population strongly agrees, 23% agrees and 13% are neutral that they are attaining Indian traditional healing methods in Rishikesh.

Table 15. Q6: Provision of exfoliation services?

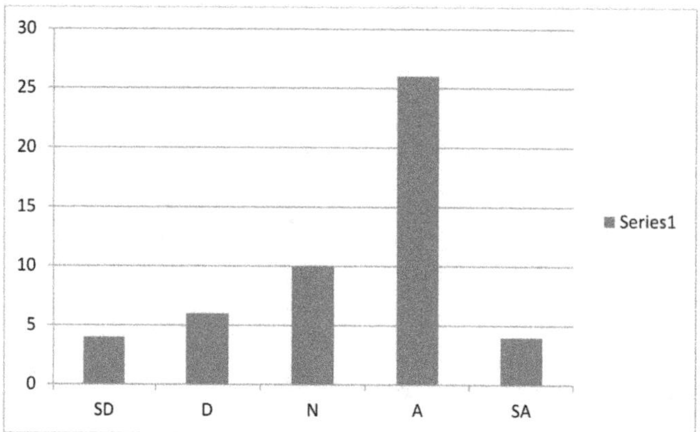

SD	D	N	A	SA
04	06	10	26	04

INTERPRETATION: The above chart is clear enough to depict that 52% of the people agree with the statement thatrishikish provide exfoliation services whereas 20% are neutral with the statement.

Table 16. Q7: Provision of traditional Indian oil massage?

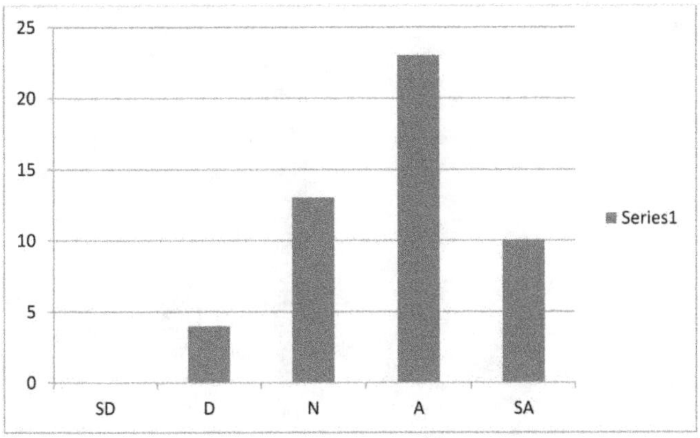

SD	D	N	A	SA
00	04	13	23	10

INTERPRETATION above chart depicts that 46% of the population Agrees that they are availing traditional Indian oil massage in rishikesh.

Relaxation

Table 17. Q1: Provision of various landscape therapies?

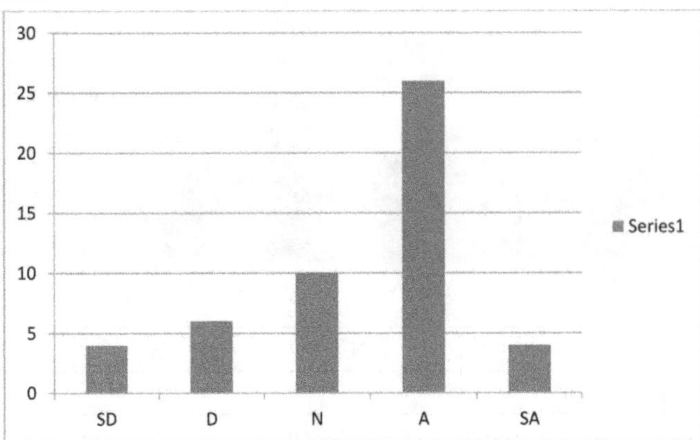

SD	D	N	A	SA
04	06	10	26	04

INTERPRETATION: The above chart is clear enough to depict that 52% of the people agree with the statement that they are avail landscape therapies in Rishikesh whereas 20% are neutral with the statement.

Table 18. Q2: Provision of relaxed atmosphere?

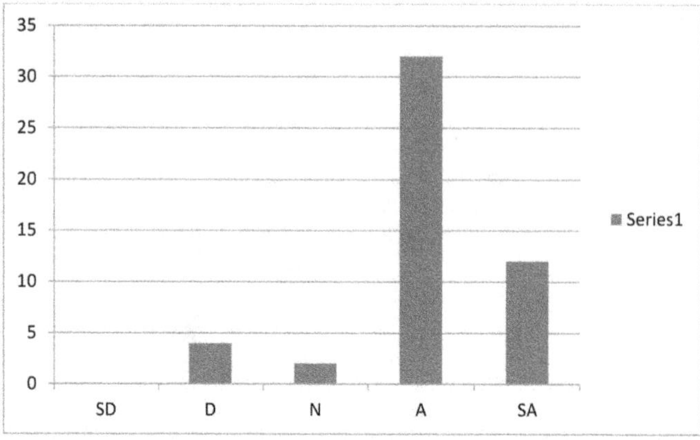

SD	D	N	A	SA
00	04	02	32	12

INTERPRETATION: The above chart depicts that 64% of the population Agree that they are getting relaxing atmosphere in Rishikesh because it is surrounded by natural beauty and the pollution is less.

Table 19. Q3: Provision of meditation activities?

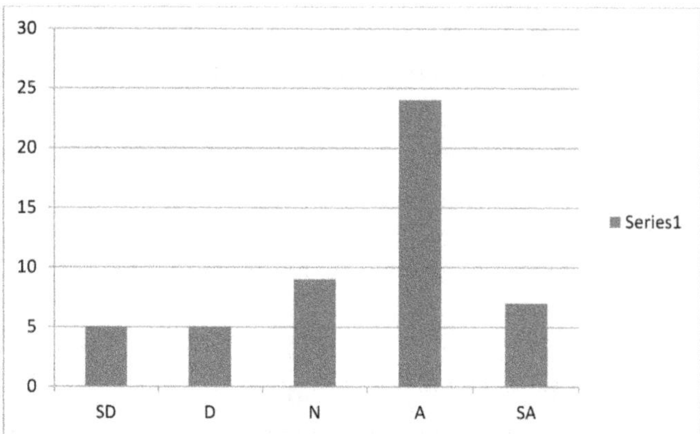

SD	D	N	A	SA
05	05	09	24	07

INTERPRETATION: The above chart reveals that 48% of the respondents agree that they would like to avail meditation activities whereas 18 are neutral to it and 14% strongly agrees with it.

Table 20. Q4: Provision of cultural customs experience

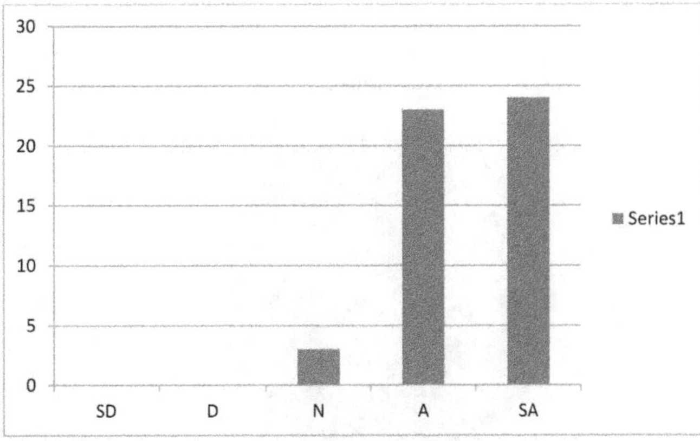

SD	D	N	A	SA
00	00	03	23	24

INTERPRETATION: The above chart depicts that 48% &46% of the population are strongly agree and agree that tourist would like to avail cultural custom experience.

Figure 3. Would you recommend Rishikesh as a wellness tourism destination to your friends and relatives

INTERPRETATION: *above pie, chat depicts that 80% population said yes that they Would recommend Rishikesh as a wellness tourism destination to their friends and relatives while 20% said no to that statement. In Rishikesh, there are end numbers of wellness centres along with the natural environment*

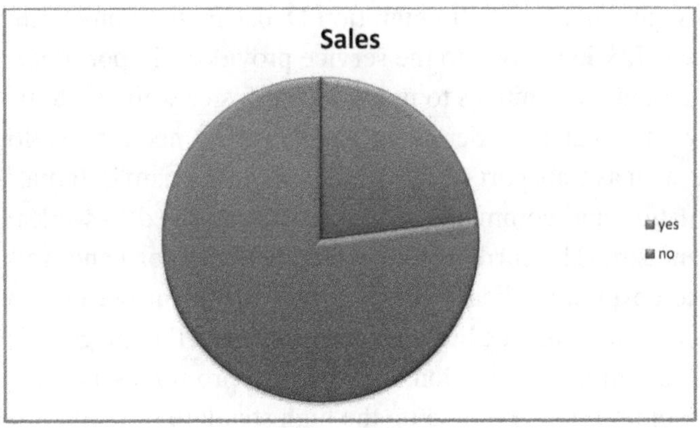

Figure 4. Is there any opportunity of wellness tourism in our state

INTERPRETATION: *the above pie chart depicts that 15% of people said yes while 85% of people said no to this statement.*

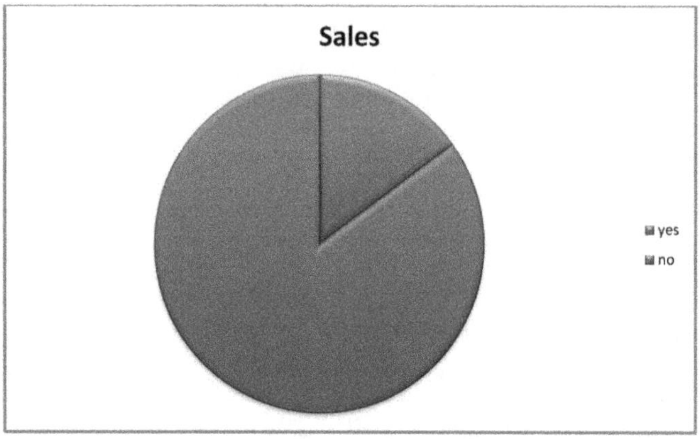

CONCLUSION

India is in an advantageous position to tap global opportunities in the yoga and wellness tourism sector. The government's role is crucial to the development of Yoga and wellness tourism. The government should take steps in the role of a regulator and also as a facilitator of private investment in healthcare. Mechanisms need to be evolved to enable quicker visa grants to foreign tourists for wellness purposes where patients can contact the Immigration Department at any point of entry for quick clearance. Tax incentives to the service providers, import duty reduction on wellness equipment, committees to promote and foster wellness tourism are some of the initiatives that can be undertaken. There is also a need to develop supporting infrastructure such as transport services to facilitate tourism in India. The tourism, health, information and communication departments need to work in tandem for efficient patient care. The current study would help the yoga and wellness tourism stakeholders to develop medical tourism strategies for further promoting medical tourism in India. These include building and promoting the image of India as a high quality wellness tourism destination, creating and promoting new combination of wellness tourism products, keeping up the high standard of quality treatments at a reasonable price, providing information online and offline materials and make them available to the potential customers. Also attaining the accreditation/standard to reassure the quality of treatments as well as emphasizing on the needs and demands of the existing target markets must be incorporated. Current study has found that yoga may offer a safe, beneficial intervention for reducing sleep and mood disturbance, perceived stress, anxiety, and blood pressure in older women and adult population.

Future Implications

Current research would help the yoga and wellness tourism stakeholders to understand the consumer buying behaviour of yoga and wellness tourists as well as would in analyzing the gap between customer expectations and experience.

Suggestions

- Yoga tourism week should be celebrated with the collaboration of wellness tourism centres.
- In India, destinations should be rightly identified where wellness tourism centres can be established.
- Policy framework for wellness tourism should be investor-friendly.
- Wellness tourism should be endorsed by the celebrity.
- Regularly, the Ministry of Tourism and the State Tourism Department should arrange a workshop and training programme for wellness instructors.
- The government should release funds for the development of infrastructure suitable for wellness tourism and also offer concession or relaxation to wellness tourism service providers.

REFERENCES

Abhyankar, A., & Dalvie, S. (2013). Growth potential of the domestic and international tourism in India. *Review of Integrative Business and Economics Research*, *2*(1), 566.

Aggarwal, A. K., Guglani, M., & Goel, R. K. (2008). *Spiritual & Yoga Tourism: A case study on experience of Foreign Tourists visiting Rishikesh*.

Bushell, R., & Sheldon, P. J. (Eds.). (2009). *Wellness and tourism: Mind, body, spirit, place*. Cognizant Communication.

Connell, J. (2006). Medical tourism: Sea, sun, sand and… surgery. *Tourism Management*, *27*(6), 1093–1100. doi:10.1016/j.tourman.2005.11.005

Hall, C. M. (2012). Medical and health tourism: The development and implications of medical mobility. In *Medical Tourism* (pp. 19–44). Routledge. doi:10.4324/9780203109458

Hernández, S. E., Suero, J., Rubia, K., & González-Mora, J. L. (2015). Monitoring the neural activity of the state of mental silence while practicing sahaja yoga meditation. *Journal of Alternative and Complementary Medicine (New York, N.Y.)*, *21*(3), 175–179. doi:10.1089/acm.2013.0450 PMID:25671603

Karar, A. (2010). Impact of pilgrim tourism at Haridwar. *The Anthropologist*, *12*(2), 99–105. doi:10.1080/09720073.2010.11891138

Konu, H., & Laukkanen, T. (2010). Predictors of tourists' wellbeing holiday intentions in Finland. *Journal of Hospitality and Tourism Management*, *17*(1), 144–149. doi:10.1375/jhtm.17.1.144

Kumar, A., Agarwal, D. K., Kumar, S., Reddy, Y. M., Chintagunta, A. D., Saritha, K. V., Pal, G., & Kumar, S. J. (2019). Nutraceuticals derived from seed storage proteins: Implications for health wellness. *Biocatalysis and Agricultural Biotechnology*, *17*, 710–719. doi:10.1016/j.bcab.2019.01.044

Lalonde, A. M. G. (2012). *Embodying asana in all new places: transformational ethics, yoga tourism and sensual awakenings* (Doctoral dissertation).

Lehto, X. Y., Brown, S., Chen, Y., & Morrison, A. M. (2006). Yoga tourism as a niche within the wellness tourism market. *Tourism Recreation Research*, *31*(1), 25–35. doi:10.1080/02508281.2006.11081244

Lemaire, J. B., Ewashina, D., Polachek, A. J., Dixit, J., & Yiu, V. (2018). Understanding how patients perceive physician wellness and its links to patient care: A qualitative study. *PLoS One*, *13*(5), e0196888. doi:10.1371/journal.pone.0196888 PMID:29763443

Liberman, K. (2004). Yoga tourism in India. *Yoga Life*, *7*(35), 23–32.

Maddox, C. B. (2015). Studying at the source: Ashtanga yoga tourism and the search for authenticity in Mysore, India. *Journal of Tourism and Cultural Change*, *13*(4), 330–343. doi:10.1080/14766825.2014.972410

Makvana, S., Patel, A., Dhingra, A., & Parmar, V. (2016). *Mental Health: A Journey from illness to wellness*. RED'SHINE Publication. Inc.

Pheng, L. T., & Husain, W. (n.d.). *IWELLNESSONLINE.Com: Application Of Knowledge-Based System In E-Marketplace For Personalized Wellness Recommendation*. Academic Press.

Sharpley, R., & Sundaram, P. (2005). Tourism: A sacred journey? The case of ashram tourism, India. *International Journal of Tourism Research*, *7*(3), 161–171. doi:10.1002/jtr.522

Smith, M. (2003). Holistic holidays: Tourism and the reconciliation of body, mind and spirit. *Tourism Recreation Research*, *28*(1), 103–108. doi:10.1080/02508281.2003.11081392

Smith, M., & Kelly, C. (2006). Holistic tourism: Journeys of the self? *Tourism Recreation Research*, *31*(1), 15–24. doi:10.1080/02508281.2006.11081243

Voigt, C., Brown, G., & Howat, G. (2011). Wellness tourists: In search of transformation. *Tourism Review*, *66*(1/2), 16–30. doi:10.1108/16605371111127206

Related Readings

To continue IGI Global's long-standing tradition of advancing innovation through emerging research, please find below a compiled list of recommended IGI Global book chapters and journal articles in the areas of medical tourism. These related readings will provide additional information and guidance to further enrich your knowledge and assist you with your own research.

Adeyinka-Ojo, S. (2019). A Strategic Framework for Managing the Challenges of Developing Rural Tourism Destination Branding. In M. A. Camilleri (Ed.), *Strategic Perspectives in Destination Marketing* (pp. 268–294). IGI Global. doi:10.4018/978-1-5225-5835-4.ch011

Ahuja, V. (2020). Promotion of Tourism Using Social Media. In S. Alavi & V. Ahuja (Eds.), *Managing Social Media Practices in the Digital Economy* (pp. 25–44). IGI Global. doi:10.4018/978-1-7998-2185-4.ch002

Ainous, R. (2018). The Benchmarking Practices as a Strategic Option to Improve the Performance of Economic Companies. In Improving Business Performance Through Effective Managerial Training Initiatives (pp. 86-113). IGI Global. http://doi:10.4018/978-1-5225-3906-3.ch005

Akoijam, S. L., & Khan, T. (2020). Prospects and Challenges of Medical Tourism. In S. Paul & S. Kulshreshtha (Eds.), *Global Developments in Healthcare and Medical Tourism* (pp. 265–276). IGI Global. doi:10.4018/978-1-5225-9787-2.ch014

Albayrak, A. (2019). Gender Discrimination in Tourism Industry. In D. Tüzünkan & V. Altıntaş (Eds.), *Contemporary Human Resources Management in the Tourism Industry* (pp. 104–129). IGI Global. doi:10.4018/978-1-5225-5760-9.ch005

Ali, R., & Pal, A. K. (2017). A Secure and Robust Three-Factor Based Authentication Scheme Using RSA Cryptosystem. *International Journal of Business Data Communications and Networking*, *13*(1), 74–84. doi:10.4018/IJBDCN.2017010107

Alves, G. M., Sousa, B. M., & Machado, A. (2020). The Role of Digital Marketing and Online Relationship Quality in Social Tourism. In J. D. Santos & Ó. L. Silva (Eds.), *Digital Marketing Strategies for Tourism, Hospitality, and Airline Industries* (pp. 49–70). IGI Global. doi:10.4018/978-1-5225-9783-4.ch003

Archondakis, S., Vavoulidis, E., Nasioutziki, M., Oustampasidou, O., Daniilidis, A., Vatopoulou, A., Papanikolaou, A., & Dinas, K. (2019). Mobile Health Applications and Cloud Computing in Cytopathology. In A. Moumtzoglou (Ed.), *Mobile Health Applications for Quality Healthcare Delivery* (pp. 165–202). IGI Global. doi:10.4018/978-1-5225-8021-8.ch008

Assad, D. B., Spiegel, T., & Silva, A. C. (2018). Improve Center of Sterilized Material Performance. In M. Ebrahimi (Ed.), *Modeling and Simulation Techniques for Improved Business Processes* (pp. 113–139). IGI Global. doi:10.4018/978-1-5225-3226-2.ch005

Attia, S., Boubetra, A., & Saoud, M. S. (2018). Prescriptive Simulation Scenarios for Hospitals Evacuation Management. In J. Tan (Ed.), *Handbook of Research on Emerging Perspectives on Healthcare Information Systems and Informatics* (pp. 368–390). IGI Global. doi:10.4018/978-1-5225-5460-8.ch016

Avram, A. C. (2020). The Impact of Rural Tourism on Wellbeing. In P. Nistoreanu (Ed.), *New Trends and Opportunities for Central and Eastern European Tourism* (pp. 281–298). IGI Global. doi:10.4018/978-1-7998-1423-8.ch015

Barker, B. (2019). *TechCreate*. IGI Global. doi:10.4018/978-1-5225-8307-3.ch004

Bashir, N. A., Balaraman, P., & Mukherjee, A. (2020). Strategic Business Enablers and Infrastructure Insights of the Saudi Arabian Tourism Industry. In D. Batabyal (Ed.), *Global Entrepreneurial Trends in the Tourism and Hospitality Industry* (pp. 33–60). IGI Global. doi:10.4018/978-1-7998-2603-3.ch003

Bayrakdaroğlu, F., & Karabulut, A. N. (2018). Marketing Mix Adaptation of Large-Scale Hotels in Turbulent Times. In R. Leon (Ed.), *Managerial Strategies for Business Sustainability During Turbulent Times* (pp. 223–240). IGI Global. doi:10.4018/978-1-5225-2716-9.ch012

Beaunoyer, E., & Guitton, M. J. (2018). Effective Use of Virtual Communities for Health-Purposes in the Elderly. In C. El Morr (Ed.), *Novel Applications of Virtual Communities in Healthcare Settings* (pp. 127–146). IGI Global. doi:10.4018/978-1-5225-2958-3.ch005

Behera, S. K. (2020). Medical Tourism in Visakhapatnam by People of South Odisha. In S. Paul & S. Kulshreshtha (Eds.), *Global Developments in Healthcare and Medical Tourism* (pp. 96–111). IGI Global. doi:10.4018/978-1-5225-9787-2.ch006

Benbelkacem, S., Kadri, F., Atmani, B., & Chaabane, S. (2019). Machine Learning for Emergency Department Management. *International Journal of Information Systems in the Service Sector, 11*(3), 19–36. doi:10.4018/IJISSS.2019070102

Berkley-Patton, J. Thompson, C. B. Ervie, K. G. Huffman, M. & Johnson, N. R. (2020). Using a Community-Based Collaborative Care Model as a Platform for Successful Interprofessional Education. In Building a Patient-Centered Interprofessional Education Program (pp. 157-182). IGI Global. http://doi:10.4018/978-1-7998-3066-5.ch009

Berry, S. (2019). The Role of Video and Text Chat in a Virtual Classroom. In J. Yoon & P. Semingson (Eds.), *Educational Technology and Resources for Synchronous Learning in Higher Education* (pp. 173–187). IGI Global. doi:10.4018/978-1-5225-7567-2.ch009

Bolgova, K. V., Kovalchuk, S. V., Balakhontceva, M. A., Zvartau, N. E., & Metsker, O. G. (2020). Human Computer Interaction During Clinical Decision Support With Electronic Health Records Improvement. *International Journal of E-Health and Medical Communications, 11*(1), 93–106. doi:10.4018/IJEHMC.2020010106

Çalişkan, C., & Dedeoglu, B. B. (2019). Sustaining Tourism and Branding. In M. A. Camilleri (Ed.), *Strategic Perspectives in Destination Marketing* (pp. 322–342). IGI Global. doi:10.4018/978-1-5225-5835-4.ch013

Camilleri, M. A. (2019). The Business of Tourism. In M. A. Camilleri (Ed.), *Strategic Perspectives in Destination Marketing* (pp. 1–27). IGI Global. doi:10.4018/978-1-5225-5835-4.ch001

Cheney, A. W., McClannon, T., Bolt, L., & Sanders, R. L. (2019). Perceptions of Presence and Community in Immersive Online Learning Environments. In K. Becnel (Ed.), *Emerging Technologies in Virtual Learning Environments* (pp. 116–131). IGI Global. doi:10.4018/978-1-5225-7987-8.ch006

Clarke, H., & Hassanien, A. (2020). An Evaluation of Toronto's Destination Image Through Tourist Generated Content on Twitter. *International Journal of Customer Relationship Marketing and Management, 11*(2), 1–16. doi:10.4018/IJCRMM.2020040101

Costanza, F. (2018). Governing Patients' Mobility to Pursue Public Value. In G. M. Azevedo, J. da Silva Oliveira, R. P. Marques, & A. D. Ferreira (Eds.), *Handbook of Research on Modernization and Accountability in Public Sector Management* (pp. 276–299). IGI Global. doi:10.4018/978-1-5225-3731-1.ch013

Costanza, F. (2020). Effects of Patient Mobility on Healthcare Systems. In G. Azevedo, J. Oliveira, R. Marques, & A. Ferreira (Eds.), *Tools, Strategies, and Practices for Modern and Accountable Public Sector Management* (pp. 227–257). IGI Global. doi:10.4018/978-1-7998-1385-9.ch009

Della Corte, V., Del Gaudio, G., & Nevola, G. (2020). The Engagement of Community and Volunteers in a Small-Scale Sport Event and the Impact on Sustainable Tourism. In A. Fotiadis & C. Vassiliadis (Eds.), *Principles and Practices of Small-Scale Sport Event Management* (pp. 45–70). IGI Global. doi:10.4018/978-1-7998-4757-1.ch003

Dinçer, H., & Yüksel, S. (2020). Defining the Strategic Impact-Relation Map for the Innovative Investments Based on IT2 Fuzzy DEMATEL. In U. Akkucuk (Ed.), *Handbook of Research on Creating Sustainable Value in the Global Economy* (pp. 103–124). IGI Global. doi:10.4018/978-1-7998-1196-1.ch007

Dogra, J., & Kale, S. S. (2020). Network Analysis of Destination Management Organization Smart Tourism Ecosystem (STE) for E-Branding and Marketing of Tourism Destinations. In C. M. Ramos, C. R. Almeida, & P. O. Fernandes (Eds.), *Handbook of Research on Social Media Applications for the Tourism and Hospitality Sector* (pp. 1–16). IGI Global. doi:10.4018/978-1-7998-1947-9.ch001

Dreisbach, S. M., Vij, M., & Dreisbach, J. L. (2020). Travel Motivations of Cancer Patients. In S. Paul & S. Kulshreshtha (Eds.), *Global Developments in Healthcare and Medical Tourism* (pp. 78–95). IGI Global. doi:10.4018/978-1-5225-9787-2.ch005

Durodolu, O. O., Mamudu, P. A., & Tsabedze, V. O. (2020). Management of Electronic Records for Service Delivery at the University College Hospital, Ibadan, Nigeria. In S. M. Keakopa & T. L. Mosweu (Eds.), *Cases on Electronic Record Management in the ESARBICA Region* (pp. 199–214). IGI Global. doi:10.4018/978-1-7998-2527-2.ch011

Elgujja, A. A. (2020). Impact of Information Technology on Patient Confidentiality Rights. In R. W. McHaney, I. Reychev, J. Azuri, M. E. McHaney, & R. Moshonov (Eds.), *Impacts of Information Technology on Patient Care and Empowerment* (pp. 365–387). IGI Global. doi:10.4018/978-1-7998-0047-7.ch018

Enakrire, R. T. (2020). Impact of ICTs in the Practice of Records Management in Ministry of Health, Nigeria. In S. M. Keakopa & T. L. Mosweu (Eds.), *Cases on Electronic Record Management in the ESARBICA Region* (pp. 1–17). IGI Global. doi:10.4018/978-1-7998-2527-2.ch001

Endong, F. P. (2019). Nation Branding and Tourism Development in Nigeria. In R. Hashim, M. H. Mohd Hanafiah, & M. Jamaluddin (Eds.), *Positioning and Branding Tourism Destinations for Global Competitiveness* (pp. 256–276). IGI Global. doi:10.4018/978-1-5225-7253-4.ch011

Evans, K. S., & Wang, E. B. (2019). Data Analysis and Integration in Healthcare. In N. Bouchemal (Ed.), *Intelligent Systems for Healthcare Management and Delivery* (pp. 220–234). IGI Global. doi:10.4018/978-1-5225-7071-4.ch010

Folorunso, G. I., Oyeyemi, A. I., Udoh, O. D., Ayodele, O. T., & Excellence-Oluye, N. O. (2020). Rethinking the Role of Traditional Media on Migration Issues in Nigeria. In N. Okorie, B. R. Ojebuyi, & J. W. Macharia (Eds.), *Handbook of Research on the Global Impact of Media on Migration Issues* (pp. 85–95). IGI Global. doi:10.4018/978-1-7998-0210-5.ch006

Gedikoglu, Z. A., Backman, S. J., Mazer, J. P., & Backman, K. F. (2020). A Conceptual Framework to Understand Online Destination Images. In C. M. Ramos, C. R. Almeida, & P. O. Fernandes (Eds.), *Handbook of Research on Social Media Applications for the Tourism and Hospitality Sector* (pp. 114–135). IGI Global. doi:10.4018/978-1-7998-1947-9.ch008

Gomes, A. M., Augusto da Costa, R., & Moreira, A. C. (2019). How Foreign Tourist Intermediaries Perceive and Sell a Destination. In M. A. Camilleri (Ed.), *Strategic Perspectives in Destination Marketing* (pp. 28–57). IGI Global. doi:10.4018/978-1-5225-5835-4.ch002

Gordin, V. Borovskaia, I. & Fedorova, E. (2020). Overtourism in Megalopolises. In Handbook of Research on the Impacts, Challenges, and Policy Responses to Overtourism (pp. 116-135). IGI Global. http://doi:10.4018/978-1-7998-2224-0.ch007

Guerra, J. M. (2019). Reactivation or Collapse. In A. C. Moreira & P. Silva (Eds.), *Handbook of Research on Corporate Restructuring and Globalization* (pp. 125–141). IGI Global. doi:10.4018/978-1-5225-8906-8.ch006

Gupta, V. P., & Arora, A. K. (2020). Automation in Healthcare Services. In R. Wason, D. Goyal, V. Jain, S. Balamurugan, & A. Baliyan (Eds.), *Applications of Deep Learning and Big IoT on Personalized Healthcare Services* (pp. 1–19). IGI Global. doi:10.4018/978-1-7998-2101-4.ch001

Hamid, S., & Jameel, S. T. (2020). A Study of Green Marketing Practices in the Selected Ayurvedic Resorts of Kerala. In S. Paul & S. Kulshreshtha (Eds.), *Global Developments in Healthcare and Medical Tourism* (pp. 176–187). IGI Global. doi:10.4018/978-1-5225-9787-2.ch010

Handayani, B., Seraphin, H., & Korstanje, M. (2019). *Halal Tourism in Bali, Why Not?* IGI Global. doi:10.4018/978-1-5225-7393-7.ch004

Handayani, B., Seraphin, H., & Korstanje, M. (2019). *Street Food as a Special Interest and Sustainable Form of Tourism for Southeast Asia Destinations*. IGI Global. doi:10.4018/978-1-5225-7393-7.ch005

Haq, F., & Medhekar, A. (2020). Strategic Indicators of the Role of Government in Developing Dubai as a Medical Tourism Hub. In S. Paul & S. Kulshreshtha (Eds.), *Global Developments in Healthcare and Medical Tourism* (pp. 52–77). IGI Global. doi:10.4018/978-1-5225-9787-2.ch004

Hege, A., Presnell, D., Reed-Ashcraft, K. B., Caldwell, K., Pyles, D. G., Bouldin, E. D., & Warren, J. (2020). Advocacy and Action in Appalachia Aimed at Adverse Childhood Experiences. In H. C. Greene, B. S. Zugelder, & J. C. Manner (Eds.), *Handbook of Research on Leadership and Advocacy for Children and Families in Rural Poverty* (pp. 125–148). IGI Global. doi:10.4018/978-1-7998-2787-0.ch006

Hudson-Flege, M. D. (2017). A Cross-Cultural Year of Service Theoretical Model. *International Journal of Civic Engagement and Social Change*, *4*(2), 13–32. doi:10.4018/IJCESC.2017040102

İnanç, Ş., & Eren Şenaras, A. (2020). Solving Nurse Scheduling Problem via Genetic Algorithm in Home Healthcare. In J. Euchi (Ed.), *Transportation, Logistics, and Supply Chain Management in Home Healthcare* (pp. 20–28). IGI Global. doi:10.4018/978-1-7998-0268-6.ch002

Jalis, M. H. (2019). Marketing and Branding Initiatives for Local Food and Tourism Identity of Terengganu, Malaysia. In R. Hashim, M. H. Mohd Hanafiah, & M. Jamaluddin (Eds.), *Positioning and Branding Tourism Destinations for Global Competitiveness* (pp. 1–22). IGI Global. doi:10.4018/978-1-5225-7253-4.ch001

Jean-Baptiste, A. M. & Asongwed, E. T. (2018). Service Learning as an Approach to Combatting the Triad of Interrelated Diseases in the District of Columbia. In Changing Urban Landscapes Through Public Higher Education (pp. 26-56). IGI Global. http://doi:10.4018/978-1-5225-3454-9.ch002

Kabadayi, N., & Dağ, S. (2020). Fuzzy Logic in Health Services. In M. Gul, E. Celik, S. Mete, & F. Serin (Eds.), *Computational Intelligence and Soft Computing Applications in Healthcare Management Science* (pp. 121–157). IGI Global. doi:10.4018/978-1-7998-2581-4.ch007

Kalambi, M. D. (2020). Caring for the Caregivers Through Healthy Human Resource Practices. *International Journal of Technology and Human Interaction, 16*(2), 1–7. doi:10.4018/IJTHI.2020040101

Karadayi-Usta, S., & Serdarasan, S. (2020). A Collaborative Framework for Medical Tourism Service Supply Chain Operations. In S. Paul & S. Kulshreshtha (Eds.), *Global Developments in Healthcare and Medical Tourism* (pp. 188–219). IGI Global. doi:10.4018/978-1-5225-9787-2.ch011

Kasemsap, K. (2017). Mastering Sustainable Tourism and Rural Tourism in the Global Economy. In P. Ordóñez de Pablos & Z. M. Aung (Eds.), *Tourism and Opportunities for Economic Development in Asia* (pp. 53–76). IGI Global. doi:10.4018/978-1-5225-2078-8.ch005

Katta, R. M., & Patro, C. S. (2019). Indian Tourism. *International Journal of Asian Business and Information Management, 10*(2), 31–54. doi:10.4018/IJABIM.2019040102

Kaukinen, D. L. (2019). JSON-LD as an Interchange Technology to Facilitate Health Information Exchange. *International Journal of Extreme Automation and Connectivity in Healthcare, 1*(1), 66–78. doi:10.4018/IJEACH.2019010107

Kaushal, V., Sharma, S., & Ali, N. (2019). Empirical Investigation of Relationship Among Destination Brand Equity Dimensions. *International Journal of Asian Business and Information Management, 10*(3), 74–90. doi:10.4018/IJABIM.2019070105

Kim, M. (2018). Implications for Poor Public Healthcare System of South Korea Revealed in MERS Outbreak. *International Journal of E-Health and Medical Communications, 9*(4), 20–28. doi:10.4018/IJEHMC.2018100103

Ko, H., Mesicek, L., Choi, J., Choi, J., & Hwang, S. (2018). A Study on Secure Contents Strategies for Applications With DRM on Cloud Computing. *International Journal of Cloud Applications and Computing, 8*(1), 143–153. doi:10.4018/IJCAC.2018010107

Kruja, A. D., & Hysi, K. (2020). Influence of Practice Management Software on Dental Services. In B. Nogalski, A. Szpitter, A. Jabłoński, & M. Jabłoński (Eds.), *Networked Business Models in the Circular Economy* (pp. 241–267). IGI Global. doi:10.4018/978-1-5225-7850-5.ch011

Luthuli, L. P., & Kalusopa, T. T. (2020). The Integration of Medical Records Management Requirements in ICTs. In S. M. Keakopa & T. L. Mosweu (Eds.), *Cases on Electronic Record Management in the ESARBICA Region* (pp. 49–67). IGI Global. doi:10.4018/978-1-7998-2527-2.ch003

Makovhololo, P., & Iyamu, T. (2020). A Framework to Guide ICT Solution for Language Barrier in South African Healthcare. *Journal of Cases on Information Technology*, *22*(2), 1–17. doi:10.4018/JCIT.2020040101

Malerba, R. C., Fernandes, C. I., & Veiga, P. (2020). What Do We Know About Destination Branding? In S. J. Teixeira & J. M. Ferreira (Eds.), *Multilevel Approach to Competitiveness in the Global Tourism Industry* (pp. 211–228). IGI Global. doi:10.4018/978-1-7998-0365-2.ch013

Martínez-Ruiz, M. P., Llodrá-Riera, I., & Jiménez-Zarco, A. I. (2018). Social Media as Information Sources and Their Influence on the Destination Image. In D. Batabyal (Ed.), *Managing Sustainable Tourism Resources* (pp. 265–283). IGI Global. doi:10.4018/978-1-5225-5772-2.ch014

Medhekar, A. (2019). Role, Rules, and Regulations for Global Medical Tourism Facilitators. In M. Chand Dhiman & V. Chauhan (Eds.), *Handbook of Research on International Travel Agency and Tour Operation Management* (pp. 81–100). IGI Global. doi:10.4018/978-1-5225-8434-6.ch006

Medhekar, A. (2020). Emerging Trends of Wellness and Medical Tourism in India. In S. Paul & S. Kulshreshtha (Eds.), *Global Developments in Healthcare and Medical Tourism* (pp. 1–22). IGI Global. doi:10.4018/978-1-5225-9787-2.ch001

Medhekar, A., & Haq, F. (2018). Urbanization and New Jobs Creation in Healthcare Services in India. In U. Benna & I. Benna (Eds.), *Urbanization and Its Impact on Socio-Economic Growth in Developing Regions* (pp. 198–218). IGI Global. doi:10.4018/978-1-5225-2659-9.ch010

Meral, Y. (2020). Health Export and Health Tourism Roles in European Union Countries. In Y. Demir Uslu, H. Dinçer, & S. Yüksel (Eds.), *Multidimensional Perspectives and Global Analysis of Universal Health Coverage* (pp. 93–115). IGI Global. doi:10.4018/978-1-7998-2329-2.ch004

Mikolič, V. (2018). Stereotyping in Tourism Discourse. In M. Bielenia-Grajewska & E. Cortes de los Rios (Eds.), *Innovative Perspectives on Tourism Discourse* (pp. 155–167). IGI Global. doi:10.4018/978-1-5225-2930-9.ch009

Mohamed, A. R. (2019). Multi-Cultural Communication is Essential for Tourism Industry. In D. Tüzünkan & V. Altıntaş (Eds.), *Contemporary Human Resources Management in the Tourism Industry* (pp. 211–236). IGI Global. doi:10.4018/978-1-5225-5760-9.ch009

Morim, A. C., Inácio, H., & Vieira, E. (2018). Internal Control in a Public Hospital. In G. M. Azevedo, J. da Silva Oliveira, R. P. Marques, & A. D. Ferreira (Eds.), *Handbook of Research on Modernization and Accountability in Public Sector Management* (pp. 77–102). IGI Global. doi:10.4018/978-1-5225-3731-1.ch005

Morim, A. C., Inácio, H., & Vieira, E. (2020). The Implementation of Internal Control in the Financial Services Expenditure in a Hospital Department. In G. Azevedo, J. Oliveira, R. Marques, & A. Ferreira (Eds.), *Tools, Strategies, and Practices for Modern and Accountable Public Sector Management* (pp. 290–323). IGI Global. doi:10.4018/978-1-7998-1385-9.ch011

Morton, M., Varghese, J., Jackson, E., & Levac, L. (2020). Principles in Practice. In A. S. Zimmerman (Ed.), *Preparing Students for Community-Engaged Scholarship in Higher Education* (pp. 322–346). IGI Global. doi:10.4018/978-1-7998-2208-0.ch016

Mosconi, E. M., Poponi, S., Fortunati, S., & Arezzo di Trifiletti, M. (2020). B Corp Certification for a Circular Economy Approach and a Sustainable Pathway. In C. Silvestri, M. Piccarozzi, & B. Aquilani (Eds.), *Customer Satisfaction and Sustainability Initiatives in the Fourth Industrial Revolution* (pp. 167–188). IGI Global. doi:10.4018/978-1-7998-1419-1.ch009

Mukherjee, T., & Nathawat-Aibas, S. S. (2017). Role of PR in Relations Management with Strategic Partners Leading to Value Co-Creation. In S. Rozenes & Y. Cohen (Eds.), *Handbook of Research on Strategic Alliances and Value Co-Creation in the Service Industry* (pp. 103–132). IGI Global. doi:10.4018/978-1-5225-2084-9.ch006

Nair, B. B. (2020). Heal and Revive. In S. Paul & S. Kulshreshtha (Eds.), *Global Developments in Healthcare and Medical Tourism* (pp. 220–235). IGI Global. doi:10.4018/978-1-5225-9787-2.ch012

Nakayama, M., Chen, C. C., & Ractham, P. (2018). Medical Tourism for Cosmetic Procedures. In J. Tan (Ed.), *Handbook of Research on Emerging Perspectives on Healthcare Information Systems and Informatics* (pp. 498–514). IGI Global. doi:10.4018/978-1-5225-5460-8.ch022

Naseehath, S. (2019). Web Resources on Medical Tourism. In S. Thanuskodi (Ed.), *Literacy Skill Development for Library Science Professionals* (pp. 174–195). IGI Global. doi:10.4018/978-1-5225-7125-4.ch008

Nsamzinshuti, A., & Ndiaye, A. B. (2018). Align Hospital Drug Delivery With Supply Chain Management. In L. C. Wood (Ed.), *Contemporary Approaches and Strategies for Applied Logistics* (pp. 170–200). IGI Global. doi:10.4018/978-1-5225-5273-4.ch007

Ojo, S. (2019). Place Consumption. In A. Gbadamosi (Ed.), *Exploring the Dynamics of Consumerism in Developing Nations* (pp. 218–242). IGI Global. doi:10.4018/978-1-5225-7906-9.ch010

Paraskou, A., & George, B. (2018). *An Overview of Reproductive Tourism*. IGI Global. doi:10.4018/978-1-5225-2694-0.ch001

Paraskou, A., & George, B. (2018). *Theoretical Framework*. IGI Global. doi:10.4018/978-1-5225-2694-0.ch002

Paraskou, A., & George, B. (2018). *Analysis of Reproductive Tourism in Greece*. IGI Global. doi:10.4018/978-1-5225-2694-0.ch004

Paraskou, A., & George, B. (2018). *The Research Method*. IGI Global. doi:10.4018/978-1-5225-2694-0.ch003

Pariatamby, A. & Bhatti, M. S. (2020). Waste Management Challenges in Malaysia. In Sustainable Waste Management Challenges in Developing Countries (pp. 186-222). IGI Global. http://doi:10.4018/978-1-7998-0198-6.ch008

Penland, J. J., & Burke, D. R. (2018). Successful Transitions From College to Career (C2C). In J. Keengwe (Ed.), *Handbook of Research on Pedagogical Models for Next-Generation Teaching and Learning* (pp. 325–344). IGI Global. doi:10.4018/978-1-5225-3873-8.ch018

Plante, J. D., Bryer, T. A., & Winston, H. G. (2019). Creating a Scale for Service. *International Journal of Adult Vocational Education and Technology, 10*(3), 54–65. doi:10.4018/IJAVET.2019070104

Preko, M., Osei-Boateng, R., & Durosinmi, A. E. (2020). Digitalising Healthcare in Developing Economies. In R. Boateng (Ed.), *Handbook of Research on Managing Information Systems in Developing Economies* (pp. 332–353). IGI Global. doi:10.4018/978-1-7998-2610-1.ch016

Punti, G., Chandiramani, N. V., & Steffens, C. M. (2018). Empowering Undergraduate Students Through Community-Based Research. In O. O. Delano-Oriaran, M. W. Penick-Parks, & S. Fondrie (Eds.), *Culturally Engaging Service-Learning With Diverse Communities* (pp. 288–307). IGI Global. doi:10.4018/978-1-5225-2900-2.ch017

Rao, N. R. (2018). Establishing Synergy Between Cloud Computing and Collaborative Technology in Medical Informatics. In Virtual and Augmented Reality (pp. 464-480). IGI Global. http://doi:10.4018/978-1-5225-5469-1.ch022

Rao, N. R. (2019). Providing Healthcare Services in the Virtual Environment. In N. Rao (Ed.), *Global Virtual Enterprises in Cloud Computing Environments* (pp. 145–170). IGI Global. doi:10.4018/978-1-5225-3182-1.ch006

Rawal, K., Sethi, G., Saini, B. S., & Saini, I. (2020). HRV. In S. Paul & S. Kulshreshtha (Eds.), *Global Developments in Healthcare and Medical Tourism* (pp. 236–264). IGI Global. doi:10.4018/978-1-5225-9787-2.ch013

Rines, O. (2020). Online Community Bonds as a Method of Mitigating Toxicity in an Interactive Livestream. In R. A. Dunn (Ed.), *Multidisciplinary Perspectives on Media Fandom* (pp. 303–322). IGI Global. doi:10.4018/978-1-7998-3323-9.ch017

Rodrigues, C. (2019). Branding Porto. In M. A. Camilleri (Ed.), *Strategic Perspectives in Destination Marketing* (pp. 198–219). IGI Global. doi:10.4018/978-1-5225-5835-4.ch008

Ryan, J., Doster, B., Daily, S., & Lewis, C. C. (2018). Aligning the Perioperative Process to Hospital Strategy. In J. Tan (Ed.), *Handbook of Research on Emerging Perspectives on Healthcare Information Systems and Informatics* (pp. 33–57). IGI Global. doi:10.4018/978-1-5225-5460-8.ch003

Sağol, G., Sariyer, G., Ekren, B. Y., & Ataman, M. G. (2019). An (s, S) Inventory Optimization Problem. In G. W. Evans, W. E. Biles, & K. G. Bae (Eds.), *Analytics, Operations, and Strategic Decision Making in the Public Sector* (pp. 187–206). IGI Global. doi:10.4018/978-1-5225-7591-7.ch009

Saha, E., & Ray, P. K. (2019). Statistical Analysis of Medical Data for Inventory Management in a Healthcare System. In G. W. Evans, W. E. Biles, & K. G. Bae (Eds.), *Analytics, Operations, and Strategic Decision Making in the Public Sector* (pp. 166–186). IGI Global. doi:10.4018/978-1-5225-7591-7.ch008

Santana, A. A., & Gil, S. M. (2018). Cooperation and Competition Among Regions. In A. Presenza & L. R. Sheehan (Eds.), *Geopolitics and Strategic Management in the Global Economy* (pp. 315–336). IGI Global. doi:10.4018/978-1-5225-2673-5.ch016

Santinha, G., Breda, Z., & Rodrigues, V. (2020). Perspectives for Medical Tourism Development in Portugal's Central Region. In S. Paul & S. Kulshreshtha (Eds.), *Global Developments in Healthcare and Medical Tourism* (pp. 112–133). IGI Global. doi:10.4018/978-1-5225-9787-2.ch007

Santo, C. A. (2017). Orchestrating Community Change through Music and Heritage. In L. N. Hersey & B. Bobick (Eds.), *Handbook of Research on the Facilitation of Civic Engagement through Community Art* (pp. 455–475). IGI Global. doi:10.4018/978-1-5225-1727-6.ch021

Saxena, N. (2020). Considerations for Stakeholders of Medical Tourism. In S. Paul & S. Kulshreshtha (Eds.), *Global Developments in Healthcare and Medical Tourism* (pp. 23–37). IGI Global. doi:10.4018/978-1-5225-9787-2.ch002

Sayan, İ. (2019). Effects of Sustainable Medical Waste Management on the Environment and Human Health. In U. Akkucuk (Ed.), *The Circular Economy and Its Implications on Sustainability and the Green Supply Chain* (pp. 265–279). IGI Global. doi:10.4018/978-1-5225-8109-3.ch015

Šebestová, J., & Palová, Z. (2017). Support of Social Innovations. In M. Lewandowski & B. Kożuch (Eds.), *Public Sector Entrepreneurship and the Integration of Innovative Business Models* (pp. 165–187). IGI Global. doi:10.4018/978-1-5225-2215-7.ch007

Setia, D., Singh, R., Sharma, A., Khosla, A., Ahuja, K., & Chand, K. (2019). Enhancing Tourism and Cultural Experience Through Gamification. In R. Hashim, M. H. Mohd Hanafiah, & M. Jamaluddin (Eds.), *Positioning and Branding Tourism Destinations for Global Competitiveness* (pp. 152–171). IGI Global. doi:10.4018/978-1-5225-7253-4.ch007

Shanmugam, M. M., & Popli, S. (2018). Quality Improvement in Real Sense or Just a Quick Fix? In A. Krishnan (Ed.), *Cases on Quality Initiatives for Organizational Longevity* (pp. 252–272). IGI Global. doi:10.4018/978-1-5225-5288-8.ch010

Shuakat, M. N., & Wickramasinghe, N. (2020). Comparative Study of Oncology Information Systems for Better Patient and Provider Outcomes. In N. Wickramasinghe (Ed.), *Handbook of Research on Optimizing Healthcare Management Techniques* (pp. 228–237). IGI Global. doi:10.4018/978-1-7998-1371-2.ch017

Shukla, P. U., & Kulshreshtha, S. K. (2020). United Arab Emirates as a Global Medical Tourism Destination. In S. Paul & S. Kulshreshtha (Eds.), *Global Developments in Healthcare and Medical Tourism* (pp. 277–290). IGI Global. doi:10.4018/978-1-5225-9787-2.ch015

Silva, T. G., Senna de Castro, C. M., Assad, D. B., Vasconcelos, A. C., & Spiegel, T. (2020). Fast Track to Reduce Patient Lead Time. In N. Wickramasinghe (Ed.), *Handbook of Research on Optimizing Healthcare Management Techniques* (pp. 238–260). IGI Global. doi:10.4018/978-1-7998-1371-2.ch018

Singh, B. K., & Thakkar, H. (2020). Recent Studies and Research on Sickle Cell Disease. In D. S. Sisodia, R. Pachori, & L. Garg (Eds.), *Handbook of Research on Advancements of Artificial Intelligence in Healthcare Engineering* (pp. 237–243). IGI Global. doi:10.4018/978-1-7998-2120-5.ch013

Sinha, H., Raj, G., Choudhury, T., & Kumar, P. (2018). Effective E-Healthcare System. *International Journal of Big Data and Analytics in Healthcare*, *3*(2), 10–27. doi:10.4018/IJBDAH.2018070102

Smith, A. D. (2019). RFID Applications in Healthcare Systems From an Operational Perspective. *International Journal of Systems and Society*, *6*(2), 1–28. doi:10.4018/IJSS.2019070101

Solórzano, J. M., Anchondo, E. L., Peinado Coronado, P., & Nogueira, L. S. (2018). A Creative Teaching Strategy to Generate Concept Designs and Their Possible Application in Tourism. In J. L. Hernández Arellano, A. A. Maldonado Macías, J. A. Castillo Martínez, & P. Peinado Coronado (Eds.), *Handbook of Research on Ergonomics and Product Design* (pp. 325–345). IGI Global. doi:10.4018/978-1-5225-5234-5.ch018

Sonuç, N. (2020). Wellness Tourism Management. In A. Akbaba & V. Altıntaş (Eds.), *Industrial and Managerial Solutions for Tourism Enterprises* (pp. 110–127). IGI Global. doi:10.4018/978-1-7998-3030-6.ch008

Sood, T. (2017). Services Marketing. In T. Sood (Ed.), *Strategic Marketing Management and Tactics in the Service Industry* (pp. 15–42). IGI Global. doi:10.4018/978-1-5225-2475-5.ch002

Tang, C. F., Zhang, M., & Gao, J. H. (2019). A Study of Place Branding of Macao. In P. Ordoñez de Pablos (Ed.), *Dynamic Perspectives on Globalization and Sustainable Business in Asia* (pp. 245–267). IGI Global. doi:10.4018/978-1-5225-7095-0.ch016

Tanniru, M. (2020). Optimization of Provider Ecosystem Through Actor-Resource Integration. In N. Wickramasinghe (Ed.), *Handbook of Research on Optimizing Healthcare Management Techniques* (pp. 103–115). IGI Global. doi:10.4018/978-1-7998-1371-2.ch007

Toylan, N. V. (2019). Strategic Alliances. In H. Dinçer & S. Yüksel (Eds.), *Handbook of Research on Managerial Thinking in Global Business Economics* (pp. 500–519). IGI Global. doi:10.4018/978-1-5225-7180-3.ch028

Tsikerdekis, M. (2017). Designing a Successful Collaborative Wiki. *International Journal of Technology and Human Interaction, 13*(2), 22–39. doi:10.4018/IJTHI.2017040102

Tyndorf, D. M. Jr. (2019). Unwarranted Stigma. In U. Gaulee (Ed.), *Global Adaptations of Community College Infrastructure* (pp. 201–221). IGI Global. doi:10.4018/978-1-5225-5861-3.ch014

Verma, J. & Verma, R. (2018). Innovation in the Provision of Medical Services in India. In Start-Up Enterprises and Contemporary Innovation Strategies in the Global Marketplace (pp. 16-27). IGI Global. http://doi:10.4018/978-1-5225-4831-7.ch002

Vinodan, A., & Meera, S. (2019). Exploring Intangible Heritage Marketing in Tourism. In S. Srivastava (Ed.), *Conservation and Promotion of Heritage Tourism* (pp. 180–201). IGI Global. doi:10.4018/978-1-5225-6283-2.ch008

Wallace, R. (2019). Ecotourism in Asia. In R. Hashim, M. H. Mohd Hanafiah, & M. Jamaluddin (Eds.), *Positioning and Branding Tourism Destinations for Global Competitiveness* (pp. 192–211). IGI Global. doi:10.4018/978-1-5225-7253-4.ch009

Wang, Z., Pei, Z., & Gu, V. C. (2019). Strategic Applications of Business Analytics to Healthcare and Hospital Management. *International Journal of Applied Research on Public Health Management, 4*(2), 47–64. doi:10.4018/IJARPHM.2019070104

Weng, P. W. (2019). Destination Competitiveness. In R. Hashim, M. H. Mohd Hanafiah, & M. Jamaluddin (Eds.), *Positioning and Branding Tourism Destinations for Global Competitiveness* (pp. 49–73). IGI Global. doi:10.4018/978-1-5225-7253-4.ch003

Yim, D., Khuntia, J., & Argyris, Y. A. (2018). User Behaviors and Knowledge Exchange in Health Infomediary. In J. Tan (Ed.), *Handbook of Research on Emerging Perspectives on Healthcare Information Systems and Informatics* (pp. 213–233). IGI Global. doi:10.4018/978-1-5225-5460-8.ch009

Yucesan, M., Mete, S., Gul, M., & Celik, E. (2020). A Fuzzy Decision-Making Model for the Key Performance Indicators of Hospital Service Quality Evaluation. In M. Gul, E. Celik, S. Mete, & F. Serin (Eds.), *Computational Intelligence and Soft Computing Applications in Healthcare Management Science* (pp. 42–62). IGI Global. doi:10.4018/978-1-7998-2581-4.ch003

Zahra, I. M. (2018). Integrated Marketing Communications (IMC). In M. N. Al-Suqri, A. K. Al-Kindi, S. S. AlKindi, & N. E. Saleem (Eds.), *Promoting Interdisciplinarity in Knowledge Generation and Problem Solving* (pp. 102–123). IGI Global. doi:10.4018/978-1-5225-3878-3.ch008

Zimmerman, A. S., & Matteson, S. M. (2020). Designing a Course for the Development of Community-Engaged Researchers in a College of Education. In A. S. Zimmerman (Ed.), *Preparing Students for Community-Engaged Scholarship in Higher Education* (pp. 84–104). IGI Global. doi:10.4018/978-1-7998-2208-0.ch005

About the Contributors

Manjeet Singh is presently working as Assistant Professor in the Department of Tourism and Travel Management, Central University of Jammu, Jammu. He is a Science graduate from the University of Jammu and completed MTM from School of Hospitality & Tourism Management, University of Jammu. He has extensive practical experience is the field of tourism and travel management and has worked with corporates like Yatra.com and Travel Boutique Online to name a few. He has participated in various trainings on entrepreneurship development, management development, business incubation and international business practices among others. He has been awarded with the IARDO RACE 2019 Bangkok Award for Best Educators.

Subbaraman Kumaran is working as Professor in Alliance School of Business, Alliance University, Bangalore. The editor has 30 years of experience (14 years in Industry and 16 years in Teaching and Research). Holds a Doctorate degree from School of Management, Alagappa University, Karaikudi. He holds MBA (Master of Business Administration), MMM (Master of Marketing Management) and M.Phil. (Master of Philosophy in Management) from reputed Universities in Tamil Nadu. Completed B.Sc (Physics) under Madurai Kamaraj University and holds Bachelor of Engineering in Agriculture in the prestigious Farm University in India, Tamil Nadu Agricultural University, Coimbatore. In 2014, completed LL.B degree from Andhra University, Vizag. Published three books (Challenges and Strategies - Tourism Management, Tourism and Water, Hills and Valleys of Tamil Nadu) on Tourism Management. Three chapters contributed in three different book publications. Also published 15 research papers published in reputed Journals and 40 research papers published in National and International Conferences. Two research scholars completed Ph.D under my guidance. Organised more than 500 business development programmes.

* * *

Wafa Alnakhi is a postdoctoral fellow at Johns Hopkins Bloomberg School of Public Health. Wafa has earned her doctorate in public health from Health Policy and Management Department in 2018 with research titled "Patients from the United Arab Emirates seeking healthcare services overseas: characteristics, motivational factors, and healthcare preferences". In her thesis, Wafa used administrative data from the Dubai Health Authority for UAE nationals who sought medical treatment oversea during 2009 – 2016. In addition, Wafa used the data from Knowledge Attitudes and Perceptions Survey 2012 that was collected in Dubai, UAE to explore views, perceptions, and experiences of UAE residents related to treatment overseas for the period 2009 – 2012.

Prem Kumar Balaraman is working in the Department of Management, Veltech Rangarajan Dr Sagunthala R & D institute of science and technology. His research interests include consumer behavior, leadership, Tourism, HR, Entrepreneurship, MIS, etc.

Nadeem Ahmed Bashir is working with the Department of Management, King Saud University, Riyadh, Saudi Arabia. His research interests include consumer behavior, leadership, Tourisms, innovation, and knowledge management.

Oğuz Doğan is an Assistant Professor in the Department of Gastronomy and Culinary Arts, Antalya Bilim University, Antalya, Turkey. He received his Ph.D degree from Akdeniz University, Institute of Social Sciences, the Department of Tourism Management in 2019. His research areas are destination management, hospitality management, tourism clusters and relationship networks, alternative tourism and future trends.

Inder Johar is an Assistant Professor in the Department of Tourism, Kashmir University Satellite Campus - Leh. Having robust corporate experience of 8 years.

Aroop Mukherjee is working with the Department of Aviation and Management, Prince Sultan University, Riyadh, Saudi Arabia. His research interest includes sustainability, agility, agribusiness, supply chain management, supply chain strategies, sustainability, innovation, and knowledge management.

Ambuj Saxena is passionate about digital marketing and loves digging research anecdotes for his research-based writing. An entrepreneur running 2 brands, an avid blogger, ferquent traveller, a book author. He has been recently roped in as a 'Specialist Trainer for Communication & Enterprise Management for Hospitality Training under World Bank funded U.P. Pro-Poor Tourism Development Project'. Post his MBA in

Brand Management from MICA, he has successfully executed various online and offline marketing campaigns for companies operating in Automobile, Fashion and Lifestyle, Travel and Tourism sectors as well as Government departments. He has provided consultancy to Hop on Hop off (HOHO) Bus services in Delhi and helped increase its ridership. He participated twice in HULT Competition, an International Annual Case study contest, in Dubai to solve an issue plaguing the society through social entrepreneurship. Earlier, as a Computer Engineer graduate, he had spent valuable time working in TCS to hone his technical skills. He has co-founded BnBNation as he believes that Tourism and Hospitality is as much online as it is offline, and he can add value to both. In the co-authored book titled, 'Indian BnBs: An emerging disruptor in the Hospitality sector', he has included snippets from BnB Nation blog and the traveller's psyche to provide the reader a taste of Indian hospitality. He has been successfully running Social Buzz, a digital marketing agency which is empanelled with Times of India and has been providing the much need buzz to brands on digital platforms. Read more about him: https://socialbuzz.org.in/team/ambujsaxena/.

G. G. Saxena, an ex-IAS officer of AGMUT Cadre, is an expert in Tourism, Infrastructure, Skill Development and Legal domains. He was a Member of 'Drafting Committee of National Tourism Policy, 2015. He served the government in various capacities including as the MD & CEO of Delhi Tourism and Secretary (Tourism) in Andaman & Nicobar Islands. During this tenure, he has worked towards developing various tourism and hospitality Infrastructure projects under PPP and non-PPP mode. He has initiated the revival of Dying Arts and Festivals of India for promoting Tourism like festivals of Magic, Itr and Sugandhi, Local Cuisines, Kite-flying etc. He has received National Tourism Award 2011 from the President of India for conducting Delhi Heritage Walks for Delhi Tourism and A&N Tourism Policy Literature prepared during his tenure was also awarded National Award. He is main author of the Book "Indian BnBs: Emerging Disruptor in Hospitality Sector". In addition, he has 6 research articles to his credit. He is visiting faculty in IITTM and other Universities and is initiating Tourism & Skill Development courses in various Universities. He has been associated with various international projects as well where he represented India. He was a speaker and Chairman of Technical Sessions in Inter international conferences organized by Indian Tourism and Hospitality Congress (ITHC) in collaboration with Tourism Departments of Universities in Bali (Indonesia) and Manila (Philippines). He is also an esteemed member of several professional societies including Indian Council of Arbitration and India Tourism & Hospitality Congress.

Priyanka Sharma is a Lecturer in School of Hospitality and Tourism Management, University of Jammu.

Index

S

T

W

Y

www.ingramcontent.com/pod-product-compliance
Lightning Source LLC
LaVergne TN
LVHW081321300926
849161LV00008B/1840
9781799834274